HESPERIA: SUPPLEMENT XXII

ATTIC GRAVE RELIEFS

THAT REPRESENT

WOMEN IN THE DRESS OF ISIS

BY

ELIZABETH J. WALTERS

AMERICAN SCHOOL OF CLASSICAL STUDIES AT ATHENS

PRINCETON, NEW JERSEY

1988

Library of Congress Cataloging-in-Publication Data

Walters, Elizabeth J.
    Attic grave reliefs that represent women in the dress of Isis / by
Elizabeth J. Walters.

        p.   cm. — (Hesperia (Princeton, N.J.). Supplement ; 22)
    Bibliography: p.
    Includes index.
    ISBN 0-87661-522-1 : $40.00
        1. Attikí (Greece)—Antiquities. 2. Greece—Antiquities. 3. Sepulchral
monuments—Greece—Attikí. 4. Relief (Sculpture), Greek—Greece—
Attikí. 5. Isis (Egyptian deity)—Cult—Greece—Attikí. I. Title. II.
Series.
    DF261.A8W35   1988
    938'.5—dc19   88-6237
                                                                    CIP

TYPOGRAPHY BY THE AMERICAN SCHOOL OF CLASSICAL STUDIES PUBLICATIONS OFFICE
C/O INSTITUTE FOR ADVANCED STUDY, PRINCETON, NEW JERSEY
PLATES BY THE MERIDEN-STINEHOUR PRESS, MERIDEN, CONNECTICUT
PRINTED IN THE UNITED STATES OF AMERICA
BY THE JOHN D. LUCAS PRINTING CO., BALTIMORE, MARYLAND

PREFACE

This publication is based on my doctoral dissertation in the Department of Fine Arts at New York University, accepted in 1982. Were it not for the excellent complete reliefs, particularly in Athens, and the exceptional if broken ones from the excavations there, this study would be without foundation or clue.

I express here my sincere appreciation for the assistance and interest of my mentor Professor Evelyn B. Harrison and Professors Peter von Blanckenhagen, Bernard V. Bothmer, Dietrich von Bothmer, and Gunter Kopcke, of the Institute of Fine Arts, New York University. This study was made possible through Dr. Harrison's encouragement, the resources of the American School of Classical Studies at Athens, and help from the staff and directors of the excavations in the Athenian Agora, Professors Homer A. Thompson and T. Leslie Shear, Jr., and the director of the excavations in the Kerameikos, Dr. Ursula Knigge. I am indebted to the Greek Archaeological Service, especially to the directors and staff of the museums, in Athens, Piraeus, and Herakleion: Dr. Olga Tzachou-Alexandri, Dr. Dina Peppas Delmousou, Dr. Basilios Petrakos, Dr. E. Touloupa, Dr. Iannis Sakellarakis, Dr. Alcmene Datsuli Stauridis, Dr. Katerina Theochari, and Dr. Nikolaos Yalouris; in Mantua: Dr. Anna Maria Tamassia; and in Trieste: Dr. G. Bravar. The knowledge and experience of Dr. Christian Habicht, Dr. Claus Baer, Dr. and Mrs. Hellmut Hager, Dr. Marian McAllister, and Mark Rose have been of great benefit. I value the encouragement from and discussions with Dr. Judith Perlzweig Binder, Dr. Robert S. Bianchi, Dr. and Mrs. Walter A. Fairservis, Dr. Michael A. Hoffman, Beth Brown, Diane W. Larkin, Yitzhak and Constance Margowski, Mona MacLellan, Patricia Lloyd, Jennifer Alden, and most of all, my parents.

ELIZABETH J. WALTERS

THE PENNSYLVANIA STATE UNIVERSITY
University Park, Pennsylvania
1987

TABLE OF CONTENTS

PREFACE iii

LIST OF ILLUSTRATIONS vii

SELECTED BIBLIOGRAPHY AND ABBREVIATIONS xiii

INTRODUCTION 1

I. ICONOGRAPHY AND EGYPTIAN-PTOLEMAIC SOURCES 5

II. ARCHAEOLOGICAL EVIDENCE AND INTERPRETATION 33

III. PRODUCTION 58

IV. STYLE AND CHRONOLOGY 67

APPENDIXES
  1: Catalogue of "Isis" Reliefs Found in the Athenian Agora 91
  2: Types of Dress for Isis on Representations in the Roman Period 112
  3: Chronological List of Attic "Isis" Reliefs 114

INDEXES
  I: General. 115
  II: Sites and Museums. 119
  III: Attic Grave Reliefs Published by A. Conze 131
  IV: Inscriptions 135

PLATES

LIST OF ILLUSTRATIONS

FIGURES IN TEXT

1 The dress of Isis 4
2 Plan of the Athenian Agora 92

PLATES

1 a Athens, E.M. 8426 (votive relief): Isis Dikaiosyne
   b London, B.M. 639 (stele): Isias (Smyrna)
   c Oxford (stele): Demetria and Sarapias (Smyrna)
   d Rhodes: Funerary altar
2 a Athens, N.M. 1224 (stele): Pompeia Isias
   b Athens (stele): Demetria
   c, d Naples, M.N. 6289 (head)
3 a, b Piraeus Museum 223 (stele): man with siren
   c, d Athens, Agora S 2443 (relief, head)
4 a **1** Agora S 1142 (relief): Fragment, left hand with situla
   b, c Boston, M.F.A. 99.347 (relief): Agrippa
5 a, b Athens, N.M. 3036 (stele): Onesiphoron
6 a, b Athens, N.M. Θησ. 140 (stele): Aphrodeisia
   c Athens, N.M. 2558 (stele): Neike
   d Athens, N.M. 1163 (stele): Ammia
7 a Athens, Kerameikos, Riemann, no. 52 (stele): Diodotos
   b Munich, Glyp. 250 (colossal statue): Isis (Rome)
   c Munich: Stele
   d Naples, M.N. 6372 (statue): dark-stone Isis
8 a, b Athens, N.M. 1296 (stele)
   c Verona, Museo Lapidario (stele): Gaius Silios Bathyllos
9 a Athens, N.M. 1250 (stele): Gaios and Hilaros
   b Athens, Kerameikos, Riemann, no. 70 (stele)
   c, d Boston, M.F.A. 01.8191 (statue)
10 a Athens, N.M. 1270 (stele)
   b, c **2** Agora S 2264 (relief): Fragment, lower legs
11 a **3** Agora S 1200 (relief): Fragment, right hand with sistrum
   b Athens, Kerameikos, Riemann, no. 58 (stele fragment)
   c Cambridge, Fitzwilliam Museum (stele): Tryphon
12 a–c Herakleion Museum 314 (statue)
13 a–d Athens, Third Ephoria (stele): Kallo and Synpheron
14 a–c Eleusis: Stele
   d Aigina (stele pediment): sistrum and situla
   e Syros (stele top): sistrum and situla

15 a Athens, Kerameikos, Riemann, no. 57 (stele): Agathostratos and Ma
     b, c Athens, N.M. 4915 (head): Titus
     d, e Athens, Agora S 1319 (head)
16 a–c 4 Agora S 315 (relief): Fragment, head
     d, e Athens, N.M. 345 (head): Domitian
17 a Athens, N.M. 3725 (stele): Titus Flavius Onesiphoros
     b–d 5 Agora S 847 (relief): Fragment, head
18 a, b 6 Agora S 455 (relief): Fragment, fringed mantle
     c 7 Agora S 2551 (relief): Fragment, right shoulder
19 a Athens, N.M. 1233 (stele): Mousaios and Amaryllis
     b Eleusis (relief): Bust
     c, d Herakleion Museum 260 + 259 (statues): Isis and Sarapis (Gortyna)
20 a, b Athens, N.M. 420 (bust)
     c 8 Agora S 202 (relief): Figure with situla
     d Athens (stele): Hilara
21 a, b Athens, N.M. 3724 (columnar relief): Melisia
     c Piraeus Museum 222 (stele): Paramonos and Alexandros
     d, e Athens, N.M. 3552 (relief, head)
     f Athens, Agora S 1118 (relief, head)
22 a Athens, Philopappos Monument: Lictors
     b Grenoble: Relief
     c 9 Agora S 437 (relief): Fragment, torso
     d Mantua, Ducal Palace 6677 (stele): Attikos
23 a Athens, E.M. 10040 (relief, ephebic decree)
     b–d Athens, Third Ephoria 1160 (stele): Methe
24 a, b Athens, N.M. 1193 (stele): Alexandra
     c Sabratha (statue): Isis (Isieion)
     d Athens, N.M. 1308 (stele): Epigonos and Elate
25 a, b 10 Agora S 486 (relief): Fragment, sistrum
     c Piraeus Museum storeroom (stele): Neikias and Aristo Euphra (Oropos)
     d Marathon Museum (stele): Zosas and Nostimos
26 a 11 Agora S 428 (relief): Fragment, torso with garland
     b 12 Agora S 1728 (relief): Fragment, torso
27 a–c Piraeus Museum 1160 (stele): Lamia Viboullia
     d Cyrene Museum (statue): Faustina the Elder
28 a Athens, N.M. Ἀπο. 237 (relief)
     b 13 Agora S 2393 (relief): Fragment, torso with garland
     c Athens, N.M. 1249 (stele): Eisias
29 a 14 Agora S 2543 (relief): Fragment, legs and hand with situla
     b Laurion Museum (stele): Sosipatros and Epiteugma
     c 15 Agora S 754 (relief): Fragment, right arm with sistrum
30 a–c Boston, M.F.A. 1971.209 (stele): Sosibia
     d 16 Agora S 1920 (relief): Fragment, fringe
31 a, b Rome, Museo Capitolino 744 (statue): Faustina the Younger as Isis
     c–e Athens, Agora S 2864 (statue fragment)
32 a Athens, N.M. 1243 (stele): Eukarpos and Philoxenos
     b Piraeus Museum (relief fragment)
     c Athens, N.M. 1303 (stele): Neike
     d Athens, N.M. 1775 (stele): Telesphoros
     e London, B.M. 630 (stele): Agathemeris and Sempronius

33 a–c **17** Agora S 1584 + S 261 (relief): Fragments, right leg and left arm
   d **18** Agora S 2544 (relief): Fragment, torso
34 a, b Naples, M.N. 124325 (Attic sarcophagus): Achilles
   c, d Athens, N.M. 1617 (statue): Isis
35 a–c **19** Agora S 2771 (relief): Fragments, left shoulder and legs
   d **20** Athens, Agora S 262 (relief): Fragment, torso
36 a **21** Agora S 297 (relief): Fragment, legs
   b Athens, N.M. 3316 (stele): Timokrates
   c Athens (stele): Praxiteles
   d Athens, E.M. 9730 (stele pediment): Cist
37 a, b Athens, N.M. ᾿Απο. 54 + 231 (stele)
   c Paros (relief): Kleitomenes
   d Salamis (stele): Aphelia and Zosimos
   e Athens, N.M. 1214 (stele): Sophia and Eukarpos (Salamis)
38 a Athens, N.M. 1223 (stele): Son of Soterion
   b Athens, N.M. 1247 (stele): Soldier
   c Athens, N.M. 1266 (stele): Soldier
   d **22** Agora I 4776 (stele): Pediment fragment (Polla Zoïlou)
39 a **23** Agora S 1917 (relief): Fragment, torso with garland
   b **24** Agora S 2029 (relief): Fragment, sistrum
   c Broom Hall (stele): Aphrodeisia
40 a Athens, Kerameikos, Riemann, no. 62 (relief fragment)
   b Tarragona (sarcophagus): Hippolytos
   c **25** Agora I 3348 + I 3532 (stele): Pediment fragment, cist
41 a Athens, Agora S 1354 (statue)
   b–d Rome, Vatican, Museo Gregoriano Egizio 83 (statue): Julia Maesa as Isis
   e **26** Agora S 2451 (relief): Fragment, torso
42 a Athens, N.M. 2014 (stele)
   b Athens, Agora S 2698 (relief fragment)
   c Brussels, Musées Royaux d'Art et d'Histoire (stele): Aphthonetos
   d Piraeus Museum (stele): Blastos
43 a, b **27** Agora S 2280 (relief): Fragment, knees
   c Trieste, Mus.Civ. 2214 (stele)
44 a, b Athens, Akropolis Museum 3194 (relief)
   c Rome, Pretextatus Catacomb (sarcophagus): Balbinus
   d Zagreb, Archaeological Museum (statue): Isis
45 a **28** Agora S 2900 (relief): Fragment, torso
   b **29** Agora S 434 (relief): Fragment, torso
   c Piraeus Museum 278 (statue): Balbinus
   d **30** Agora S 984 (relief): Fragment, torso with garland
46 a Athens, N.M. 1176 (sarcophagus): Pelops
   b Athens, N.M. 3256 (stele)
   c Athens, Kerameikos, Riemann, no. 59 (relief fragment)
   d Verona, Museo Lapidario: Relief
47 a **31** Agora S 2396 (relief): Fragment, torso with garland
   b, c Thessaloniki, Arch.Mus. 1247 (Attic sarcophagus): Dionysiac scenes
48 a Naples, M.N. (sarcophagus): "Brother"
   b Athens, N.M. 3669 (stele): Julios Ephebos
   c Athens, E.M. 10038 (relief, ephebic decree)
49 a, b **32** Agora S 341 (two-figure relief): Fragment, lower part
   c. Rome, Piazza Venezia (colossal statue): Isis

50 a **33** Agora S 1987 (relief): Fragment, torso
   b, d Athens, N.M. 1244 (stele): Parthenope
   c Athens, Kerameikos, Riemann, no. 61 (relief fragment)
51 a **34** Agora S 1281 (relief): Fragment, pediment with cist
   b Athens, Kerameikos, Riemann, no. 46 = N.M. 1210 (relief)
   c Naples, M.N. 2929 (stele): Balullia Varilla
   d Athens, N.M. 274 (statue): Athena (Epidauros)
   e Rome, Vatican, Loggia Scoperta (stele): Galatea
   f Palermo, M.N. 704 (statue)
52 a Alexandria, Graeco-Roman Museum 25783 (statue): Isis (Ras-el-Soda)
   b Tunis, Bardo Museum C 982 (statue): Isis
   c Naples, M.N. (statue): black-stone Isis
   d Luxor, Sarapieion (statue): Isis-Fortuna (Upper Egypt)
   e Naples, M.N. (statue): Isis Barberini

PHOTOGRAPHIC CREDITS:

Sources of photographic prints supplied for the illustrations (the photographer where known) are listed below.
Agora Excavations: 15:d, e; 28:b; 50:a
   Vanderpool: 40:c
   Vincent: 4:a; 10:b, c; 11:a; 16:a–c; 17:b, d; 18; 20:c; 22:c; 25:a, b; 26:a, b; 29:a, c; 30:d; 31:c–e; 33:a–d;
      35:b–d; 36:a; 38:d; 39:a, b; 41:a, e; 42:b; 43:a, b; 45:a, b, d; 47:a; 49:a, b; 51:a
   Walker: 35:a
British Museum: 1:b
DAI Athens: 7:a; 9:b; 11:b; 15:a; 40:a; 46:a, c; 47:c; 50:c; 51:b
   Rome: 27:d; 40:b; 44:c; 48:a; 52:b, c, e
Walters: 1:a; 2:c, d; 3; 4 b, c; 9:c, d; 12; 13:c, d; 14:a–c; 19:c, d; 21; 22:d; 23; 24:a, b; 25:c; 27:a–c; 28:a; 30:a–c;
   31:a, b; 32:e; 34; 36:d; 37:a, b; 41:b–d; 44:a, b; 45:c; 47:c; 48:c; 50; 51:c; 52:a, d

Other sources of photographs:

W. Amelung, *Die Sculpturen des Vaticanischen Museums* II, Berlin 1908, pl. 82, no. 19: 51:e
Ἀρχαιολογικὴ Ἐφημερίς 1939/1940, p. 12, fig. 16: 17:a
                           1960, Χρονικά, pl. Θ: 37:c
Ἀρχαιολογικὸν Δελτίον 11, 1927/1928 (1930), p. 10, fig. 17: 48:b
                           33, 1978 (1985), pl. 155: 15:b, c
Annuario della Scuola Archeologica di Atene 1–5, 1939–1943, p. 206, fig. 44: 22:a
N. Bonacasa, *Ritratti greci e romani della Sicilia*, Palermo 1964, pl. 58, cat. no. 128: 51:f
M.-C. Budischovsky, *La Diffusion des cultes isiaques autour de la Mer Adriatique*, Leiden 1977, pl. XXXIX:
   44:d; pl. LVI: 46:d
A. Conze, *Die attischen Grabreliefs* IV, Berlin/Leipzig 1911–1922: 2:a, b; 6:d; 7:c; 8:c; 9:a; 11:c; 13:a; 19:b;
   20:d; 22:b; 24:a; 25:d; 29:b; 32:a–d; 36:c; 37:d; 38:b, c; 39:c; 42:a, c, d; 43:c; 46:b
F. Dunand, *Le Culte d'Isis dans le Bassin oriental de la Méditerranée*, Leiden 1973, I, pl. XXX: 7:b.
                           II, pl. III: 28:c; pl. VI: 38:a; pl. VIII: 24:d; pl. XL: 14:d, e
Jahreshefte des österreichischen archäologischen Instituts 21–22, 1922–1924, p. 175, fig. 58: 20:a, b
Mitteilungen des Deutschen Archäologischen Instituts, Römische Abteilung 85, 1978, pl. 155: 15:a
Monumenti antichi 28, 1922, cols. 157–170: 52:e
G. Pesce, *Il Tempio d'Iside in Sabratha*, Rome 1953, fig. 28: 24:c
E. Pfuhl and H. Möbius, *Die ostgriechischen Grabreliefs* I, Mainz 1977, pl. 118, fig. 813: 1:d; pl. 131,
   fig. 878: 1:c

V. Tran Tam Tinh, *Le Culte des divinités orientales en Campanie*, Leiden 1972, pl. II: 7:d
R. Witt, *Isis in the Graeco-Roman World*, Ithaca 1971, p. 169, fig. 32: 51:c

PERMISSIONS:

Permission for the publication of certain illustrations has been granted as follows:
Dr. Olga Tzachou-Alexandri: 13; 14:a–c; 23:b–d
Alexandria, Graeco-Roman Museum: 52:a
Athens, Akropolis Museum and the Greek Archaeological Service, Athens: 44:a, b
Athens, Greek Archaeological Service: 37:c
Athens, National Museum and the Greek Archaeological Service: 5; 6:a–c; 8:a, b; 10:a; 16:d, e; 17:a; 19:a; 21:a, b, d, e; 24:a, b, d; 28:a, c; 34:c, d; 36:b; 37:a, b, e; 38:a; 46:b; 50:b, d
Boston, Museum of Fine Arts: 4:b, c; 9:c, d; 30:a–c
DAI Athens: 7:a; 9:b; 11:b; 15:a; 40:a; 46:a, c; 47:c; 50:c; 51:b
DAI Rome: 27:d; 40:b; 44:c; 46:a; 48:a; 52:b, c, e
Dr. Dina Peppas Delmousou (Athens, Epigraphical Museum) and the Greek Archaeological Service: 1:a; 23:a; 36:d; 48:c
Leiden, E. J. Brill: 7:b, d; 14:d, e; 24:d; 28:c; 38:a; 44:d; 46:d
London, Trustees of the British Museum: 1:b; 32:e
Mainz, Philipp von Zabern: 1:c, d
Naples, Museo Nazionale: 2:c, d; 34:a, b
Palermo, Banco di Sicilia: 51:f
Dr. Basilios Petrakos: 25:c
Piraeus Museum and the Greek Archaeological Service: 3:a, b; 21:c; 27:a–c; 45:c
Rome, "L'Erma" di Bretschneider: 24:c
Rome, Museo Capitolino: 31:a, b
Rome, Vatican, Museo Gregoriano Egizio: 41:b–d
Dr. Iannis Sakellarakis (Herakleion Museum) and the Greek Archaeological Service, Herakleion: 12:a–c; 19:c, d
Dr. Alcmene Datsuli Stauridis: 15:b, c
Dr. Anna Maria Tamassia (Superintendent of Art, Mantua, Ducal Palace): 22:d
Thessaloniki, Archaeological Museum: 47:b, c

PLAN (Figure 2):

Drawn by John Travlos. Revised by William B. Dinsmoor, Jr.

BIBLIOGRAPHY AND ABBREVIATIONS

SELECTED BIBLIOGRAPHY

Adam, *Technique* = S. Adam, *The Technique of Greek Sculpture* (British School of Archaeology at Athens *Supplementary Vol.* 3), London 1966

Alexandri, Δελτ 22, B′ 1 = O. Alexandri, «᾽Ελευσίς», Δελτ 22, 1967, B′ 1 (1968), pp. 122–130

Andreae, *Art of Rome* = B. Andreae, *The Art of Rome*, New York 1977

*ARV*² = J. D. Beazley, *Attic Red-figure Vase-painters*, 2nd ed., Oxford 1963

Bianchi, *BES* 2, 1980 = R. S. Bianchi, "Not the Isis Knot," *BES* 2, 1980, pp. 9–31

Bieber, *Ancient Copies* = M. Bieber, *Ancient Copies*, New York 1977

BMC = *A Catalogue of Coins in the British Museum*, 1873– (*Alexandria; Ptolemies*)

Bonnet, *Reallexikon* = H. Bonnet, *Reallexikon der ägyptischen Religionsgeschichte*, Berlin 1952

Bothmer, *ESLP* = B. V. Bothmer *et al.*, *Egyptian Sculpture of the Late Period 700 B.C. to A.D. 100: an Exhibition held at the Brooklyn Museum 18 October 1960 to 9 January 1961*, Brooklyn 1960

Bradeen, *Agora* XVII = D. Bradeen, *The Athenian Agora*, XVII, *Inscriptions: The Funerary Monuments*, Princeton 1974

Brückner, *Eridanos* = A. Brückner, *Der Friedhof am Eridanos bei der Hagia Triada zu Athen*, Berlin 1909

Budischovsky, *Diffusion* = M.-C. Budischovsky, *La Diffusion des cultes isiaques autour de la Mer Adriatique*, I, *Inscriptions et monuments*, Leiden 1977

Clinton, *TAPS* 64 = K. Clinton, *The Sacred Officials of the Eleusinian Mysteries* (*Transactions of the American Philosophical Society* 64, part 3), Philadelphia 1974

Comstock and Vermeule, *Sculpture in Stone* = M. Comstock and C. Vermeule, *Sculpture in Stone: the Greek, Roman and Etruscan Collections of the Museum of Fine Arts, Boston*, Boston 1976

Conze = A. Conze, *Die attischen Grabreliefs* IV, Berlin/Leipzig 1911–1922

Diepolder, *Die attischen Grabreliefs* = H. Diepolder, *Die attischen Grabreliefs des 5. und 4. Jahrhunderts v. Chr.*, Berlin 1931

DarSag = C. Daremberg and E. Saglio, *Dictionnaire des antiquités grecques et romaines*, Paris 1877–1919

Dow, *HThR* 30, 1937 = S. Dow, "The Egyptian Cults in Athens," *Harvard Theological Review* 30, 1937, pp. 183–232

Dow and Vermeule, *Hesperia* 34, 1965 = S. Dow and C. Vermeule, "The Statue of the Damaskenos at the American School at Athens," *Hesperia* 34, 1965, pp. 273–297

Dunand, *Le Culte d'Isis* = F. Dunand, *Le Culte d'Isis dans le Bassin oriental de la Méditerranée* I–III, Leiden 1973

Dunand, *Religion populaire* = F. Dunand, *Religion populaire en Égypte romaine; les terres cuites isiaques du Musée du Caire*, Leiden 1979

Follet, *Athènes* = S. Follet, *Athènes au IIe et au IIIe siècle: études chronologiques et prosopographiques*, Paris 1976

Fraser, *OpusAth* 3, 1960 = P. M. Fraser, "Two Studies on the Cult of Sarapis in the Hellenistic World," *OpusAth* 3, 1960, pp. 1–54

Fraser,
  OpusAth 7, 1967
= P. M. Fraser, "Current Problems concerning the Early History of the Cult of Sarapis," *OpusAth* 7, 1967, pp. 23–45

Fraser, *Ptolemaic
  Alexandria*
= P. M. Fraser, *Ptolemaic Alexandria*, Oxford 1972

Fraser, *Rhodian
  Funerary Monuments*
= P. M. Fraser, *Rhodian Funerary Monuments*, Oxford 1977

Graindor, *Athènes
  sous Hadrien*
= P. Graindor, *Athènes sous Hadrien*, Cairo 1934

Grenier, *L'Autel
  funéraire isiaque*
= J.-C. Grenier, *L'Autel funéraire isiaque de Fabia Stratonice*, Leiden 1978

Griffiths, *De Iside*
= J. G. Griffiths, *Plutarch's De Iside et Osiride*, Wales 1970

Griffiths, *The Isis Book*
= *Apuleius of Madauros. The Isis-Book (Metamorphoses, Book XI)*, J. G. Griffiths, ed., Leiden 1975

Guarducci,
  Epigrafia greca
= M. Guarducci, *Epigrafia greca*, I, *Caratteri e storia della disciplina: la scrittura greca dalle origini all'età imperiale*, Rome 1967; II, *Epigrafi di carattere pubblico*, Rome 1969; III, *Epigrafi di carattere privato*, Rome 1974; IV, *Epigrafi sacre pagane e cristiane*, Rome 1978

Harrison, *Agora* I
= E. B. Harrison, *The Athenian Agora*, I, *Portrait Sculpture*, Princeton 1953

Helbig⁴
= W. Helbig, *Führer durch die öffentlichen Sammlungen klassischer Altertümer in Rom*, 4th ed. supervised by H. Speier, Tübingen 1963–1972

Heyob, *Cult of Isis*
= S. K. Heyob, *The Cult of Isis Among Women in the Graeco-Roman World*, Leiden 1975

Hornbostel, *Sarapis*
= W. Hornbostel, *Sarapis: Studien zur Überlieferungsgeschichte, den Erscheinungsformen und Wandlungen der Gestalt eines Gottes*, Leiden 1973

IG II²
= *Inscriptiones graecae*, II–III, *editio minor*, J. Kirchner, ed.

Johnson, *Corinth* IX
= F. P. Johnson, *Corinth*, IX, *Sculpture 1896–1923*, Cambridge, Mass. 1931

Klebs, *ZäS* 67, 1931
= L. Klebs, "Die verschiedenen Formen des Sistrums," *Zeitschrift für ägyptische Sprache und Altertumskunde* 67, 1931, pp. 60–63

Koumanoudes,
  Δελτ 25, 1970
= S. N. Koumanoudes, «Ἐπιγραφαὶ ἐξ Ἀθηνῶν», Δελτ 25, 1970, A (1971), pp. 54–86

Kourouniotis,
  Ἀρχ Ἐφ, 1913
= K. Kourouniotis, «Αἰγίνης μουσεῖον», Ἀρχ Ἐφ, 1913, pp. 86–98

Kurtz and Boardman,
  Greek Burial Customs
= D. Kurtz and J. Boardman, *Greek Burial Customs*, Ithaca 1971

Kyparissis,
  Δελτ 10, Παράρ.
= N. Kyparissis, «Ἐξ Ἀθηνῶν καὶ Ἀττικῆς», Δελτ 10, 1926 (1929), Παράρτημα, pp. 55–85

Lafaye,
  DarSag III, i
= G. Lafaye in DarSag III, i, 1900, pp. 577–586

Lattanzi, *Cosmeti*
= E. Lattanzi, *I Ritratti dei Cosmeti nel Museo Nazionale di Atene*, Rome 1968

Lenormant, DarSag I, ii
= F. Lenormant in DarSag I, ii, 1908, pp. 1205–1208

Lexikon der Ägyptologie I–III, Wiesbaden 1975–1980

Lichtheim,
  JNES 6, 1947
= M. Lichtheim, "Situla No. 11395 and Some Remarks on Egyptian Situlae," *JNES* 6, 1947, pp. 169–179

Malaise, *Conditions*
= M. Malaise, *Les Conditions de pénétration et de diffusion des cultes égyptiens en Italie*, Leiden 1972

Marcadé, *Délos*
= J. Marcadé, *Au Musée de Délos*, Paris 1969

Matz, *ASR* IV, i
= F. Matz, *Die antiken Sarkophagreliefs*, IV, i, *Die dionysischen Sarkophage*, Berlin 1968

Mau, *RE* III
= A. Mau in *RE* III, 1889, cols. 2591–2592

Muehsam, = A. Muehsam, "Attic Grave Reliefs from the Roman Period," *Berytus* 10, 1952,
  Berytus 10, 1952   pp. 51–114
Needler, = W. Needler, "Some Ptolemaic Sculptures in the Yale University Art Gallery,"
  Berytus 9, 1949   *Berytus* 9, 1949, pp. 129–141
Niemeyer, *Studien* = H. G. Niemeyer, *Studien zur statuarischen Darstellung der römischen Kaiser*,
      Berlin 1968
Ohly, *AA* (*JdI* 80), 1965 = D. Ohly, "Kerameikos-Grabung. Tätigkeitsbericht 1956–1961," *AA* (*JdI* 80),
      1965, pp. 278–375
Pfuhl and Möbius, *Die ost-* = E. Pfuhl and H. Möbius, *Die ostgriechischen Grabreliefs* I, Mainz 1977
  griechischen Grabreliefs I
Polaschek, *TrZ* 35, 1972 = K. Polaschek, "Studien zu einem Frauenkopf im Landesmuseum Trier und
      zur weiblichen Haartracht der iulisch-claudischen Zeit," *Trierer Zeitschrift*
      für Geschichte und Kunst des Trierer Landes und seiner Nachbargebiete,
      1972, pp. 141–210
Quaegebeur, = J. Quaegebeur, "Documents concerning a Cult of Arsinoe Philadelphos at
  JNES 30, 1971   Memphis," *JNES* 30, 1971, pp. 239–270
Quaegebeur, = J. Quaegebeur, "Ptolémée II. en adoration devant Arsinoé II. divinisée,"
  BIFAO 69, 1970   *BIFAO* 69, 1970, pp. 191–217
Quaegebeur, "Reines = J. Quaegebeur, "Reines ptolémaïques et traditions égyptiennes," in *Das ptolé-*
  ptolémaïques"   *mäische Ägypten*, Mainz am Rhein 1978, pp. 245–262
RE = Pauly-Wissowa, *Real-Encyclopädie der classischen Altertumswissenschaft*
Riemann = H. Riemann, *Kerameikos*, II, *Die Skulpturen*, Berlin 1940
Roullet, *Monuments* = A. Roullet, *The Egyptian and Egyptianizing Monuments of Imperial Rome*,
      Leiden 1972
Roussel, *Cultes* = P. Roussel, *Les Cultes égyptiens à Délos du IIIe au Ier siècle avant J.-C.*,
  égyptiens   Nancy 1916
SEG = *Supplementum epigraphicum graecum*
Stricker, = B. H. Stricker, "Graeco-Egyptische private sculptuur," *OMRL* 41, 1960,
  OMRL 41, 1960   pp. 18–30
Thompson, = D. B. Thompson, *Ptolemaic Oinochoai and Portraits in Faience*, Oxford 1973
  Ptolemaic Oinochoai
Tran Tam Tinh, = V. Tran Tam Tinh, *Le Culte des divinités orientales en Campanie*, Leiden
  Campanie   1972
Tran Tam Tinh, *Essai* = V. Tran Tam Tinh, *Essai sur le culte d'Isis à Pompéi*, Paris 1964
Tran Tam Tinh, = V. Tran Tam Tinh, *Isis Lactans*, Leiden 1973
  Isis Lactans
Travlos, = J. Travlos, *Pictorial Dictionary of Ancient Athens*, New York 1971
  Pictorial Dictionary
Vidman, = L. Vidman, *Isis und Sarapis bei den Griechen und Römern*, Berlin 1970
  Isis und Sarapis
Vidman, *Sylloge* = L. Vidman, *Sylloge inscriptionum religionis Isiacae et Sarapiacae*, Berlin 1969
Walker, *BSA* 74, 1979 = S. Walker, "A Sanctuary of Isis on the South Slope of the Athenian Acropolis,"
      Annual of the British School at Athens 74, 1979, pp. 243–257
Walters, *AAA* 12, 1979 = E. J. Walters, "Two Attic Grave Reliefs of the Roman Period," *Athens Annals*
      of Archaeology 12, 1979, pp. 215–221
Wegner, *Die* = M. Wegner, *Das römische Herrscherbild*, II, iv, *Die Herrscherbildnisse in*
  Herrscherbildnisse   *antoninischer Zeit*, Berlin 1939
Witt, "Isis-Hellas" = R. E. Witt, "Isis-Hellas," *ProcCamPhilSoc* 192, 1966, pp. 48–69
Witt, *Isis* = R. E. Witt, *Isis in the Graeco-Roman World*, Ithaca 1971

Wycherley, *Stones*   = R. E. Wycherley, *The Stones of Athens*, Princeton 1978
   of Athens
Yalouris *et al.*, *Alexander* = N. Yaloùris, *The Search for Alexander* (Exhibition, Washington, D.C.,
                    November 16—San Francisco, May 16, 1981), Washington, D.C. 1980

PERIODICAL ABBREVIATIONS

AA   = *Archäologischer Anzeiger*
AJA   = *American Journal of Archaeology*
AM   = *Mitteilungen des Deutschen Archäologischen Instituts, Athenische Abteilung*
ʼΑρχʼΕφ   = *Ἀρχαιολογικὴ Ἐφημερίς*
BCH   = *Bulletin de correspondance hellénique*
BES   = *Bulletin of the Egyptological Seminar*
BIFAO   = *Bulletin de l'Institut français d'Archéologie Orientale*
Δελτ   = *Ἀρχαιολογικὸν Δελτίον*
JdI   = *Jahrbuch des Deutschen Archäologischen Instituts*
JNES   = *Journal of Near Eastern Studies*
OMRL   = *Oudheidkundige Mededelingen uit het Rijksmuseum van Oudheiden te Leiden*
OpusAth   = *Opuscula atheniensia*
RM   = *Mitteilungen des Deutschen Archäologischen Instituts, Römische Abteilung*

INTRODUCTION

There is striking conformity in the praise of the Egyptian goddess Isis in Egypt and beyond to the Mediterranean. As early as the early 1st century B.C., the hymns of Isidorus inscribed on the antae of the temple of Isis-Hermouthis at Medinet Madi[1] in the Fayyum of Egypt had much in common with the contemporary aretalogy of Isis from the island of Andros in the Aegean.[2] Isis was considered the source of all good, life, and salvation. Her endless powers continued to be recorded in aretalogies of Roman date from Ios, Kyme, and Thessaloniki.[3] In the *Metamorphoses* XI.5 by Apuleius in the 2nd century after Christ, Isis announces her all-encompassing powers and various identities as the goddess most revered by other peoples.[4]

The popularity of Isis, so well attested in the Roman Empire, may well have been established in the Mediterranean as early as the 2nd century B.C., as suggested by Fraser.[5] The popularity of Isis, particularly in Athens, is of interest to us here. The inscriptions from Athens and its environs indicate that her cult may have been known there as early as the late 4th century B.C. and that participation in it continued to the middle of the 3rd century after Christ.[6] Because the inscriptions concerning the cult of Isis in Athens are few, its popularity and importance can be better assessed when careful consideration is also given to an important group of monuments. These are grave reliefs from Athens that represent women in the dress of Isis, the subject of this publication.

Attic grave reliefs showing women in the dress of Isis are of Roman date, produced from at least as early as the last quarter of the 1st century B.C. to the beginning of the 4th century after Christ.[7] There are 106 known, some only by fragments, representing approximately one third of the published Attic grave reliefs of the Roman period. Owing to the number and generally high quality of the "Isis" reliefs, this series provides the basis for a valid chronology to which the other, contemporary grave reliefs may be related.[8]

Graindor is the only scholar who has recognized the artistic as well as the cult significance of Attic grave reliefs showing women in the dress of Isis. Although he included few

---

[1] Fraser, *Ptolemaic Alexandria*, pp. 670–671: four hymns that date to 96 B.C. are the earliest of the preserved praises of Isis; *SEG* VIII, pp. 536–537 and pp. 548–551; see also V. F. Vanderlip, *The Four Greek Hymns of Isidorus and the Cult of Isis (American Studies in Papyrology* XII), Toronto 1972.

[2] W. Peek, *Der Isishymnus von Andros und verwandte Texte*, Berlin 1930; Fraser, *Ptolemaic Alexandria*, pp. 670–671 and *OpusAth* 3, 1960, p. 3, note 2; Dunand, *Le Culte d'Isis* II, pp. 116–118.

[3] *Ibid.* See also Dunand, *Le Culte d'Isis* II, p. 215 (Ios), p. 188 (Thessaloniki), and III, p. 86 (Kyme); for Thessaloniki, see S. Pelekidis, Ἀπὸ τὴν πολιτεία καὶ τὴν κοινονία τῆς ἀρχαίας Θεσσαλονίκης, Thessaloniki 1934.

[4] Griffiths, *The Isis Book*, p. 75.

[5] Fraser, *Ptolemaic Alexandria*, p. 672.

[6] Vidman, *Sylloge*, nos. 1–33; Dunand, *Le Culte d'Isis* II, pp. 4–17, 133–153.

[7] See **1, 34**, and Chapter IV.

[8] See footnote 1 below, p. 58.

of these Attic "Isis" reliefs in his research on Athens,[9] he did draw attention to them:

> Among the funerary stelai of the Roman period one of the richest series is
> that of the deceased as a devotee of Isis. . . . No doubt the numerousness of
> the devotees of the Egyptian goddess corresponds to a period when Egypt
> and her cult were particularly in favor.[10]

More recently, the cult significance of these reliefs has been clarified by Dunand, the most thorough of the few scholars to cite some of the Attic "Isis" reliefs in their studies on the cult of Isis in Athens.[11]

In reviewing the arguments of Graindor and Dunand, and the less convincing ones of Heyob and Vidman,[12] several questions arise. Who are these women in the dress of Isis on Attic grave reliefs? Priestesses have often been suggested. What is the origin of the costume and what is its significance? Do the majority of these grave reliefs belong to the 2nd century after Christ, particularly to the reign of Hadrian (A.D. 117–138) as proposed by Graindor?[13] Few scholars have questioned the dates offered by Graindor, yet from other monuments with inscriptions concerning the cult of Isis in Athens, it is clear that it was not fostered by any Roman emperor.[14]

The large number and surprising quality of Attic "Isis" reliefs strongly suggest the importance of these monuments to the individuals and families to whom they belonged, as well as the importance of their role in the cult of Isis in Athens; this study is the first to be devoted to them. I have attempted here to define the place of the "Isis" reliefs amid contemporary sculpture as well as in the long history of figured grave reliefs from Athens. A valid chronology is essential. Information concerning the original provenience, however, is often limited or lacking, the accompanying inscriptions are difficult to date, and the persons named in them can seldom be identified.[15] All these factors will be considered, but the chronology must be based chiefly on style.

Attic grave reliefs with women in the dress of Isis from the Agora Excavations are the heart of this study. We are fortunate to have 34 of them, catalogued below in Appendix 1, among which are examples of the earliest and latest of this series. Although the "Isis" reliefs from the Agora are fragmentary, some are of surprisingly high quality. Others are so distinctive in style and execution that close comparisons have been found with other pieces of sculpture suggesting the possibility of the same workshop and, at the least, contemporaneity.

---

[9] P. Graindor, *Athènes sous Auguste*, Cairo 1972, p. 206, note 7; *idem, Athènes de Tibère à Trajan*, Cairo 1931, p. 203, notes 2 and 6; and Graindor, *Athènes sous Hadrien*, p. 283.

[10] Graindor, *Athènes sous Hadrien, loc. cit.*

[11] Dunand, *Le Culte d'Isis* II, p. 145; for the opinions of other scholars, see pp. 54–56 and 59–60 below.

[12] Graindor, *Athènes sous Hadrien, loc. cit.*; Dunand, *Le Culte d'Isis* II, pp. 145–149; Heyob, *Cult of Isis*, pp. 90–92; Vidman, *Isis und Sarapis*, pp. 48–49.

[13] Graindor, *Athènes sous Hadrien, loc. cit.*

[14] Dunand (*Le Culte d'Isis* II, p. 152) agrees with Dow (*HThR* 30, 1937, p. 232) that the inscriptions of the cult in Athens do not indicate patronage from any emperor. Dunand's chart of 22 "Isis" reliefs (pp. 146–148), however, has only two revisions for dates proposed by Graindor. Only four reliefs are cited by Vidman and Heyob, resulting in incorrect conclusions: Vidman, *Sylloge*, nos. 13, 18, 23, 24 and *Isis und Sarapis*, pp. 48–49; Heyob, *Cult of Isis*, pp. 90–92. See also pp. 54 and 60 below.

[15] See footnote 1 below, p. 58. Most helpful are two catalogues containing "Isis" reliefs: Conze, 1868, 1954–1972, 2077, 2139–2142 and Riemann, nos. 57–59, 61, and 62.

The better preserved Attic "Isis" reliefs in the other museums of Athens and the Piraeus have been essential to reconstructing the Agora fragments, but only together with the Agora examples do they form a continuous series from which a valid chronology for Attic grave reliefs of Roman date can be determined.

The Attic "Isis" reliefs in this study belong to a period of heightened production of figured grave reliefs in Athens, from the third quarter of the 1st century B.C. through the 60's of the 3rd century after Christ.[16] A few were made after the invasion of the Heruli in A.D. 267.[17] These centuries may also be significant for the cult of Isis in Athens.

The "Isis" grave reliefs may indicate a period of renewed or increased interest in the cult. It may not be mere coincidence that the first appearance of these reliefs occurred at the time when the island of Delos was being abandoned by the Athenians. Delos had not only been an important crossroads in sea trade and a possession of Athens from 166 B.C. but also had served as a showcase for Athenian participation, often by members of the most prominent families, in the cult of Isis.[18] With the rapid decline of Delos in the first century B.C., the Athenians may have renewed their attentions to local sanctuaries of Isis.

The numerous and continuous series of "Isis" reliefs indicates a broader participation in the cult beginning in the late 1st century B.C., contemporary with Roman rule. The question of the role in the cult of the individuals depicted on the monuments is tantalizing. It is as much of a problem as the identity and place of each in Athenian society. The information most helpful for the solution may lie with the "Isis" reliefs themselves.

Definition of costume and all features that permit identification of the often very fragmentary "Isis" reliefs are discussed first, establishing the Athenian arrangement of the most popular dress of Isis in the Roman Empire. The history of this costume, as well as the characteristic hairstyle and hand-held attributes, leads back to her homeland of Egypt and to recognition of the enrichment of the iconography by the Greeks and the Romans.

Archaeological evidence concerning the "Isis" reliefs, as grave monuments and through the accompanying inscriptions, provides a basis on which to assess the importance of these monuments, the status of the persons named, and finally their role in the cult of Isis in Athens. The last two chapters are concerned with the production of the reliefs and the developments in style which together establish the chronology for this series. The importance of these reliefs to the cult of Isis in Athens is reflected in the sculptors and workshops that created them.

The text of this study is followed by the catalogue of fragmentary reliefs from the excavations of the Athenian Agora (indicated in the text by bold numbers), a table of the versions of the Isis costume represented in sculpture of Roman date, and a chronological table of all the "Isis" reliefs. In the text and on the plates, the sculpture is identified by museum inventory number and inscribed name, if possible; Conze references are given for pieces not illustrated in the plates. The concordance of Conze numbers given in Index III provides locations in Index II or internal references.

---

[16] See pp. 59–60 below.
[17] See pp. 88–89 below.
[18] See pp. 61–62 below.

4

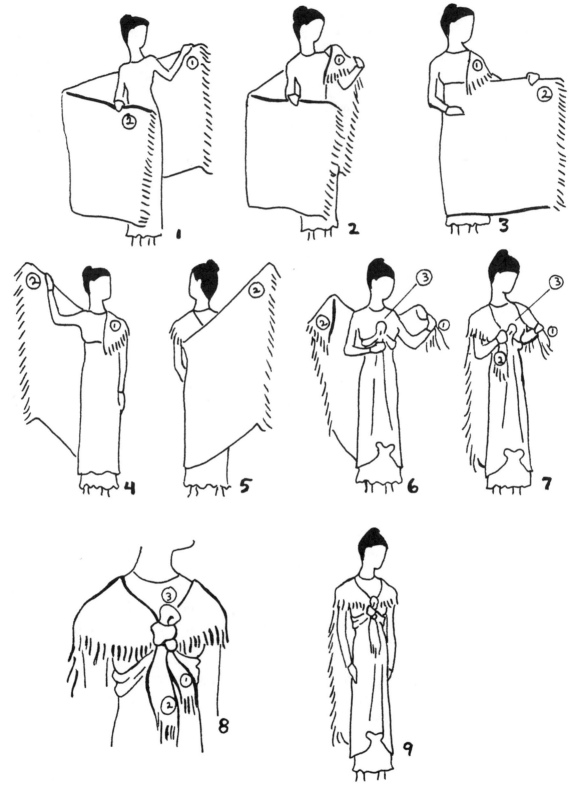

FIG. 1. The dress of Isis

I

ICONOGRAPHY AND EGYPTIAN-PTOLEMAIC SOURCES

In seeking the significance of the costume and hand-held cult objects displayed on Attic grave reliefs, we are led first to Egypt. Costume and cult articles will be found to have a long and often separate history, complicated by developments in Egypt under Greek and, finally, Roman rule. It is the Egyptian goddess Isis whose representations have been considered the model for the costume and whose cult the source for the hand-held articles, but clarification is needed to determine when each became her property.

COSTUME

A rather exotic, feminine costume, thought to be that of the Egyptian goddess Isis, is worn by women on grave reliefs in Athens.[1] It consists of two garments of which the more noticeable is the mantle with long fringe, often snugly draped and always knotted at the chest. It is worn over a sleeved gown.

This form of dress is Egyptian in origin.[2] It was worn by queens, noblewomen, and some commoners at least as early as the New Kingdom (1570–1085 B.C.)[3] and continued to be in fashion in Egypt into the 4th century after Christ.[4]

With the seemingly endless array of titles for the goddess Isis in the Hellenistic and Roman periods, she was represented in the Mediterranean in a variety of dress as well as in the guise of other goddesses.[5] The attire for Isis included this Egyptian costume with fringed

[1] Tran Tam Tinh, *Essai*, p. 96; V. von Gonzenbach, "Der griechisch-römische Scheitelschmuck und die Funde von Thasos," *BCH* 93, 1969 (pp. 885–945), p. 902, note 1; Dunand, *Religion populaire*, p. 21, notes 41, 42 and *Le Culte d'Isis* II, pp. 144–149; for the reliefs, see Conze 1868, 1954–1972. On the dress of Isis, see footnote 2 below; for this Egyptian goddess, see J. Bergmann in *Lexikon der Ägyptologie* III, ii, Wiesbaden 1978, pp. 186–204.

[2] H. Schäfer, "Das Gewand der Isis," in *Janus*, I, *Festschrift zu C. F. Lehmann-Haupts sechzigsten Geburtstage*, Vienna 1921, p. 200; Needler, *Berytus* 9, 1949, pp. 137–141. See also bibliography in A. Adriani, *Repertorio d'arte dell'Egitto greco-romano. Scultura* A I, II, Palermo 1961, p. 38.

[3] *Ibid.* This costume served as a ceremonial dress for queens: see Quaegebeur, "Reines ptolémaïques," New Kingdom relief, fig. M and Ptolemaic queens, p. 254, figs. C and K; S. Sauneron, "Un Document égyptien relatif à la divinisation de la reine Arsinoé II," *BIFAO* 60, 1960, p. 85.

[4] In the Roman period, women are represented in this form of dress on funerary monuments, such as numerous mummy masks cited by Dunand, *Religion populaire*, p. 21; G. Grimm, *Die römischen Mumienmasken aus Ägypten*, Wiesbaden 1974, pls. 11:2–4, 12:1, 15:1, 114:2, 116:5, 117:4 and 8, 118:3. One of the latest, probably Coptic, is an unpublished limestone grave relief, Brooklyn 70.132: compare with Louvre E 25908 (J. Vandier, "Nouvelles acquisitions," *La Revue du Louvre* 23, 1973, p. 250, fig. 5). A date early in the 4th century after Christ is likely; for a similar hairstyle and geometric treatment of the figure and face, see a grave relief in the Rijksmuseum, Leiden (A. Badawy, *Coptic Art and Archaeology*, Cambridge, Mass. 1978, pp. 129–130 and fig. 3:24) and mummy mask, Cairo CG 33281 (G. Grimm, *Kunst der Ptolemäer- und Römerzeit im Ägyptischen Museum Kairo*, Mainz am Rhein 1975, p. 26, no. 56, pl. 95).

[5] The titles and various representations of Isis are outlined by Dunand, *Le Culte d'Isis* I, pp. 80–108 and

mantle knotted at the chest. It was the most popular and distinctive form of dress for representations of Isis in the Roman Empire.[6]

Why did Athenians wear this garb on their grave reliefs? Did they emulate the Egyptian goddess Isis, or was this costume worn by women in the cult of Isis in Athens? Its appearance on 106 Athenian grave reliefs strongly suggests not only local interest in the cult but also use of this dress by its worshipers.

ARRANGEMENT OF THE FRINGED MANTLE

Women in the dress of Isis on Attic grave reliefs wear a fringed mantle over a sleeved garment. The mantle is cross-draped on the back of the figure while the two ends are drawn over the shoulders and caught in the knot at the chest (Fig. 1, views 1–9). The cross-draping is as follows: the end [1] of the mantle is held before the chest while the rest is drawn over the proper left shoulder and down the back to pass under the right arm (view 2). It passes the front of the figure below the breasts (view 3) and under the left arm to cross the back on the opposite diagonal (views 4, 5). The mantle is then drawn over the right shoulder with the second end [2] held before the chest. A slip-knot is then formed by looping the two ends [1 and 2] around part of the folds [3] below the breasts, drawing up the mantle over the legs with characteristic, often thick, center folds (views 6–9).

The cross-draping of the fringed mantle follows a basic Egyptian arrangement, particularly popular in the Ptolemaic and Roman periods.[7] On the Egyptian examples, the mantle has only one end caught in the knot at the chest while the second end lies free over the left shoulder.[8] The catching of two ends in the knot at the chest and the fringing of these two edges are distinctive to Attic monuments; they are due neither to a misunderstanding of the Egyptian dress nor to an artistic preference for symmetry.

The Athenian arrangement of the fringed mantle is a more practical way to wear this Egyptian form of dress. To knot the ends together anchors the mantle securely. To have two fringed edges on the mantle is not difficult. A second fringe for the other end of the mantle is readily made. One must simple loosen the strands from the fabric of the mantle and tie several as tufts, forming a fringe. With both edges caught in the knot and fringed, additional attention is given to this elegant dress.

---

pls. X–XII, XV–XVII, XLIV; II, pls. XVI, XXII, XXIII, XXVII, XXIX, XXXII, XXXIV–XXXVIII, XLII; III, pls. I–III, V, VIII, XII, XV, XVI, XX. See also the summary by Witt (*Isis*, pp. 111–129, figs. 4–8, 13–19, 24, 28); Witt, "Isis-Hellas," pp. 48–69; Bonnet, *Reallexikon*, pp. 328–329; Lafaye, DarSag III, i, pp. 579–585.

[6] Dunand, *Religion populaire*, p. 21.

[7] Needler, *Berytus* 9, 1949, p. 138; Bianchi (*BES* 2, 1980, pp. 9–23) reaffirms the Egyptian origin of this costume, but his explanation of the draping is not valid. Other arrangements of the fringed linen mantle are possible, such as the New Kingdom examples: E. Riefstahl, "A Note on Ancient Fashions: Four Early Egyptian Dresses in the Museum of Fine Arts, Boston," *Bulletin of the Museum of Fine Arts, Boston* 68, 1970 (pp. 244–259), p. 246, fig. 3 and the coffin lid of Iyanafery, New York, M.M.A. 86.1.6a from the tomb of Sennedjem at Deir el Medineh (Dynasty XIX, early in the reign of Ramses II) to be published by Y. Margowsky.

[8] Needler, *Berytus* 9, 1949, p. 138. A number of Egyptian statues with this form of dress of the Ptolemaic and Roman periods are published by Stricker (*OMRL* 41, 1960, pp. 18–30, pls. XVII–XXII).

The knotting of the two ends of a double-fringed Egyptian mantle seems to be exclusive to the Athenians and is best explained as the way in which the Egyptian dress was worn in Athens. Two ends falling from the knot at the chest are clearly shown on the most carefully carved of figures on Attic grave reliefs, as well as on a few statues from Attic workshops of the Roman period.[9] The cross-draping of the fringed mantle on the latter is shown in the round. Like the Egyptian version, the fringed mantle on Attic grave reliefs was made of linen.[10] Its characteristic texture is repeatedly shown on grave-relief figures from Athens, regardless of size or workmanship.[11]

The undergarment worn by women in this garb is a chiton. Its fullness is seen in the looping folds that fall from and frame the breasts and in the narrow folds at the feet of the figure below the mantle which covers this undergown to mid-calf. The long sleeves of the chiton fit snugly and cover the wrists, usually with a cuff. The unusual effect of a second sleeve at mid-upper arm on three relief figures of the early Antonine period (A.D. 140–160) is simply a fold from the fullness of the chiton that has fallen across the arm.[12]

The use of the Greek dress, the chiton, as the undergown for the knotted, fringed mantle does occur among representations of the goddess Isis in Egypt.[13] In the Mediterranean under Roman rule, the knotted, fringed mantle with the chiton was the most characteristic costume for the goddess Isis.[14] Was it exclusive to the Egyptian goddess Isis at any time in the long history of Egypt and the Mediterranean? The reason for the representation of non-Egyptian women[15] in such dress on gravestones in Athens and the environs may well depend on the origin and history of the costume as well as on its use in Athens.

[9] Athens, N.M. 1270 (Pl. 10), Athens, N.M. 1214 (Pl. 37), Mantua, Duc.Pal. 6677 (Pl. 22), and the heavily rasped Athens, N.M. 1308 (Pl. 24). The statues include Herakleion 314 (Pl. 12), Rome, Mus.Cap. 744 (Pl. 31), Vatican, Mus.Greg.Eg. 83 (Pl. 41), and from Dalmatia, Zagreb, Arch.Mus. 34 (Pl. 44).

[10] D. B. Thompson, "A Bronze Dancer from Alexandria," *AJA* 54, 1950 (pp. 371–385), p. 380 and *Ptolemaic Oinochoai*, p. 30. On the literary references to linen, see footnote 78 below, p. 16.

[11] The rasp may be used to suggest the texture of linen, but the short slash marks cutting across the main folds represent its crinkle. See **8, 9, 13, 14, 17, 28,** and **31**; cf. Boston, M.F.A. 1971.209 (Pl. 30) and London, B.M. 630 (Pl. 32).

[12] Lamia Viboullia, Piraeus 1160 (Pl. 27), Athens, N.M. Ἀπο. 237 + **13** (Pl. 28), and **12** (Pl. 26).

[13] Terracotta figurines, assigned to the late Hellenistic and Roman periods: Dunand, *Religion populaire,* pls. XV:21, XXIII, XLIV; and statues of Isis of Ptolemaic and Roman periods: Dunand, *Le Culte d'Isis* I, pls. VII:2, X:1, XI:1, XVI, XXIX:1; XXXIII.

[14] Although the knotted, fringed mantle is emphasized by Dunand (*Religion populaire,* p. 21), the chiton is evident in her examples (see footnote 13 above) and repeatedly occurs in examples of Roman date, such as statues of Isis from the Sarapieion at Luxor and from the Isieion at Ras-el-Soda (Pl. 52) and of Isis-Fortuna from upper Egypt, Alexandria 4780 (T. Kraus, "Alexandrinische Triaden der römischen Kaiserzeit," *Mitteilungen des deutschen archäologischen Instituts, Abteilung Kairo* 19, 1963 [pp. 97–105], p. 100 and pl. XVI:a). Other examples of Roman date include statues from Italy and North Africa (Pls. 7 and 52); votive relief, Rome, Mus.Cap. 4371 (Hornbostel, *Sarapis,* pl. CXV); in Athens, Isis from the south slope of the Akropolis (p. 63); from Attic workshops, see footnote 9 above; from Macedonia, two statues of Isis-Fortuna (T. Janakievski, *Macedonia Acta Archaeologica* 2, 1976, pp. 176 and 194).

[15] See the discussion of the inscriptions (pp. 48–51). Only one name for an individual on an Attic "Isis" grave relief has been suggested as possibly Egyptian: "Anaitis" (*IG* II², 10182) as the root of the garbled name for the woman in the dress of Isis on the Broom Hall relief (Pl. 39).

HISTORY OF THE FRINGED MANTLE AND UNDERGARMENT

In Egypt one of two garments is worn under the fringed mantle: a sheathlike dress which has a long history in Egypt[16] or a Greek dress, the chiton. The sheath often has short sleeves as seen on Egyptian statues of the Ptolemaic and Roman periods.[17] The mantle is tightly draped over the sheath and reveals much of the torso.

In contrast to this snug arrangement is that of the figures who wear the fringed mantle over a Greek dress, the chiton. On Ptolemaic oinochoai,[18] the queens in this dress have a bell-like or pyramidal form resulting from the greater fullness of the chiton. The mantle is worn higher, draped to mid-calf over the chiton rather than completely covering the lower edge of the undergown, as seen in the traditional Egyptian statues[19] with a sheath as the undergarment.

It appears that either of these versions was appropriate for the Ptolemaic queens of Egypt and that each was tied to an artistic tradition in Egypt. When the queens wear the fringed mantle over a sheath, the monument is a traditional Egyptian work, such as the statues of Arsinoe II[20] and temple reliefs and stelai of other Ptolemaic queens.[21] When these queens wear the fringed mantle over a chiton, they are represented in works of Greek heritage such as the relief figures on a few oinochoai of the second half of the 3rd and early 2nd centuries B.C.[22] These figures appear to be essentially Greek in style with some influence from Egyptian monuments in the abstract patterning of folds and facial features.[23] A

[16] Needler, *Berytus* 9, 1949, p. 138; see the statues in Stricker, *OMRL* 41, 1960, pp. 18–30, pls. XVII–XXII. When the sheath has sleeves, it is a bag-tunic which is known from the Middle Kingdom; see the definition by Riefstahl (footnote 7 above, p. 6), pp. 253–259 and fig. 8.

[17] Stricker, *OMRL* 41, 1960, pls. XVII–XXII.

[18] Thompson, *Ptolemaic Oinochoai*, nos. 122–124 and a fourth example, Amsterdam 7588: *eadem*, "More Ptolemaic Queens," in *Eikones: Studien zum griechischen und römischen Bildnis* (*Antike Kunst* Beiheft 12), Bern 1980 (pp. 181–184), pp. 182–183, pl. 61:3.

[19] Stricker, *OMRL* 41, 1960, pls. XVII–XXII, particularly XXI:1–4.

[20] This costume reaches the feet of Arsinoe II on two examples: a small limestone statue, M.M.A. 20.2.21, inscribed on the back pillar "Arsinoe, divine brother-loving" like the Greek Θεὰ Φιλαδελφός (H. Kyrieleis, *Bildnisse der Ptolemäer*, Berlin 1975, pp. 82 and 178, no. J 1, pl. 71), and a fragment of a large granite statue (base with feet and lower edge of drapery) inscribed to Arsinoe in hieroglyphs and Greek, Chicago Oriental Institute 10158 (P. M. Fraser, "Inscriptions from Ptolemaic Egypt," *Berytus* 13, 1960 [pp. 123–161], pp. 133–134, pl. XXIX:2a and 2b).

[21] Berenike II on the propylon of the Temple of Khonsu at Karnak and on the stele from Kôm el Hisn, Cairo CG 22186: Quaegebeur, "Reines ptolémaïques," p. 254, fig. K and p. 247, fig. C. See also the relief on the west pylon inscribed to Ptolemy X at Qus: A. Kamal, "Le pylône de Qous," *Annales du Service des Antiquités de l'Égypte* 3, 1902 (pp. 215–235), pp. 227–228. Needler (*Berytus* 9, 1949, p. 138, note 4) cites the relief of Ptolemy VII between the two Cleopatras at Kom Ombo for a variation of the dress, but these two queens wear a small kerchieflike shawl over a sheath. One example that barely shows a slight edge of the sheath below the lower edge of the knotted mantle is a statue, Cairo CG 27472 (Bianchi, *BES* 2, 1980, p. 19, fig. 12); on this example the garments are above the ankles, higher than the lower edge of the two garments that reach the ankles on figures in the reliefs cited here. This Cairo statue should be early Ptolemaic, according to Bianchi, by comparison with Alexandria 1332 (Bothmer, *ESLP*, no. 95).

[22] Thompson, *Ptolemaic Oinochoai*, nos. 122–124; *eadem*, "More Ptolemaic Queens" (footnote 18 above), pp. 182–183, pl. 61:3 (Amsterdam 7583).

[23] *Ibid.*; on Egyptian elements, Thompson, *Ptolemaic Oinochoai*, pp. 104–106, 116, nos. 25, 30, 109, 118, and discussion pp. 87 and 89.

blending of these two artistic traditions did occur in Egypt, but it seems to have been rare among major monuments. To my knowledge, a mixture seems to have occurred in six Egyptian monuments which show the folds of a chiton below the mantle.[24] Several of these monuments appear to be unusual and may have been made in the Ptolemaic or Roman period.[25]

It is important to observe that none of the representations of the queens wearing fringed mantle and the traditional Egyptian sheath bear the title of Isis.[26] This form of dress may always have been ceremonial, as evident from the temple reliefs,[27] which may well explain why the queens on the oinochoai wear the fringed mantle over a chiton. These vases appear to have been gifts in honor of the queens and may have been used in their festivals.[28] If both versions of the costume with the knotted, fringed mantle were ceremonial, then a precedent existed in Egypt for the use of the knotted, fringed mantle for festivals, adopted later in Athens for those of the goddess Isis.[29]

The Egyptian form of dress worn by women on Attic grave reliefs seems to have borrowed features from both of the Egyptian versions. The Athenians wear the fringed mantle over a chiton to mid-calf like the figures on the Ptolemaic oinochoai, but the snugness and the nearly symmetrical folds of the mantle are closer to the traditional Egyptian statues of the Ptolemaic and Roman periods.[30] The close resemblance to the latter may indicate that the Athenians were emulating an important representation, possibly made in Egypt. A statue or series of statues may have served as their model and possibly as a model for statues of the goddess Isis in Roman times.

If we look for a model among the preserved Egyptian statues of Ptolemaic and Roman

[24] The chiton worn by Arsinoe III has an unusual flared hem hanging below the mantle on a stele from Tanis, B.M. 1054 (W. M. Flinders Petrie, *Tanis* II, London 1889, no. 164); it was mislabeled as Arsinoe II by E. A. Budge (*A Guide to the Egyptian Galleries, Sculpture*, London 1909, p. 257, no. 955), corrected by T. G. H. James (review of B. V. Bothmer, *Egyptian Sculpture of the Late Period*, *JEA* 48, 1962 [pp. 169–171], p. 171), and cited by Quaegebeur (*BIFAO* 69, 1970, p. 201, note 2). The second example is the fragmentary statue from Tanis with unmistakable chiton folds: P. Montet, "Un chef-d'oeuvre de l'art gréco-égyptien. La statue de Panemerit," *Monuments et mémoires. Fondation E. Piot* 50, 1955, p. 9, fig. 4; it does not belong with statues of mantled men as assigned by R. S. Bianchi (*The Striding Male Figure of Ptolemaic Egypt*, diss. Institute of Fine Arts, New York University 1976, pp. 130–131, no. IX E). These two monuments from Tanis are of Ptolemaic date, possibly products of a hybrid art made for or influenced by Greek settlers in the eastern Delta, while two other examples (Vatican, Mus.Greg.Eg. 107 and Belgium, Mariemont E 51) with exaggerated figures may be adaptations made in Egypt under Roman rule: see pls. 109 and 112 in Roullet, *Monuments*, p. 94, notes 103 and 106. The last two examples, less stylized, may have been made in Egypt early in the Roman period: a colossal statue from Rhacotis near the so-called Pompey's pillar, Alexandria 14941 (see Bothmer, *ESLP*) and the small queen beside the legs of a colossal striding Pharaoh, east of Alexandria at Ma'amra in the Delta (Bothmer, *ESLP*, and J. Leclant, "Fouilles et travaux en Égypte. 1954–1955," *Orientalia*, n.s. 25, 1956 [pp. 251–268], pl. LIII, fig. 22).

[25] Particularly two statues: Vatican, Mus.Greg.Eg. 107 and Brussels, Mariemont E 51; see footnote 24 above.

[26] The statues of Arsinoe II are the only ones to preserve the name and titles (see footnote 20 above, p. 8 and footnote 33 below, p. 10).

[27] See footnote 21 above, p. 8.

[28] Thompson, *Ptolemaic Oinochoai*, pp. 74–75, 117–119.

[29] The peculiar Athenian arrangement of the mantle (see pp. 6–7 above) does suggest an actual, practical use of the costume; see also pp. 31–32 below.

[30] See footnote 8 above, p. 6.

date, difficulties arise in trying to identify who is represented.[31] If these were known to represent Isis and could be dated, then there would be important assistance in determining when Isis first appeared in the knotted, fringed mantle. The majority of these statues, uninscribed and headless, escape identification. They are so varied in style and execution that they have not been dated.[32] From the four statues with inscriptions preserved, we learn that they may simply represent the queen or a private person.[33]

It has been all too tempting to identify these Egyptian statues of Ptolemaic and Roman date as Isis or a queen in the role of Isis,[34] but the inscribed statues mentioned above indicate the need for caution. Could the ceremonial use of this knotted, fringed mantle, long important in Egypt,[35] be sufficient explanation for its popularity in representations of the goddess Isis in the Roman Empire?

The interpretation of these Egyptian statues with knotted, fringed mantle as queens in the form of Isis stems from the frequent assimilation of the Ptolemaic queens to Isis.[36] Difficulties repeatedly arise in trying to determine which queen emphasized her role as Isis. With which queen was this role so important that a costume could be associated with it?

There is little evidence to identify any queen who promoted herself as Isis and wore a specific costume for that role. One should remember that in Egypt under the Ptolemies deification of kings and queens was customary after death. The second queen, Arsinoe II, was the first queen to be deified, after her death in 270 B.C.[37] From the inscriptions, we learn that Arsinoe II, dead and deified, was the first to be called Isis.[38] The inscriptions preserved

---

[31] *Ibid.* The confusion concerning the identification of these statues is mentioned by Dunand (*Religion populaire*, p. 21, note 40) and by Bianchi (*BES* 2, 1980, pp. 18–19).

[32] Stricker, *OMRL* 41, 1960, pp. 24–30, pls. XVII–XXII.

[33] Two statues bear the name and titles of Arsinoe II without any reference to Isis and show Arsinoe in the knotted mantle: Chicago Oriental Institute 10158 (Fraser, *loc. cit.* [footnote 20 above, p. 8]) and M.M.A. 20.2.21 (Bothmer, *ESLP*, no. 123). A third statue of a queen in this costume, M.M.A. 89.2.660 (Bothmer, *ESLP*, no. 113), simply has the name Cleopatra in a cartouche. The fourth statue is Leiden F 1960/3,1 (Stricker, *OMRL* 41, 1960, p. 20, pls. XIX, XX), but it is inscribed in Greek as a dedication *to* Isis, not as a representation *of* Isis. It is a votive statue given by a man named Dionysios in thanks to Isis for having heard (his prayer): Ἴσιδι ἀκοῖς Διονύσιος υἱός Ἀπαουήρ εὐχαριστῶ. It seems unlikely that the name of the woman in the knotted costume was to have been included in the inscription because the latter, in two lines covering the back pillar, is complete. The Leiden votive would then be a statue of an unnamed woman similar to the late Antonine statue given to Isis and found in the sanctuary of Isis at Tauromenium: Palermo, M.N. 704 (Pl. 51).

[34] Concerning the confusion, see footnote 31 above.

[35] See footnote 21 above, p. 8.

[36] Fraser, *Ptolemaic Alexandria*, pp. 221, 239, 240, chap. 5, note 249; Dunand, *Le Culte d'Isis* I, pp. 36, 38, 40–41.

[37] Fraser, *Ptolemaic Alexandria*, p. 236 and Dunand, *Le Culte d'Isis* I, pp. 35–36. The traditional date for Arsinoe's deification, 270 B.C., is maintained by Quaegebeur ("Reines ptolémaïques," p. 262 and *JNES* 30, 1971, p. 242). Fraser (*op. cit.*, pp. 216–217) proposes that Arsinoe II was deified with her husband as Theoi Adelphoi in 272/1 B.C. on the basis of the Hibeh papyri 199 and 99, a theory accepted by Thompson (*Ptolemaic Oinochoai*, p. 56, note 3), although Fraser's date is questioned by A. E. Samuel (*American Studies in Papyrology*, II, *Yale Papyri*, New Haven/Toronto 1967, pp. 66–67, no. 28).

[38] Fraser, *Ptolemaic Alexandria*, pp. 236–237. Thompson (*Ptolemaic Oinochoai*, pp. 58–59) draws attention to the Pithom stele (Cairo CG 22183) of 264/3 B.C. (after the queen's death), on which Arsinoe is called "Arsinoe image of Isis and Hathor", and represents Arsinoe in the knotted mantle as "costumed as Isis", hence assimilated with the goddess Isis, but the identification with two goddesses again negates the exclusiveness of the dress to Isis at that time.

for Arsinoe II are not only extensive but also clearly indicate that the epithet Isis was simply one of this queen's titles, appropriate in sanctuaries sacred to Isis and rarely used else-where.[39] From Ptolemy III on, after 243/2 b.c., queens were regularly deified with their husbands shortly after accession to the throne.[40] The names of numerous divinities used for Arsinoe II may well have continued as customary titles for following generations.

If assimilation to the goddess Isis was an important and noteworthy step for the Ptolemaic queens, then it may not have occurred until late.[41] One possible candidate for the event is Cleopatra III (born *ca.* 160–155 b.c.), who in the inscriptions and papyri seems to have had the greatest accumulation of titles of Isis.[42] A second possibility is the last queen, Cleopatra VII (69–30 b.c.). According to Plutarch, this one, the famous Cleopatra, called herself the New Isis and wore the dress of Isis on several occasions.[43] This flamboyant ruler may seem to be the most likely to have been responsible for the promotion and establishment of the knotted, fringed mantle as the dress of Isis. Plutarch, however, writing in the 2nd century after Christ, does not describe the dress of Isis worn by Cleopatra. Unfortunately, there are no statues preserved that are inscribed to this or any Ptolemaic queen which show her wearing the knotted, fringed mantle and also give her the name of Isis.[44]

THE HELLENISTIC COSTUME AND HAIRSTYLE OF ISIS

It is difficult to assess the frequency and importance of the various costumes worn by Isis prior to the Roman Empire, either within or beyond Egypt in the 3rd through 1st centuries b.c., when the cult of Isis was being established in the Mediterranean.

There are Greek (Hellenistic) monuments in Egypt which, for the purpose of this study, should be considered first. The diversity of artistic styles represented increases the difficulties in assessing this material. Under the Ptolemies, the monuments of Egypt included those reflecting their Greek heritage or Hellenistic art, various mixtures of Greek

---

[39] Isis was one of the epithets of Arsinoe II. Her various epithets correspond to the queen as "σύνναος θεά", sharing altar and sanctuary with other gods: Quaegebeur, *JNES* 30, 1971, pp. 242–243 and "Reines ptolé-maïques," pp. 249–254; Fraser, *Ptolemaic Alexandria*, pp. 235–243; Thompson, *Ptolemaic Oinochoai*, pp. 58–59. Four of the 61 hieroglyphic inscriptions which include the name of Isis vary in formula: "Isis (Arsinoe)" on the naos from Sais, Louvre C 123 (Quaegaebeur, *BIFAO* 69, 1970, pp. 202 and 212, doc. 19); "(Isis-Arsinoe)" on a Ma'sara relief (*ibid.*, p. 212, doc. 20); "(Arsinoe) thea philadelphos, Isis" on a Memphis stele, B.M. 379 (*ibid.*, p. 210, doc. 17); "(Arsinoe) image of Isis and Hathor" on the Pithom stele, Cairo CG 22183 (*ibid.*, p. 210, doc. 9); stele of priest of Isis and Arsinoe at Memphis, Louvre C 124 (Quaegebeur, *JNES* 30, 1971, pp. 254–256). Similarly there are only four Greek inscriptions to Isis-Arsinoe from Egypt: *Orientis graeci inscriptiones selectae* 31, SB 601 and 602; and one from Canopus (Dunand, *Le Culte d'Isis* I, p. 35, note 6, p. 113, note 4 and II, p. 33; Quaegebeur, *BIFAO* 69, 1970, p. 202). On the oinochoai inscribed to "Agathe Tyche, Arsinoe Philadelphos, Isis", Arsinoe appears to have been represented in the common dress of chiton and plain mantle (Thompson, *Ptolemaic Oinochoai*, pp. 142–149, no. 1).

[40] Fraser, *Ptolemaic Alexandria*, pp. 219–220.

[41] *Ibid.*, p. 244.

[42] *Ibid.*

[43] *Ibid.*; Plutarch, *Antonius*, 54; Dunand, *Le Culte d'Isis* I, pp. 42–43; Heyob, *Cult of Isis*, p. 20.

[44] One should note that a fragmentary statue in a finely pleated linen dress at Karnak, a queen of the New Kingdom, is reinscribed to Cleopatra II in a cartouche; no reference to Isis was made. See Bianchi, *BES* 2, 1980, p. 11; J. Lauffray, "Rapport sur les travaux de Karnak," *Kêmi* 20, 1970, p. 71, fig. 13, pl. XV; *idem*, "Communication: les activités du Centre franco-égyptien des Temples de Karnak en 1969," *Comptes rendus des séances de l'Académie des Inscriptions et Belles-lettres*, 1970, p. 142, fig. 1.

and Egyptian, and traditional Egyptian works of art. Little is known concerning the Hellenistic Isis in Egypt. The earliest securely dated representation of Isis is on coins of Ptolemy V (221–204 B.C.); here the head of her consort, Sarapis, overlaps that of Isis and permits only her profile (with the hair parted over the forehead) and the emblem of Isis to be seen.[45]

The emblem of Isis and the corkscrew hairstyle are the only features characteristic of the Hellenistic Isis in Egypt. The former, a sun disk framed by horns and topped by two feathers, is a crown worn by several Egyptian goddesses and queens from the New Kingdom on;[46] it seems, however, to have been used to designate Isis in Hellenistic representations from Egypt and is a feature exclusive to Isis in the Mediterranean under Roman rule.[47] The second feature specific to Isis is the hairstyle with thick corkscrew locks set in tiers.[48] It is also of Egyptian origin, recalling the various Egyptian ceremonial wigs.[49] These two features are known from a few monuments of the 2nd and 1st centuries B.C., such as a seal impression from Edfu and three marble heads of Isis in Alexandria and Cairo.[50] Unfortunately these monuments preserve only the head of Isis.

[45] Hornbostel, *Sarapis*, pp. 141–142, pl. XLIII, fig. 68; this type also appears on the coins of Ptolemy VI: see E. Breccia, *Alexandrea ad Aegyptum*, Bergamo 1922, p. 303, fig. 218.

[46] M. Münster ("Untersuchungen zur Göttin Isis vom Alten Reich bis zum Ende des Neuen Reiches," *Münchner ägyptologische Studien* 11, 1968, pp. 118–119) observes that the Hathor emblem of disk and horns is also worn by Isis in the Middle Kingdom; the crown of disk, horns, and feathers is worn by several goddesses and queens in the New Kingdom, but they remain separate unless inscriptions or literary evidence indicate that they have been assimilated to one another (p. 146). The latter crown is worn by all the Ptolemaic queens except Arsinoe II: Quaegebeur, "Reines ptolémaïques," p. 257, note 85.

[47] For Hellenistic examples, see footnote 64 below, p. 14. For representations of Isis in the Roman Empire, see imperial coins from Alexandria: R. S. Poole, *BMC Alexandria*, pls. XIV and XVI; see Dunand, *Le Culte d'Isis* I, pp. 80–81 and II, p. 148 for a discussion of the emblem of Isis. A lotus is worn on archaizing representations of Isis in the Roman period, such as the terracotta plaque from the site of the Temple of Apollo on the Palatine in Rome (W. von Sydow, "Archäologische Funde und Forschungen im Bereich der Soprintendenz Rom 1957–1973," *AA* [*JdI* 88], 1973 [pp. 521–647], p. 605, fig. 50) and dated by Andreae (*Art of Rome*, pp. 39–40) to *ca.* 28 B.C. A feather is the most whimsical Isiac emblem; see the contemporary paintings and stucco ceiling reliefs from the villa found below the Farnesina in Rome: *ibid.*, p. 379, fig. 286 and figs. 281, 282.

[48] The long corkscrew locks are thought to be natural hair worn by Egyptian women: Needler, *Berytus* 9, 1949, pp. 138–139. On the other hand, the traditional ceremonial wigs (that fall deep over the shoulders and often have tiny corkscrew locks set in tiers) are the best prototype for the tiered hairstyle popular for Ptolemaic queens and Hellenistic representations of Isis: see a statue of Ptolemaic or Roman date in Amsterdam (Stricker, *OMRL* 41, 1960, pp. 25 and 27, pl. XXI, fig. 1) and the New Kingdom examples, Nefertiti on a relief from Tell el Amarna, CG 54517 (C. Aldred, *Art in Ancient Egypt*, London 1972, fig. 110) and a statue of queen Tiye, Cairo JE 38257 (*ibid.*, figs. 83 and 84).

[49] See the imperial coins from Alexandria, Poole (footnote 47 above), pls. XIV and XVI. See statues of Isis throughout the Roman Empire, such as that from the south slope of the Akropolis (see p. 63 below), from Gortyna, Crete (Pl. 19), from Ras-el-Soda, Egypt (Pl. 52), and from Laodicea ad Lycum, Asia Minor (L. Kahil in J. des Gagniers *et al.*, *Laodicée du Lycos*, Paris 1969 [pp. 187–244], pp. 189–192, pls. LXI–LXIII).

[50] Edfu seal: Kyrieleis (footnote 20 above, p. 8), pp. 115–117, pl. 100, fig. 3. The marble heads of Isis, Hellenistic in style and execution, are briefly discussed by A. Adriani, *Testimonianze e momenti di scultura alessandrina*, Rome 1948, p. 14, pls. IV–VI (Alexandria); p. 26, pl. X:2 (Alexandria 25724); pl. X:3, 4 (Cairo JE 39517). On the latter, see Grimm (footnote 4 above, p. 5), p. 18, no. 10, pl. 11. The first head has a dowel hole for the attachment of a diadem and a second hole for the emblem of Isis, while the others have a hole for the emblem but the diadem carved; Alexandria 25724, however, has not been fully described or photographed.

For the pose and dress of Isis, we must look to the baffling array of terracotta figurines from Egypt.[51] Because these figurines have not been dated individually, it is hard to determine which is the most popular type of Isis in Egypt either prior to or during Roman rule. They have been considered to have been made at the earliest in the 1st century B.C. and to have been produced in greatest number in the 1st through 3rd centuries after Christ.[52]

In Egypt under the Ptolemies, there may have been a cult statue of Isis as a companion to that of her consort Sarapis. According to literary tradition, the statue of Sarapis was the work of an Athenian sculptor, Bryaxis, active in the 4th century B.C.[53] Although Fraser and Hornbostel discredit this attribution, they convincingly argue for a date in the early 3rd century B.C. for the commission and creation of the cult statue of the god Sarapis for the Sarapieion in Alexandria.[54] Müller suggested that the companion statue to Sarapis may have been of Isis seated and breastfeeding her child Harpokrates.[55] His suggestion seems unlikely as the only representation of this type of Isis with Sarapis is found on a gold relief plaque in the Louvre, a late and obviously eclectic work.[56] Whenever the two deities are shown together, Isis is standing.[57] It may be that if there was a companion statue, it was an

[51] See Dunand, *Religion populaire*, pp. 18–29 and *Le Culte d'Isis* I, pls. XVII–XXIX, XXXIV–XLIV; Tran Tam Tinh, *Isis Lactans*, pp. 31–35; Hornbostel, *Sarapis*, p. 254. Although the chronology of these figurines is poorly defined owing in part to the fact that few are from dated contexts, the variety is amazing, and only a few repeat types found elsewhere, such as Isis-Demeter (Dunand, *Religion populaire*, pl. XXVI:41) or Isis-Fortuna (pl. XXX:48). Isis breastfeeding Harpokrates is particularly numerous: see Tran Tam Tinh, *Isis Lactans*.

[52] *Ibid.*

[53] This attribution was made by Athenodoros of Tarsus, cited by Clement of Alexandria, *Protrepticus* IV.8; on this sculptor, see Hornbostel, *Sarapis*, pp. 36–58, 103–126 and G. M. A. Richter, *The Sculpture and Sculptors of the Greeks*, New Haven 1941, pp. 279–281.

[54] Fraser, *OpusAth* 7, 1967, pp. 23–35 and p. 36, note 55 on the establishment of the cult in Egypt; Hornbostel, *Sarapis*, pp. 35–59 and 103–126.

[55] H. W. Müller, "Isis mit dem Horuskinde," *Münchner Jahrbuch der bildenden Kunst* 14, 1963 (pp. 7–38), p. 13. Tran Tam Tinh (*Isis Lactans*, pp. 31–35) considers the original of this Isis to be of the 3rd century B.C.; artist and place of the original are unknown to him. Joint dedications found in foundation deposits of the Sarapieion suggest that statues of Sarapis and Isis were in this temple: Fraser, *OpusAth* 7, 1967, p. 38 and *Ptolemaic Alexandria*, pp. 267–268.

[56] Louvre E 14.268 is placed in the early 3rd century after Christ by Müller (*op. cit.*, pp. 31–32, fig. 27). A 2nd-century date given by Tran Tam Tinh (*Isis Lactans*, pp. 68–70, pl. XXXVII) is unlikely, considering the broad figures and paratactic arrangement popular in the 3rd century, e.g., a relief of Alexandrian gods, Rome, Mus.Cap. 4371 (Hornbostel, *Sarapis*, pl. CXV) and the Capitoline gods on the arch of Septimius Severus at Lepcis Magna (A. M. McCann, *The Portraits of Septimius Severus [A.D. 193–211]* [Memoirs of the American Academy in Rome XXX], 1968, pl. XX:1).

[57] Hellenistic reliefs: Hornbostel, *Sarapis*, pl. CCVI, fig. 355 (Rhodes) and fig. 356 (Erythai); Dunand, *Le Culte d'Isis* II, pl. XXXVII (Delos) and III, pl. I (Xanthos). On the imperial coins from Alexandria of the reign of Trajan, Isis and Sarapis stand (Poole [footnote 47 above, p. 12], pl. XIV, no. 448); Isis stands beside Sarapis enthroned (*ibid.*, no. 449); and Sarapis is enthroned and flanked by standing figures of Demeter and Tyche in a naos (G. Dattari, *Monete imperiali Greche numi Augg. Alexandrini. Catalogo della collezione G. Dattari, compilato dal proprietario*, Cairo 1901, nos. 1152–1154). Imperial coins from Asia Minor: W. Drexler, "Der Isis- und Sarapis-cultus in Kleinasien," *Numismatische Zeitschrift* 11, 1889, pp. 1–234; D. Magie, "Egyptian Deities in Asia Minor in Inscriptions and on Coins," *AJA* 57, 1953 (pp. 163–187), p. 181. Reliefs of Roman date from Egypt show an enthroned Sarapis flanked by Demeter and Isis standing: Hornbostel, *Sarapis*, pl. CXCIV, figs. 319, 320 and pl. CCXX, fig. 373. A lamp from Athens of the 3rd century after Christ shows Isis in chiton and mantle standing beside an enthroned Sarapis in a temple façade: J. Perlzweig, *The Athenian Agora*, VII, *Lamps of the Roman Period*, Princeton 1961, no. 805, pp. 121–122, pl. 18.

Isis distinguished only by emblem and hairstyle. The latter suggestion seems likely, to judge from the numerous and varied terracotta figurines of Isis from Egypt, which have only been assigned to the time between the 1st century B.C.(?) and the 3rd century after Christ.[58]

Beyond Egypt, the Hellenistic representations of Isis in the Mediterranean also present a wide variety of dress and hairstyle.[59] The few that wear the knotted mantle need not have the distinctive corkscrew locks nor the most helpful feature for identification, the emblem of Isis atop the head.[60] The variety corresponds well to the wide range of epithets for Isis popular in the Hellenistic period.[61] Local iconographic inventions for the different types of Isis, such as Isis-Aphrodite and Isis-Nike, seem to explain the diversity of and few parallels for terracotta figurines of Isis from the islands of Thera and Delos and from the cities of Priene and Myrina, which at the earliest should be dated to the end of the 2nd century B.C.[62]

It may not be coincidental that the earliest preserved representations of Isis in the Mediterranean are from the island of Rhodes, a major sea power in Hellenistic times.[63] They should be dated to the third quarter of the 2nd century B.C. and are followed by slightly later replicas from the islands of Kos and Delos and from the port cities of Cyrene in North Africa and Corinth on the Greek mainland.[64] This majestic figure with arms set outwards like a

[58] Few are from dated contexts, and no chronology has thus far been determined; see footnote 51 above, p. 13.

[59] See Dunand, *Le Culte d'Isis* II, pls. XXXII, XXXIV–XXXVII (Delos), XLII (Thera); III, pls. V (Rhodes); VIII (Priene); XII (Myrina).

[60] For the corkscrew locks and the emblem of Isis, see p. 12 above. For the various types of the Hellenistic Isis, see Dunand, *Le Culte d'Isis* II, pl. XLII (Thera), III, pl. VII (Priene); from Delos, see Marcadé, *Délos*, pl. LVII: A 378, A 2255, A 5370, A 5373; from Kos, see L. Laurenzi, "Sculture inedite del Museo di Coo," *Annuario della Scuola Archeologica di Atene* 17–18, 1955–1956 (1957; pp. 59–156), pp. 92–93, no. 48; from western Crete, Athens N.M. 224 (R. Horn, *Stehende weibliche Gewandstatuen in der hellenistischen Plastik*, *RM*, Ergänzungsheft II, 1931, p. 40, pl. 17:1). There is an unusual statuette from Rhodes: see G. Kostantino-poulos, «Ἀρχαιοτήτες καὶ μνημεῖα Δωδεκανήσου», Δελτ 22, 1967, Β' 2 (1969; pp. 514–540), p. 533, pl. 389:B. Belonging with these representations of Isis is a statuette in Turin of unknown provenience; it has a dowel hole for the attachment of the emblem of Isis: A. J. B. Wace, "Some Sculptures at Turin," *Journal of Hellenic Studies* 26, 1906, pp. 240–241 and Horn, *op. cit.*, pl. 17:2.

[61] For various titles and types of Isis, see Dunand, *Le Culte d'Isis* I, pp. 80–108; II, pls. XVI, XXII, XXIII, XXVII, XXIX, XXXII, XXXIV–XXXVIII, XLII; III, pls. I–III, V, VIII, XII, XV, XVI, XX. See also Witt, "Isis-Hellas," pp. 48–69 and *Isis*, pp. 111–129.

[62] Dunand, *Le Culte d'Isis* II, pl. XLII (Thera), Isis-Aphrodite, p. 129, pls. XXIV, XXV (Delos); III, pl. VIII (Priene), Isis-Nike, p. 60; pl. XII (Myrina), Isis-Aphrodite, p. 263. Isis figurines from Delos have been dated to the 2nd and 1st centuries B.C. by A. Laumonier (*Exploration archéologique de Délos*, XXIII, *Les Figurines de Terre Cuite*, Paris 1956, pp. 140–143), but they could be later; he does consider some figurines to be of Roman date (p. 190, no. 655, pl. 66). The Isis figurines from Delos should be contemporary with figurines from Myrina that compare well with those by Diphilos, A.D. 20–70: D. B. Thompson, *Terra-cottas from Myrina*, Vienna 1934, pp. 10–13, 33, fig. 8 and pl. IV:9. Isis figurines from Thera and Priene should be of the late 1st century B.C. as they compare well with the Myrina Cupid and Psyche (*ibid.*, pp. 36–37, pl. VI) and the Muse relief of Archelaos, *ca.* 130 B.C. (D. Pinkwart, "Das Relief des Archelaos von Priene," *Antike Plastik* 4, 1965, p. 64, pls. 28–35).

[63] Two votive reliefs from Rhodes and a statue from Catajo in Vienna; Laurenzi considers the last a copy of Roman date of a Hellenistic original similar to the Isis on the reliefs: L. Laurenzi, "Rilievi e statue d'arte Rodia," *RM* 54, 1939, pp. 44–50, figs. 3–5 and pl. 13.

[64] *Ibid.* Statuettes from Kos, Delos, and Cyrene should be slightly later than the Rhodian statue (see footnote 63 above) owing to the flattened pose and simplified drapery: see Laurenzi (footnote 60 above),

Hellenistic ruler may have originated on Rhodes, as suggested by Laurenzi,[65] and would be appropriate for Isis in her role as mistress of the sea.[66] Isis is known from inscriptions as protectress ($\sigma\acute{\omega}\tau\epsilon\iota\rho\alpha$) on Rhodes and Delos, as provider of good sailing ($\epsilon\mathring{v}\theta\pi\lambda o\hat{\iota}a$), and as mistress of the open sea ($\pi\epsilon\lambda\alpha\gamma\acute{\iota}a$) at Corinth.[67]

The few representations of cult statues of Isis that have come down to us are not very helpful concerning a possible prototype for the Isis popular in the Roman Empire. The cult statue seems to have been a conservative image hardly distinguishable from other Greek goddesses. The fragmentary, colossal statue of Isis occupying the Isieion on Delos, 128/7 B.C., has the appearance of Aphrodite, leaning to her left and dressed in a chiton with a heavy mantle draped low about her hips.[68] Apparently, a common cult image of Isis was a standing figure in chiton and plain mantle, diagonally draped from her left shoulder. This type is known as early as 117/6 B.C., to judge from the representation of Isis on coins from Athens,[69] and as late as the emperor Vespasian (A.D. 69–79), on coins from Rome.[70] The latter show the cult statue for the Iseum Campense in Rome, the most important sanctuary of Isis in the Roman Empire.[71]

The earliest preserved examples of Isis in the Roman period, which show the goddess in her most popular dress with knot and fringe and corkscrew wig, are three statues in Rome,

pp. 92–93, no. 48; Marcadé, *Délos*, pl. LVII: A 378; E. Paribeni, *Catalogo delle Sculture di Cirene*, Rome 1959, p. 143, pl. 180, fig. 414. The fragment from Corinth has not been dated (Johnson, *Corinth* IX, p. 68, no. 123) but may belong to the Roman period. None of the other Isis types are earlier than those from Rhodes. The statuette from Crete, Athens, N.M. 224, should be of the late 2nd century B.C. by close comparison with the Muse relief of Archelaos (Pinkwart [footnote 62 above, p. 14] pp. 55–56, pls. 28–35) and not of the late 3rd century B.C. as suggested by Thompson (*Ptolemaic Oinochoai*, pp. 88 and 113).

[65] Laurenzi (footnote 63 above, p. 14), pp. 44–50.

[66] The concept of mistress of the sea is explained by Dunand, *Le Culte d'Isis* II, pp. 118, 120; III, pp. 110, 116, 256.

[67] Inscriptions: Rhodes, Dunand, *Le Culte d'Isis* III, p. 24 and Vidman, *Sylloge*, no. 198; Delos, Dunand, *Le Culte d'Isis* II, pp. 113–114 and Roussel, *Cultes égyptiens*, nos. 147 and 194; Corinth, Dunand, *Le Culte d'Isis* II, pp. 156–157 and Vidman, *Sylloge*, no. 34. Concerning Corinth, Pausanias (II.4.6) in the 2nd century after Christ mentions a sanctuary of Isis Pelagia and one of the Egyptian Isis, but what is meant by the latter and where these sanctuaries were is unknown (Dunand, *Le Culte d'Isis* II, p. 18). The Isis from Rhodes has a commanding, regal pose and is not holding forth the sails as found on representations of Isis Pelagia; for the latter, see P. Bruneau, "Isis Pélagia à Délos," *BCH* 85, 1961, pp. 435–446 and "Isis Pélagia à Délos (Compléments)," *BCH* 87, 1963, pp. 301–308; E. R. Williams, "Isis Pelagia and a Roman Marble Matrix from the Athenian Agora," *Hesperia* 54, 1985, pp. 109–119. Isis Pelagia is a title that may be of the early 1st century B.C. at the earliest (Dunand, *Le Culte d'Isis* III, p. 98, note 5). Dunand (*Le Culte d'Isis* I, pp. 94–95) suggests that Isis as mistress of the sea may be the harbor goddess of Alexandria in Egypt, but Fraser (*Ptolemaic Alexandria*, p. 20) has identified that harbor goddess with Isis Pharia who is first known in the Roman period and is represented with a sail like Isis Pelagia: see Bruneau, *BCH* 85, 1961, *loc. cit.* and *BCH* 87, 1963, pp. 306–308.

[68] Dunand, *Le Culte d'Isis* II, pls. XXXI, XXXII and Marcadé, *Délos*, p. 429, pl. LVII; for inscription and date, see Roussel, *Cultes égyptiens*, no. 86, p. 134.

[69] Coins from Athens are cited by Dow (*HThR* 30, 1937, p. 207) and by Dunand, *Le Culte d'Isis* II, p. 12, note 1). See J. N. Svoronos, *Trésor de la numismatique grecque ancienne*, Munich 1923-1926, pl. 70, nos. 15–19 and M. Thompson, *The New Style Silver Coinage of Athens*, New York 1961, p. 372, pl. 131, nos. 1169b, 1173–1178, of 117/6 B.C.

[70] Roullet, *Monuments*, pp. 23–26, pl. XV, fig. 22.

[71] *Ibid.* and F. Le Corsu, *Isis: mythe et mystères*, Paris 1977, pp. 186–187.

Naples, and Athens.[72] I would date them no earlier than the reign of Caligula, the 40's of the 1st century after Christ.[73] In Egypt, the earliest dated imperial representations of Isis are found on coins of Domitian.[74] Although these two emperors promoted the Egyptian cults,[75] the cited statues of Isis of the 1st century after Christ do not seem likely candidates for the prototype of the popular image of Isis in the Roman period.

LITERARY DESCRIPTIONS OF THE COSTUME OF ISIS

In the literature that has come down to us, neither the dress nor the ornamentation of the goddess Isis is well defined.[76] In the Hymn from the island of Andros from the first third of the 1st century B.C., the dress of Isis is linen, and flowers adorn the thick tresses of her hair.[77] Linen is mentioned by successive Roman authors,[78] but according to Plutarch and Apuleius[79] the dress is also one of many colors.

The only lengthy passage describing the goddess is that written by Apuleius (*Metamorphoses* XI.3–4) in the second half of the 2nd century after Christ. It produces a rich, if confusing, image which J. G. Griffiths attempts to clarify in his translation.[80] Two garments are worn by Isis: a tunic of many colors, *tunica multicolor*, and a very black cloak, *palla nigerrima*. The latter, according to Griffiths, may have been the knotted, fringed

[72] Statue of Isis and Harpokrates from Palazzo Barberini, Rome: Munich, Glyp. 250 (Pl. 7); statue in gray marble, Naples, M.N. 6372 (Pl. 7); fragmentary statue in dark Eleusinian limestone from the south slope of the Akropolis, Athens: I. Meliades, «Ἀνασκαφαὶ νοτίως τῆς Ἀκροπόλεως», Πρακτικά, 1955 (1960; pp. 36–52), p. 49.

[73] See p. 70 below; the Isis in Naples, M.N. 6372 (Pl. 7) is less bulky than the other two. It also belongs to the 40's because of the figure proportions, short-waisted and with a thick torso, and especially because of the equal treatment of every feature and detail, drapery and hairstyle, rendering all clear and ornamental. The high placement of the knot of the fringed mantle is characteristic of Tiberian and Caligulan figures in this dress (Pls. 6, 7). In view of the drapery, worn snug to and revealing her legs, this Naples Isis could be a forerunner of the popular Isis type in the Flavian period (p. 72 below, Pls. 13–17); the snug folds are symmetrically arranged and decorative, lacking the Flavian characteristic of taut folds pulling against the figure curiously as if to contain and restrict the figure's movement.

[74] Dattari (footnote 57 above, p. 13), pl. XVII, no. 503; on the coins of Galba (*ibid.*, pl. XVII, no. 378) a similar bust of Isis is shown, but the image is worn, obscuring any trace of the fringed mantle, if indeed she wore it. The latter is cited by Adriani ([footnote 50 above, p. 12] p. 84) as the earliest example of Isis in the corkscrew wig on imperial coins from Alexandria.

[75] See Hornbostel, *Sarapis*, pp. 368–369 (Caligula) and 375–377 (Domitian); Heyob, *Cult of Isis*, pp. 25 (Caligula) and 27–28 (Domitian).

[76] Lafaye (DarSag III, i, 1908, p. 579) cites the Hymn from Andros I.1 and 18; Tibullus, *Elegies* I.3.27; *Anthol. Pal.* VI.231.1; Plutarch, *de Is. et Os.*, 77; Apuleius, *Metamorphoses* XI.3–4.

[77] Hymn from Andros I.1 (linen) and 18 (flowers); Lafaye, DarSag III, i, p. 579, notes 5 and 7; Dunand, *Le Culte d'Isis* II, pp. 116–118; Peek (footnote 2 above, p. 1); *IG* XII 5, 739.

[78] Tibullus, *Elegies* I.3.27, reign of Augustus: Stricker, *OMRL* 41, 1960, p. 22, note 10 and Griffiths, *De Iside*, p. 270. Seneca, *de vita beata* XXVI.8, reign of Tiberius: Dunand, *Le Culte d'Isis* III, p. 218. Apuleius, *Metamorphoses* XI.3, second half of the 2nd century after Christ. Ovid, *Metamorphoses* I.570: see Tran Tam Tinh, *Essai*, p. 74, note 3. Lafaye (DarSag III, i, p. 579) names the linen dress: λινόπεπλος, λινόστολος, and *linigera*. Lafaye (*loc. cit.*, note 7) also cites *Anthol. Pal.* VI.231.1 (Phillip of Thessaloniki).

[79] Plutarch, *de Is. et Os.*, 77 and Apuleius, *Metamorphoses* XI.3, 2nd century after Christ; Lafaye, DarSag III, i, p. 579; Griffiths, *De Iside*, p. 562; Griffiths, *The Isis Book*, p. 127.

[80] Griffiths, *The Isis Book*, pp. 124–130.

mantle, which we have mentioned repeatedly as the most popular dress of Isis in the Roman Empire. If we follow the description of Apuleius in this passage, we find that a knot and fringe are mentioned directly after the draping of the black mantle, but owing to the incompleteness of the wording, it is not clear to which garment the knot and fringe belong.[81]

Apuleius' description may have blended together features of several garments worn by the goddess. Fringe occurs on two other garments as found on the extant representations of Isis: a short veil worn over the head and a narrow stole.[82] The stole is often black in Pompeian wall paintings, including one from the Iseum.[83] Cosmic designs, mentioned by Apuleius as decoration for the black mantle worn by Isis, are also found as decoration of the stole.[84]

The rich attire of Isis described by Apuleius may have been chosen to evoke the wealth, power, and great beauty with which Isis was thought to be endowed.[85] His description recalls the numerous epithets and the variety in appearance of the goddess in Hellenistic representations. Like the flower-laden locks of Isis in the late Hellenistic Hymn from Andros,[86] flowers almost magically appear in her hair and dress in Apuleius' description.

According to Griffiths, there is no exact parallel for the elaborate crown worn by Isis as described by Apuleius.[87] It resembles, however, a variety of decorations atop the goddess' head in terracotta figurines from Egypt, assigned to the late Hellenistic and Roman periods.[88] The description may have been a mixture of several costumes and headdresses, intended to evoke the immediacy as well as the impressiveness of her appearance, rather than a specific attire of this goddess.

[81] Griffiths, *The Isis Book*, pp. 70–75 and 124–130.

[82] Isis with veil: see Tran Tam Tinh, *Campanie*, p. 64, note 2. The following statues should be added to his list: Isis from the Terme at Lepcis Magna (R. Bartoccini, *Le Terme di Lepcis*, Bergamo 1929, p. 162, fig. 173); Rome, Pal.Cons. (H. Stuart Jones, *The Sculptures of the Palazzo dei Conservatori*, Oxford 1926, p. 84, no. 15, pl. 30); Vatican, Mus.Greg.Eg. 83 (Pl. 41); Rome, Mus.Cap. (H. Stuart Jones, *The Sculptures of the Museo Capitolino*, Oxford 1912, p. 320, no. 14, pl. 77; the head has been incorrectly restored as traces of the veil on the shoulders indicate that the head should be veiled). Lafaye (DarSag III, i, p. 579) suggests that the veil represents concealment of the mysteries. On the stole, see Griffiths, *The Isis Book*, pp. 128–129 and 130–131, Tran Tam Tinh, *Campanie*, p. 82, note 1, and Tran Tam Tinh, *Essai*, pp. 74–75; see also the relief of Galatea in the Vatican (Pl. 51).

[83] Tran Tam Tinh, *Essai*, pp. 75 and 143, note 47, pl. X:1 from the Iseum; p. 127, note 13, pl. XIX:1 from Casa delle Amazoni (VI, 2, 14); and p. 129, note 17, pl. XV:1 from Casa degli Amorini dorati (VI, 16, 7).

[84] Although four representations cited by Griffiths (*The Isis Book*, p. 130) cannot be identified as Isis, a fifth can: a terracotta from Abella, Campania (London, B.M. D 285; Tran Tam Tinh, *Campanie*, pp. 81–82, pl. XXI), where the stole is decorated with dots and has fringe. The other representation in the round showing Isis with a stole is the statue known as Isis-Barberini, Naples, M.N.: A. Levi, "L'Iside Barberini," *Monumenti antichi* 28, 1922, cols. 157–170, figs. 1–3; the stole is plain (Pl. 52). Griffiths (*loc. cit.*) suggests that designs could have been painted on the stole; there are traces of red paint on the dress of the votive statue of Isis from the Iseum at Pompeii: J. B. Ward-Perkins and A. Claridge, *Pompeii A.D. 79*, New York 1978, pp. 128–129, no. 191. See also the colossal statue of Isis from Rome: Munich, Glyp. 250 (Pl. 7).

[85] See Vanderlip (footnote 1 above, p. 1), pp. 5–7; Witt, "Isis-Hellas," pp. 48–69.

[86] Hymn from Andros 1.18; *IG* XII 5, 739: Peek (footnote 77 above, p. 16); Lafaye, DarSag III, i, p. 579, note 7; Dunand, *Le Culte d'Isis* II, pp. 116–118. On the vast powers, numerous epithets, and varied representations of Isis, see Witt, "Isis-Hellas" and *Isis*, and especially Dunand, *Le Culte d'Isis* II, pp. 80–106.

[87] Griffiths, *The Isis Book*, pp. 124–131, esp. p. 126 and *De Iside*, p. 252.

[88] Dunand, *Religion populaire*, pp. 18–30.

When did the iconography of Isis that was popular in the Roman Empire become established? We have explored a variety of possible prototypes without a final answer to this question. It is clear that the exotic appearance of the Egyptian fringed mantle and hairstyle thick with corkscrew locks appealed to Greek and Roman taste, but was that sufficient reason for its popularity for representations of Isis in the Roman Empire? We only know for certain that the knotted, fringed garment in Egypt may have served as a form of ceremonial dress as late as the 2nd century B.C.[89]

The dilemma remains unresolved. We may have to await the identification and chronology of the Egyptian statues showing the knotted, fringed mantle before understanding the history of this Egyptian dress in the critical time when the cult of Isis was spreading into the Mediterranean, the 4th through 1st centuries B.C.[90] These Egyptian statues are the best parallel for the dress worn by women on Attic grave reliefs and the best candidate for a possible prototype for the iconography of Isis under the Roman Empire.

HAIRSTYLE OF WOMEN IN THE DRESS OF ISIS

On Attic grave reliefs, women in the dress of Isis usually wear a simple, timeless hairstyle.[91] Waved strands of hair are parted in the center of the forehead and drawn back over the ears to frame the face. A few wear coiffures fashionable in any given period during the Roman Empire.[92]

These women, regardless of coiffure, have long locks of hair that fall to their shoulders. The long locks are important features, recalling the numerous corkscrew locks of the

[89] See the relief on the west pylon inscribed to Ptolemy X at Qus: Kamal (footnote 21 above, p. 8), pp. 227–228.

[90] On the spread of the cult of Isis, see Fraser, *OpusAth* 3, 1960, pp. 1–5.

[91] Muehsam, *Berytus* 10, 1952, pp. 70 and 105; Dunand, *Le Culte d'Isis* II, p. 148. This hairstyle, popular since the 5th century B.C. (see examples on Attic grave reliefs in Diepolder, *Die attischen Grabreliefs*, pls. 10, 26, 30, 42, and 51), was worn by women in the Mediterranean in the Hellenistic period: Attic grave relief (Conze 1869); grave reliefs from Delos (M.-T. Couilloud, *Exploration archéologique de Délos*, XXX, *Les Monuments funéraires de Rhenée*, Paris 1978, pl. 11, no. 56; pl. 13, no. 58; pl. 21, no. 87); from Smyrna (Pfuhl and Möbius, *Die ostgriechischen Grabreliefs* I, pl. 66, nos. 405, 406); in Thessaloniki (P. M. Fraser, *Archaeological Reports*, 1970–1971, p. 19, fig. 36); from Alexandria (G. Grimm and D. Wildung, *Götter Pharaonen* [Essen, Villa Hugel exhibition, 2 June—17 September, 1978], Essen 1978, nos. 103, 104). It is found less frequently in Athens in the Roman period: Athens, N.M. 3725 (late Flavian, Pl. 17); Conze 1951 (Hilara, Trajanic, Pl. 20); and Athens, N.M. 3669 (60's of the 3rd century after Christ, Pl. 48). Women on classicizing reliefs also wear this hairstyle, e.g. Conze 1939–1943; these reliefs are considered to be of the 1st century B.C. by F. Hauser (*Die neu-attischen Reliefs*, Stuttgart 1889, p. 142) and Muehsam (*Berytus* 10, 1952, p. 83, note 4 and p. 108, note 3), but they may be later. Conze 1940 has an inscription dated to the 2nd century after Christ by letter forms (*IG* II², 7042), and a fragment, Agora S 2698 (Pl. 42), is definitely of the second quarter of the 3rd century in style and execution.

This hairstyle is also used for idealized portraits, especially in the 1st century after Christ, and is the standard hairstyle for Greek and Roman goddesses: Polaschek, *TrZ* 35, 1972, pp. 142–143, note 26; see also P. Noelke, "Zum Kopf der 'Meter' Doria-Pamfili," *Bonner Jahrbücher* 167, 1967, pp. 39–57. It continues to be worn by goddesses into the Byzantine period: see Coptic bone carvings (L. Marangou, *Bone Carvings from Egypt*, I, *Graeco-Roman Period, Benaki Museum, Athens*, Tübingen 1976, pl. 55:a–c, nos. 187–189).

[92] Athens, Third Ephoria (Pl. 13); Boston, M.F.A. 1971.209 (Pl. 30); Salamis relief (Pl. 37).

goddess Isis.[93] A few individuals like Lamia Viboullia (Piraeus Museum 1160; Pl. 27) have shoulder-length hair worn loose, which may have been a hairstyle for girls and young women but also bears a resemblance to the thick tresses of Isis.[94]

Usually the long locks are slightly curled and are one to three in number at each side of the neck. They appear to be strands of natural hair not caught up in the waves encircling the head.[95] Exceptionally long locks, such as those on late Hadrianic relief figures, are an artistic convention, an archaizing element.[96]

The long locks may refer to the mourning locks of Isis. According to Plutarch, Isis in mourning for Osiris cut and dedicated a lock of her hair at Coptos, the major temple of Isis in Upper Egypt since the Ptolemies.[97] The gesture is thought to be Greek, although to cut, tear, or pull one's hair in mourning may have been an ancient custom in Egypt as well.[98]

[93] Von Gonzenbach (footnote 1 above, p. 5), p. 902. The corkscrew locks of Isis have been called Libyan locks (Adriani [footnote 50 above, p. 12], p. 9; Needler, *Berytus* 9, 1949, pp. 138–139; Tran Tam Tinh, *Campanie*, p. 33; Thompson, *Ptolemaic Oinochoai*, p. 61), but the latter term is inappropriate, as the two types of locks differ in shape and arrangement. The locks of Isis are long, reaching the shoulders, while short ones frame the face and are often set in tiers: see p. 12 above and Cairo JE 39517 (Grimm [footnote 4 above, p. 5], pls. 11, 12). So-called Libyan locks are sharply pointed and of equal length arranged on a slope starting with the level of the chin: Magas, *ca.* 280 B.C. (R. S. Poole, *BMC Ptolemies*, p. 38, pl. VI, no. 8). In marble these locks are rare: from Egypt, Louvre MA 3546 (Kyrieleis [footnote 20 above, p. 8], p. 185, M 12, pl. 104, figs. 1, 2); those on a bronze bust from Herculaneum (Villa dei Papyri, Naples, M.N. 6141) have been restored (A. Hekler, *Die Bildniskunst der Griechen und Römer,* Stuttgart 1912, pl. 74).

[94] Lamia Viboullia has a "shag-cut" for the locks framing the face, somewhat like the tiered locks of Isis. Such loose hair is also worn by a small figure on a contemporary relief of the early Antonine period (Athens, N.M. 1249, Pl. 28) and by another figure in the dress of Isis on a Claudian relief (Athens, N.M. 1296, Pl. 8). On the latter, a mature woman is seated on the left and may represent the mother of the young woman in the dress of Isis on the right. A little girl on a Hellenistic grave relief from Tarsus (Athens, N.M. 1158) has a similar hairstyle with soft curls: Pfuhl and Möbius, *Die ostgriechischen Grabreliefs* I, pl. 64, fig. 395. For references to the thick tresses of Isis in literature and inscriptions, see Griffiths, *The Isis Book,* p. 124.

[95] See Sosibia (Boston, M.F.A. 1971.209, Pl. 30) and Agathemeris (London, B.M. 630, Pl. 32).

[96] Alexandra (Athens, N.M. 1193, Pl. 24); Elate (Athens, N.M. 1308, Pl. 24). The long locks of Alexandra are considered by K. Parlasca ("Ein Isiskultrelief in Rom," *RM* 71, 1964 [pp. 195–205], pp. 201–202) to be classicizing, but the ornamental arrangement and length recall the long locks of Archaic korai, such as Akropolis 680 and 674: see B. S. Ridgway, *The Archaic Style in Greek Sculpture,* Princeton 1977, p. 107, figs. 20 and 30.

[97] *De Is. et Os.,* 14; Griffiths, *De Iside,* pp. 314–315 and *The Isis Book,* p. 124; Dunand, *Le Culte d'Isis* I, p. 143, note 2 (Coptos). Possibly locks of Isis were also dedicated at Memphis: Lucian, *Adversus indoctum,* 17 and Griffiths, *De Iside,* pp. 314–315; Dunand, *Le Culte d'Isis* I, p. 123; Thompson, *Ptolemaic Oinochoai,* p. 61. The locks dedicated by Berenike II and Arsinoe III, according to Dunand (*op. cit.,* p. 38) and Thompson (*loc. cit.*), may have been patterned on the locks dedicated by Isis. The locks of these two Ptolemaic queens were votives in the temples of Arsinoe II and Artemis respectively. The references to locks of Isis at Coptos and Memphis are of the 2nd century after Christ.

[98] M. Werbrouck (*Les Pleureuses dans l'Égypte ancienne,* Brussels 1938, pp. 142–159) would define the pose of the majority of mourners as that known in the hieroglyphs for mourning and supplication (A. Gardiner, *Egyptian Grammar,* London 1973, A 28 and A 4), but the active wailing women, such as those in the tomb of Nebamun and Ipuky, Thebes (see A. Mekhitarian, *Egyptian Painting,* Geneva 1954, p. 130), could be pulling their hair. Offerings of hair are found in Egyptian graves: see Bonnet, *Reallexikon,* pp. 267–268. Griffiths (*De Iside,* pp. 314–315) considers the cutting and dedication of locks of hair a Greek custom but notes (p. 314, note 5) that a wreath of hair was found on the coffin of Tutankhamun. On Greek customs, see C. Sittl, *Die Gebärden der Griechen und Römer,* Leipzig 1890, pp. 65–67.

SISTRUM AND SITULA

Women in the dress of Isis on Attic grave reliefs clearly belong to the cult of this Egyptian goddess. In the upraised right hand they hold the sistrum, an Egyptian musical instrument, and in the lowered left hand they hold the situla, a suspended vase. These hand-held attributes are specific to the cult of Isis in the Mediterranean and were used during the Hellenistic and Roman periods.[99] In Egypt, the sistrum and situla were not exclusive to the cult of Isis but rather served in a number of religious ceremonies, at least as early as the New Kingdom.[100]

The loop sistrum is a rattle with disks on prongs set loosely within a loop on a handle.[101] The simple version is represented on Attic grave reliefs. It has three prongs with hooked ends to prevent them from falling out of the sistrum. The usual knob shown on top of the loop may have been a simple decoration or a knob to fasten the curving sides of the loop in place. The latter would be necessary if the loop of actual sistra were not of cast metal. Most extant examples are made of bronze, and they often have an ornament on top of the loop.[102]

Sistra with a loop and broad prongs that appear to be flat are characteristic of reliefs in Athens of the early 3rd century after Christ.[103] Only a few on Attic grave reliefs are decorated. One of these sistra, on a relief of the mid-1st century after Christ, has a twisted handle (Pl. 11), while four of the 2nd century have a lotus on top.[104] Two of the latter also

[99] These objects are the most common attributes of Isis in the Roman period: Lafaye, DarSag III, i, p. 579; Magie (footnote 57 above, p. 13), p. 167; Dunand, *Religion populaire*, p. 31. R. Krause (in *Lexikon der Ägyptologie* II, 1977, p. 602) mentions that the use of the sistrum spread into the Mediterranean with the cult of Isis. Hellenistic reliefs repeatedly show both items, the sistrum and situla: see two grave reliefs from Smyrna of the 2nd century B.C. (Pl. 1) and a relief from Thasos of the same time (Dunand, *Le Culte d'Isis* II, pp. 62–63, pl. XX:2). Wall paintings from the Iseum at Pompeii and from Herculaneum show these items held by participants in the cult as well as by priests and possible priestesses: Witt, *Isis*, figs. 27 and 26 respectively; Tran Tam Tinh, *Essai*, p. 76; *idem, Le Culte des divinités orientales à Herculanum*, Leiden 1971, pp. 29–40, 83–86, pl. 27, fig. 35 and pl. 28, figs. 40, 41; and **14, 24, 36, 40**. On these attributes, see S. de Ricci, DarSag IV, ii, pp. 1355–1357; A. Grenier in *ibid.*, pp. 1357–1360; Bonnet, *Reallexikon*, pp. 716–720; Griffiths, *The Isis Book*, pp. 132–133, 186–187, 208–209; G. Grimm, *Die Zeugnisse ägyptischer Religion und Kunstelemente im römischen Deutschland*, Leiden 1969, pp. 184–185; Grenier, *L'Autel funéraire isiaque*, p. 5, note 10.

[100] For the sistrum in Egypt, see Münster (footnote 46 above, p. 12), pp. 115–118 and C. Ziegler, "Le Sistre d'Henouttaouy," *La Revue du Louvre* 27, 1977, pp. 1–4. Concerning the situla, see Lichtheim, pp. 169–179; J. Monnet, "Un Vase à libation royal du culte d'Amon-Ré de Gematon," *Revue d'égyptologie* 9, 1952, pp. 90–99; C. Evrard-Derricks and J. Quaegebeur, "La Situle décorée de Nesnakhtiou au Musée Royal de Mariemont," *Chronique d'Égypte* 54, 1979, pp. 26–56.

[101] Egyptian sistra often have metal disks that slide; see the bronze one of chantress Tapenu, of Saite period according to Y. Margowsky, M.M.A. 68.44. Others have prongs that slide: see Klebs, *ZÄS* 67, 1931, pp. 60–63 and B. Söderberg, "The Sistrum: a Musicological Study," *Ethnos*, 1968, pp. 91–133.

[102] See footnote 101 above. Simple looped sistra with plain rod handles as well as ornate ones with figured handles and top finial cast of bronze have been found in Athens; see footnote 105 below, p. 21.

[103] See **22** (Pl. 38); mended relief, Athens, N.M. Ἀπο. 54 + 231 (Pl. 37); Athens, N.M. 1214 (Pl. 37); Athens, N.M. 1223 (Pl. 38).

[104] **3** has the twisted handle. Those with lotus finial are Athens, N.M. 1308, late Hadrianic (Pl. 24); **15**, middle Antonine (Pl. 29); Boston, M.F.A. 1971.209, middle Antonine (Pl. 30); and Broom Hall relief, middle Severan (Pl. 39).

have a floral or figured base, recalling ornate Egyptian sistra of the Saite to Roman periods.[105]

In Egypt, the sistrum was associated with the goddess Hathor at least as early as the Old Kingdom, but it also served other gods and divine royalty from the New Kingdom on.[106] The earliest type seems to have been in the shape of a naos or temple,[107] while the loop sistrum is known from texts beginning in the Middle Kingdom.[108] The prongs are often in the shape of snakes.[109] Sistra of any material could have been played if the prongs or disks were metal and either were loose.[110] The representations of sistra in reliefs and on wall paintings in the New Kingdom show the snake-shaped prongs fixed while the disks on them slip and rattle.[111]

There are two instances of the sistrum not held but shown instead on the pediment of an Attic "Isis" relief.[112] Of these, the fully preserved relief of Methe in Athens (Pl. 23) of late Hadrianic date[113] provides one possible reason for this change in placement. Methe is shown with her right arm around the shoulder of the accompanying man and her hand resting on his shoulder. Because of the close positions of the figures, her sistrum was not included. The importance of the sistrum was not diminished but rather made more prominent by its position in the pediment and careful carving.

The situla on Attic grave reliefs is a pendent vase with a knob at the bottom. It usually has a short neck and a lip as broad as the shoulder. This necked situla appears to have been

[105] **15** (Pl. 29) and Boston, M.F.A. 1971.209 (Pl. 30). For ornate Egyptian sistra, see Klebs, *ZÄS* 67, 1931, pp. 60–63 and bronze sistrum, Louvre E 11201, probably of Saite period (Ziegler [footnote 100 above, p. 20], pp. 1–4). Plain sistra, frequent on Attic reliefs, resemble those found in Athens and Pompeii (Ward-Perkins and Claridge [footnote 84 above, p. 17], no. 186). Ornate ones with Hathor head and Bes on the handle and cat nursing kittens on top of the loop have also been found in Athens and Pompeii (*ibid.*, no. 187) and may be imports from Egypt: compare with Cairo CG 69316 (H. Hickmann, *Catalogue générale: Instruments de Musique*, Cairo 1949, pp. 80–81, pls. 65, 66).

[106] Klebs, *ZÄS* 67, 1931, pp. 60–63; Münster (footnote 46 above, p. 12), pp. 115–118; F. Daumas in *Lexikon der Ägyptologie* II, 1977, p. 1028.

[107] Klebs, *ZÄS* 67, 1931, pp. 60–63; Bonnet, *Reallexikon*, pp. 716–720; Söderberg (footnote 101 above, p. 20), pp. 122–127. The earliest preserved example is the alabaster sistrum of King Teti "beloved of Hathor, Mistress of Dendera," Dynasty IV (M.M.A. 26.7.1450): S. Allam, *Beiträge zum Hathorkult (bis zum Ende des Mittl. Reiches)* (*Münchner ägyptologische Studien* 4), Berlin 1963, p. 50, pl. IV and H. G. Fischer, *Dendera in the Third Millennium B.C.*, New York 1968, p. 37 and frontispiece.

[108] Klebs, *ZÄS* 67, 1931, p. 61 and Bonnet, *Reallexikon*, p. 717; both types of sistra are cited in literary texts of the Middle Kingdom, but the loop sistrum is first represented in the New Kingdom.

[109] Klebs, *ZÄS* 67, 1931, pp. 60–62: two types of snake form the prongs, a viper and a cobra. Swan heads for the hooked ends of the prongs are on two sistra, in Athens and Pompeii (Ward-Perkins and Claridge [footnote 84 above, p. 17], p. 81, nos. 186, 187); these may be Ptolemaic or Roman in date: compare with Cairo CG 69316 (Hickmann [footnote 105 above], pp. 80–81, pls. XLV, XLVI).

[110] Söderberg (footnote 101 above, p. 20), p. 97, fig. 3 and pp. 122–127.

[111] Klebs, *ZÄS* 67, 1931, pp. 61–62.

[112] In Aigina, only the pediment is preserved (possibly Flavian in date, footnote 41 below, p. 73; Pl. 14): Kourouniotis, Ἀρχ᾽Ἐφ, 1913, p. 97, fig. 20. The second example is the unpublished relief of Methe, Athens, Third Ephoria 1160.

[113] For the date of Methe's stele, see p. 76 below.

the characteristic vase in the Mediterranean for the cult of Isis during the Hellenistic and Roman periods.[114]

The earliest known examples of situlae in the Greek world, according to D. von Bothmer, are two silver vases of the mid-6th century B.C. One, said to be from the Troad, is a necked, deep bowl, Achaemenid in type if not an import from Persia.[115] The second, which is said to be from Lydia, at that time a Persian satrapy, is a copy of the common Egyptian ovoid situla.[116] Neither is the prototype for the vase on Attic grave reliefs, nor does this vase resemble any of the various types of situlae made in Greece, often found in tombs, and dating from the late 6th century B.C.[117] No resemblance is found to the numerous and varied Etruscan situlae from the 7th century B.C.,[118] which had a broad range of use, domestic and ceremonial.[119] One may think of the Greek amphora-situla, but its large size and lid,

[114] See two grave reliefs from Smyrna, 2nd century B.C. (Pl. 1), and one from Eretria, mid-1st century B.C. (Δελτ 23, 1968, pl. 49). At Pompeii near the Palaestra were found a silver situla and two matching beakers; each is decorated with odd Egyptiànizing figures, one of whom holds a necked situla and a sistrum: Munich, Mus.Ant.Kl. 512 (*5000 Jahre ägyptische Kunst* [Essen exhibition, 15 May–27 August], Essen 1961, no. 264) and Naples, M.N. (H. Fuhrmann, "Archäologische Funde," *AA* [*JdI* 56], 1941, pp. 591–598, figs. 108–115). This necked situla recurs on wall paintings from the Iseum at Pompeii (Tran Tam Tinh, *Essai*, nos. 29, 31, and 35) and in scenes before a temple of Isis on wall paintings from Herculaneum (Tran Tam Tinh, *Le Culte des divinités orientales* [footnote 99 above, p. 20], pl. 27, fig. 35 and pl. 28, figs. 41 and 43). From Syros, a funerary relief (Pl. 14), possibly Flavian (Dunand, *Le Culte d'Isis* II, pl. XL:2); in the Vatican the early Antonine relief of Galatea (Pl. 51); the late Antonine statue of Isis from her temple at Ras-el-Soda, Egypt (Pl. 52): A. Adriani, "Sanctuaire de l'Époque romaine à Ras el Soda," *Annuaire du Musée Gréco-romain Alexandrie*, 1935–1939, p. 147; compare with the late Antonine statue Palermo, M.N. 704 (Pl. 51).

[115] M.M.A. 1972.118.157: D. von Bothmer, *Ancient Art in New York Private Collections* (Metropolitan Museum of Art exhibition, December 17, 1959—February 28, 1960), New York 1961, no. 56, pl. 100. Compare to Achaemenid bowls: D. E. Strong, *Greek and Roman Gold and Silver Plate*, London 1966, pp. 99–100, fig. 23.

[116] M.M.A. 1973.11.10: Sotheby and Co., *Sale Catalogue*, July 10, 1972, p. 17, no. 60d, pl. 16. The lip of this vase is too broad to be an Egyptian ovoid situla: see Lichtheim, *JNES* 6, 1947, pp. 170–171 and pl. IV, figs. 1–5, 7–12, and 16. The chain, which may have been attached to a lid, may be a later addition, but if original, this vase would be the earliest example of a lidded situla. This small vase could have been a perfume vase, again unlike Egyptian situlae. See the small silver alabastron with lid from Vergina: Yalouris *et al.*, *Alexander*, p. 184, no. 165.

[117] Greek situlae are rare prior to the 4th century B.C.: see four Archaic situlae of the pail shape dedicated at the sanctuaries at Delphi, at Olympia, of Athena at Lindos, and of Athena at Mantinea (K. Lehmann, "A Bronze Pail of Athena Alalkomenia," *Hesperia* 28, 1959, pp. 153–161, pls. 31–34) and the contemporary amphora-situla, M.M.A. 60.11.2 (D. von Bothmer, "Newly Acquired Bronzes—Greek, Etruscan and Roman," *Bulletin of the Metropolitan Museum of Art* 19, 1960/1961, pp. 140–141). None are in terracotta, and few are depicted in Attic vase painting: D. A. Amyx, "A New Pelike by the Geras Painter," *AJA* 49, 1945 (pp. 508–518), p. 514. Fourth-century examples in silver and bronze are from Macedonia and Thrace: Yalouris *et al.*, *Alexander*, p. 156, no. 107 (pail situla); p. 157, no. 109 and p. 169, no. 134 (amphora-situla); p. 159, no. 116 (krater-kador); p. 161, no. 122 (spouted situla); p. 162, no. 123 and p. 170, no. 135 (concave-sided situla); p. 181, no. 157 (stamnoid situla).

[118] M. V. Giuliani-Pomes, "Cronologia delle situle rinvenute in Etruria," *Studi etruschi* 23, 1954, pp. 149–194; S. Boucher, "Trajets terrestres du commerce étrusque aux Ve et IVe siècles avant J.-C.," *Revue archéologique* 1973, pp. 79–96; L. G. Eldridge, "A Third Century Etruscan Tomb," *AJA* 22, 1918, pp. 251–294.

[119] Giuliani-Pomes (footnote 118 above), pp. 150–153 and p. 173, fig. 10; Boucher (footnote 118 above), pp. 85–96.

possibly because it held wine,[120] argue against it as the prototype for the situla held by women in the dress of Isis on Attic grave reliefs. These situlae are small and light weight to judge from the ease with which women hold them.[121]

The situla on Attic grave reliefs is based on two popular Egyptian situlae, the common ovoid vase popular since the New Kingdom[122] and the mammiform situla frequent in the Saite-to-Roman period,[123] but the addition of the neck shows a Greek preference for articulated vases.[124] In Egypt, necked situlae with a mammiform or knobbed body are rare and may have occurred only in the Roman period.[125] The necked, mammiform situla seems to have come to the Mediterranean with the spread of the cult of Isis and was probably designed for or by Greeks specifically for this cult. The earliest example known to me is represented on a grave relief from Smyrna of a girl named Isias (Pl. 1), which should be dated to the beginning of the 2nd century B.C.[126]

On Attic grave reliefs, the closest parallel for the Egyptian necked, mammiform situla is the long situla held by Lamia Viboullia (Pl. 27) of the early Antonine period.[127] Poor workmanship need not account for the simple cuplike situlae on two late Severan reliefs.[128] These vases may have been patterned on or could possibly be contemporary with similar situlae of bronze in Cairo.[129] A more surprising explanation may be true for the very small situla represented on the earliest Attic grave relief of a woman in the dress of Isis (1, Pl. 4), last quarter of the 1st century B.C.[130] Such abbreviated vases were made in bronze or blown glass.[131] A representation of the latter best explains the lowness of relief and the illusionistic

[120] See the late 6th-century bronze amphora-situla, M.M.A. 60.11.2: Bothmer (footnote 117 above, p. 22), pp. 140–141. Other lidded examples are from the 4th century B.C.: Yalouris *et al.*, *Alexander*, p. 157, no. 109 and p. 169, no. 134. Bothmer (*op. cit.*, p. 144) notes that the loop on the bail handle is for the rope to lower the vase into a well, as seen on an Attic red-figured column krater in Madrid, *ARV²*, p. 1097, no. 17. The lid attached by a chain to this loop makes these vases containers, possibly for wine like the bronze psykter, a wine-cooler (M.M.A. 60.11.3: Bothmer, *op. cit.*, pp. 140–141). Hydriai, water vases by name and as seen in vase painting, are not lidded in bronze or terracotta: H. Gericke, *Gefässdarstellungen auf griechischen Vasen*, Berlin 1970, pp. 48–54.

[121] On Attic grave reliefs the situla is usually as long as the hand of the woman and the grasp is loose: see **1** (Pl. 4). The forefinger and little finger are often extended, e.g., Mantua, Duc.Pal. 6677 (Pl. 22), **14** (Pl. 29), and Boston, M.F.A. 1971.209 (Pl. 30).

[122] For ovoid Egyptian situlae, see Lichtheim, *JNES* 6, 1947, pp. 170–173, pl. IV, figs. 1, 3, 9 (New Kingdom) and figs. 10, 11, and 16 (Saite to Roman).

[123] *Ibid.*, p. 178, pl. IV, figs. 17 and 6; and pl. VI:A.

[124] See G. M. A. Richter and M. Milne, *Shapes and Names of Athenian Vases*, New York 1935, p. xi; R. M. Cook, *Greek Vase Painting*, London 1972, p. 217; D. von Bothmer, "Greek Vase Painting, an Introduction," *Bulletin of the Metropolitan Museum of Art* 31, Fall 1972, p. 9.

[125] Lichtheim, *JNES* 6, 1947, p. 174, note 45: a sunken relief on a limestone offering table, Cairo, CG 2317 (A. Kamal, *Catalogue général des antiquités égyptiennes: Tables d'Offrandes*, Cairo 1909, p. 149, "Roman period"). The other example is a late Antonine statue of Isis from her temple at Ras-el-Soda (footnote 114 above, p. 22; Pl. 52).

[126] London, B.M. 639. For the date, see pp. 53–54 below.

[127] Piraeus Mus. 1160.

[128] Broom Hall relief (Pl. 39) and Athens, N.M. Ἀπο. 230 (Conze 1964).

[129] Compare with bronze situlae, Cairo, CG 3547 and 3582 (F. W. von Bissing, *Metallgefässe*, Vienna 1901, pp. 22 and 35); the latter has an inscription in Greek and Demotic.

[130] **1** is the work of a master sculptor; see pp. 67–69 below.

[131] Compare with bronze situlae, Cairo, CG 3560 and 3562 (Von Bissing [footnote 129 above], pp. 23–24),

blurring of the edges of the situla as well as the unusual handle. This tilted handle could be a glass bail handle which would swing.[132] A cord, ribbon, or wire could also be attached to the body of a glass situla to serve as a handle, but a lip would be necessary to keep the tied cord in place.[133] How the handle was attached is not shown on this Attic grave relief. More important is the movement, the handle tilting as well as the free swing of the body of the vase, which is masterfully if minimally carved.

The only ornate situla that I have discovered is that held by Amaryllis (Pl. 19) on the unusual three-figure relief, Athens, N.M. 1233, of Trajanic date. This vase is fluted from neck to shoulder and from shoulder to bottom, above and below a horizontal groove. It may have been modeled on a situla of precious metal or mold-blown glass.[134] On one of the last Attic grave reliefs, Parthenope (Athens, N.M. 1244; Pl. 50) once held a sistrum and a situla of bronze.[135]

The necked, mammiform situla, the most common type on Attic grave reliefs, may have been the μαστίον recorded in the inventories for the temple of the Egyptian gods Isis and Sarapis known as Sarapieion C on the island of Delos before 166 B.C.[136] The mammiform shape would be appropriate for libations of milk which, according to Apuleius in the 2nd century after Christ, were made from a breast-shaped vase of gold for the cult of Isis.[137] Water libations are another possibility.[138] The fact that so few situlae have been found in

---

a glass situla from Pompeii (G. Eisen, *Glass*, New York 1927, p. 278, fig. 126), and glass vessels, possibly amphoriskoi, that could be suspended from a cord (p. 295, fig. 133).

[132] See a glass situla in Köln of the 2nd to 3rd century after Christ: F. Fremersdorf, *Die Denkmäler des römischen Köln* V, Köln 1959, p. 54, N 126, pl. 65 and O. Doppelfeld, *Römische und frankische Glas in Köln*, Köln 1966, no. 119.

[133] The earliest example of a glass vase suspended from a cord or ribbon depicted by the Greeks, according to D. von Bothmer, is on an Attic red-figured cup signed by Brygos, *ca.* 480 B.C. (*ARV²*, p. 398) in the Geneva market; it is an aryballos marked with zigzag lines clearly meant to be of colored glass, possibly an import from the Near East or Egypt where examples are known since the New Kingdom: see S. Auth, *Ancient Glass at the Newark Museum*, Newark 1976, pp. 15–16 and 27. For suspension chains, see silver Etruscan vases from Chiusi (Eldridge [footnote 118 above, p. 22], pp. 264–265) and numerous examples of Roman date, such as a glass aryballos of the 2nd to 3rd century after Christ: M.M.A. 17.194.193. A lip would hold the cord, ribbon, or chain in place, but it has been omitted on the grave relief, **1**; a simply shaped situla similar to **1** with a broad lip and suspended by two ribbons is held by a priest of Isis on a wall painting from Casa di Lorio Tiburtino, Pompeii (II, 2, 5): Tran Tam Tinh, *Essai*, pl. VII:4.

[134] See the silver situla from Pompeii: Munich, Mus.Ant.Kl. 512 (*5000 Jahre ägyptische Kunst* [footnote 114 above, p. 22], no. 264). Fluted or ribbed Greek vases of gold or silver are fairly common: paterae from the 7th century B.C. (Strong [footnote 115 above, p. 22], pp. 55–56) and 4th-century examples such as a silver bottle (Yalouris *et al.*, *Alexander*, p. 157, no. 111) and a cup (*ibid.*, p. 160, no. 120). Mold-blown bases could be ornate such as that of the blue bottle of the 1st century after Christ, M.M.A. 13.198.6, which has ivy in relief on the body, a ribbed shoulder, and a paneled area above the base.

[135] Athens, N.M. 1244 (Conze 1954); Conze observed that the dowel holes in her hands are for the attachment of bronze sistrum and situla.

[136] Dunand, *Le Culte d'Isis* II, p. 107, note 4 and III, p. 219; *IG* XI 1307, line 9; Roussel, *Cultes égyptiens*, pp. 209 and 286.

[137] *Metamorphoses* XI.10; Griffiths, *The Isis Book*, p. 210.

[138] Apuleius (*Metamorphoses* XI.20) also mentions that water libations were made in the sanctuary of Isis, but the vase employed is not described; see Griffiths, *The Isis Book*, p. 276. Griffiths (p. 210) discusses the possibility of both kinds of libation.

the Mediterranean may be due to re-use of the metal or to poor preservation of those made of glass.

In Egypt, situlae may have served for libations of water or milk.[139] They were used in the temples as well as in the cult of the dead.[140] The earliest preserved example is a necked situla with carinated body, which is inscribed to the Pharaoh Amenemhet I, "beloved of Hathor Mistress of Dendera", and dates to the Middle Kingdom.[141] The situlae of the New Kingdom have many forms, but it is not certain whether any particular shape or type corresponds to a libation of milk or water.[142] Lichtheim observed that the variety of New Kingdom situlae suggests neither a single origin nor a single function.[143]

There is one other example of a situla on Attic grave reliefs. This bucketlike vase is held by a youth standing with his dog on a relief probably dating to the second quarter of the 1st century after Christ.[144] The long locks that fall to his shoulders indicate that the youth belonged to a mystery cult, such as the Eleusinian Mysteries, the cult of Dionysos, or that of Isis, or that he venerated one of the gods of the Phratria.[145] The vase that he holds is a large bucket with broad mouth and spreading flat bottom, totally unlike the mammiform situla belonging to the cult of Isis. His situla resembles the pail-situla that appears to have been used in the cult of Dionysos, to judge from Attic and South Italian red-figured vase painting.[146]

[139] Lichtheim, *JNES* 6, 1947, pp. 172–173; Griffiths, *The Isis Book*, pp. 208–210.

[140] *Ibid.*; Evrard-Derricks and Quaegebeur ([footnote 100 above, p. 20], p. 41 and p. 50, note 9) cite libations of water as an offering to the gods and also in the cult of the dead; the inscription on the situla that they present emphasizes the use of water as an offering to the god Osiris, while milk and other gifts are mentioned.

[141] Berlin 18492: H. Schäfer and W. Andrae, *Die Kunst des alten Orients*, Berlin 1925, p. 299, fig. 5. Lichtheim (*JNES* 6, 1947, p. 170) cites it as the earliest example; see also Fischer (footnote 107 above, p. 21), pp. 37, 52, note 209 and frontispiece.

[142] Lichtheim, *JNES* 6, 1947, pp. 170–173, pl. IV, figs. 2, 4, 5, 7, 8, and 12 (New Kingdom); ovoid situlae popular in the Saite-to-Roman period, pl. IV, figs. 1, 3, and 9 (New Kingdom) and figs. 10, 11, and 16 (Saite to Roman); mammiform situlae (without the short neck popular on Attic grave reliefs) are frequent in the Saite-to-Roman period, pl. IV, figs. 6 and 17, and pl. VI:A.

[143] Lichtheim, *JNES* 6, 1947, p. 173.

[144] Athens, N.M. 1867 (Conze 1987), *IG* II², 8837:

Ἐπαφρόδιτος | Ἀπίστωνος Θεσ|πιεύς

Dated by Riemann (p. 52) to the last quarter of the 1st century B.C. A date in the second quarter of the next century is more likely, as this relief shows a development from that of Diodotos, definitely Tiberian in figure proportions, style, and composition (p. 69, Pl. 7). Epaphroditos would still precede Theophilos (Riemann, p. 53, no. 50, pl. 13) which is a Claudian relief, in view of the generalized treatment of the figure, shallowly carved sheer drapery, and broadly spaced composition, agreeing with Riemann's observation (p. 52) that the letter forms of this relief correspond to those of inscriptions dated A.D. 40–50.

[145] Von Gonzenbach (footnote 1 above, p. 5), pp. 885–927: long locks as a sign of veneration; an emblem for the cult of Isis or Dionysos (p. 917); dedication of locks to the gods of the Phratria (p. 925); in imitation of the child gods Eros, Horus, and Dionysos (p. 925). Wreathed heads of boys in the Agora (pp. 926–927) have been identified by Clinton (*TAPS* 64, pp. 101–107) as hearth initiates in the Eleusinian Mysteries. Griffiths (*The Isis Book*, pp. 186–187) cites the locks dedicated to the Dionysiac Mysteries as a possible source for the "Horus lock" in the cult of Isis. More important, the long locks of youths appear to have been a fairly common sign of veneration in the Roman Empire; earlier impetus may stem from local customs such as the "Horus lock", a traditional Egyptian child's hairstyle known since the Middle Kingdom: see C. Müller in *Lexikon der Ägyptologie* III, 1980, pp. 273–274.

[146] Pail-situlae are held by the companions of Dionysos. See an Attic red-figured pelike by the Geras

GARLANDS

A few women in the dress of Isis on Athenian grave reliefs wear a long garland. It is draped over the left shoulder and reaches just below the right knee. It is usually made of flowers, although fruit may be included. Of the 12 extant examples, 3 date to the 2nd century after Christ and 6 to the 3rd.[147]

A garland of laurel leaves alternating with roses is fairly common, occurring on one relief of the 2nd century after Christ and two of the 3rd.[148] On the large relief figure (**13** + Athens, N.M. Ἀπο. 237) preserved in two pieces (Pl. 28), the garland is more carefully carved than the drapery. This peculiar contrast in execution and detail is characteristic of early Antonine reliefs and sculpture in the round.[149] Similarly, on two contemporary reliefs, a plain ropelike garland contrasts with the shallow, evenly carved drapery.[150]

More elaborate garlands seem to appear on Attic grave reliefs in the 3rd century after Christ. The massive figure **30** (Pl. 45) has the richest garland with grape clusters followed by two sets of buds bound by a fillet. A small figure, Athens, N.M. 3256 (Pl. 46), also from the 40's of the 3rd century, has a surprisingly delicate garland of flowers bound by a broad fillet.

Flowers are lightly scalloped, barely indicated on a flat, bandlike garland worn by the large figure **31** (Pl. 47), from the 50's of the 3rd century. This oddly textured, flat garland, which seems to conflict with the bold modeling and twisting pose of the figure, is a careless abbreviation. Its cottonlike texture is used repeatedly on floral moldings of certain Attic sarcophagi, where the bold contours of the figures are more important than the details or execution.[151]

One might suggest that because these examples are few, the wearers of the garland might have had a special status or role in the cult of Isis in Athens. There are, however, two facts that argue against this interpretation. First, these reliefs are not isolated chronologically, but rather occur in groups. Second, contemporary monuments differ in size, quality, and execution, betraying limited interest in the garland. It might be more helpful to suggest that these Attic examples belong to two periods in particular when women in Athens wore a long garland over the dress of Isis: the 40's of the 2nd century after Christ and more frequently in the 40's and 50's of the 3rd century.

Painter, *ca.* 480 B.C. (*ARV²*, p. 286): Amyx (footnote 117 above, p. 22); South Italian vases of the 4th century B.C.: A. D. Trendall, *The Red-Figured Vases of Lucania, Campania and Sicily*, Oxford 1967, pls. 10:2, 83:4 and 5, 234:3.

[147] Three fragmentary reliefs in the Akropolis Museum I have not seen (Conze 1957 b–d); the other (dated) nine are as follows: Piraeus Mus. 1160 (Pl. 27), **11, 13, 23, 30, 31**, Akropolis Mus. 3194 (Pl. 44), Athens, N.M. 3256 (Pl. 46), and Trieste, Mus.Civ. 2214 (Pl. 43).

[148] See **13** of early Antonine date (Pl. 28), and Trieste, Mus.Civ. 2214 (Pl. 43) and Akropolis Mus. 3194 (Pl. 44), both of the 40's of the 3rd century.

[149] **13**; see p. 78 below. The statues include two portrait statues from Cyrene (footnote 78 below, p. 79) of which one has been conclusively identified as the empress Faustina the Elder (Pl. 27).

[150] See the small figure **11** (Pl. 26) and the large figure of Lamia Viboullia, Piraeus Mus. 1160 (Pl. 27).

[151] Compare the cottony garland with the cursorily carved acanthus molding on the short sides of the Attic Amazonomachy sarcophagus, Thessaloniki, Arch.Mus. 1245: A. Giuliano and B. Palma, "La maniera ateniese di età romana: i maestri dei sarcofagi attici," *Studi miscellanei* 24, 1978, pl. XLIII, fig. 103.

Representations of the goddess Isis with similar long garlands could lend support to the idea that the garlands were worn by these Athenians to emulate the goddess. The evidence is limited to five examples outside Egypt[152] and one statue from Egypt,[153] all of Roman date. The innumerable terracotta figurines with garlands from Egypt, assigned to the late Hellenistic and Roman periods, include Isis and her consort Sarapis, but the use of garlands in Egypt was so prevalent that Breccia referred to it as *ghirlandomania*.[154]

Garlands need not be exclusive to Isis or her cult. Wreaths and garlands were used for religious and secular decoration throughout the Mediterranean in the Hellenistic and Roman periods.[155] Garlands not only decorated altars in sanctuaries but also funerary and votive altars. The origin of these customs is unknown.[156]

In Egypt, the use of flowers as gifts to the gods, divine royalty, the deceased, and the living has a long and rich tradition, particularly evident in the representations of the New Kingdom.[157] Flowers were placed in temples, on graves and houses, and were carried in a variety of processions.[158] In tombs of the New Kingdom, garlands decorate the upper border of the wall paintings.[159] Although flowers were given to Isis at Philae, the major temple to Isis near Aswan, dated to the late Ptolemaic and Roman periods, flowers were a common sign of devotion in religious ceremonies in Egypt and throughout the Mediterranean.[160] Neither garlands nor flowers were exclusive to any god or cult.

Wreaths freely worn by individuals on all occasions, according to Thompson, may have originated in Egypt, the land famous for wreath and garland making.[161] Wreaths adorn the heads of innumerable terracotta figurines from the 4th century B.C. onwards throughout the

---

[152] Two Delos and Myrina terracotta figurines of Isis with garlands (Dunand, *Le Culte d'Isis* II, pls. XXXV and XII:3) should date to the 1st century by close comparsion with figurines by Diphilos, A.D. 20–70 (see Thompson [footnote 62 above, p. 14], pp. 10–13, fig. 8 and p. 33, pl. IV:9); one of the two Trajanic statues of Isis from Gortyna, Crete; one statuette from Gortyna, possibly of the late 3rd century considering the geometric treatment of figure and drapery (see footnote 164 below, p. 28): G. Oliverio, "Santuario delle Divinità Alessandrine," *Notiziario archeologico dei Ministero delle Colonie* 4, 1927, pp. 166–167, pl. 23:9. An Istanbul figurine, possibly of the 60's of the 3rd century in view of the Gallienian shell-like drapery (see pp. 87–88 below) is published by Laumonier (footnote 62 above, p. 14), pl. 106:b.

[153] Alexandria Mus. 4780: Kraus (footnote 14 above, p. 7), p. 100.

[154] E. Breccia, "Ghirlandomania alessandria," *Musée Égyptienne* 3, 1909, pp. 13–25; see footnote 161 below.

[155] M. Honroth, *Stadtrömische Girlanden*, Vienna 1971, pp. 7–11; Fraser, *Rhodian Funerary Monuments*, p. 27 and note 136 with earlier references.

[156] An Egyptian origin based on Alexandrian material from the 3rd century B.C. is suggested by Honroth (*op. cit.*, pp. 7–8), while Fraser (*Rhodian Funerary Monuments*, p. 27, note 136) suggests a Greek origin based on evidence from Attic vase painting of the 4th century B.C.: see J. D. Beazley, "Excavations at Al Mina, Sueidia, III. The Red-figured Vases," *Journal of Hellenic Studies* 59, 1939 (pp. 1–44), pp. 35–36. The use of flowers in sanctuaries has the longer tradition in Egypt; see below.

[157] E. Brunner-Traut in *Lexikon der Ägyptologie* I, 1975, pp. 834–839.

[158] *Ibid.*, p. 838.

[159] M. Vallogia in *Lexikon der Ägyptologie* I, 1975, p. 602.

[160] Brunner-Traut (footnote 157 above); Griffiths, *The Isis Book*, p. 132.

[161] D. B. Thompson, *Troy, the Terracotta Figurines of the Hellenistic Period*, Princeton 1963, pp. 44–46 with references to earlier literature; Thompson, *Ptolemaic Oinochoai*, pp. 37 and 71 for the use of garlands in secular and religious processions.

Mediterranean, but garlands are rarely represented outside Egypt.[162] A variety of figurines from Egypt, generally dated to late Hellenistic and Roman times, are virtually encased in garlands.[163]

Wreaths or garlands may not have been a constant feature in the cult or dress of Isis.[164] Representations of women in the dress of Isis and wearing a garland are few: from Cyrene two portrait statues of early Antonine date;[165] from Athens 11 grave reliefs; and from Egypt two grave reliefs, possibly Coptic.[166] From Eretria north of Athens, an isolated example has been found of a young woman wearing a wreath on her head and a long garland diagonally draped over a plain mantle and chiton. This monument is a Hellenistic grave relief, probably dating to the beginning of the 1st century B.C.[167] The situla identifies her as a member of the cult of Isis.

Wreaths and garlands added to the color and pomp of the Isis processions. Apuleius mentions women wearing wreaths and a priest carrying a circlet of roses in these processions, as well as people bringing boughs, greenery, and garlands to the sanctuary of Isis.[168]

[162] Thompson, *loc. cit.*

[163] See E. Breccia, *Monuments de l'Égypte gréco-romaine* II, ii, Bergamo 1934, pl. VII, figs. 24–26 (Isis); pl. XLII, figs. 208, 209 (Sarapis); pl. LV, fig. 271 (woman with basket). Dunand, *Religion populaire*, pls. LXXIX (Harpokrates), XCIV and XCV (garlands on shrine beside Harpokrates).

[164] Of two Trajanic statues of Isis from Gortyna, Crete, the one from the Prytaneion wears a thick floral garland and originally held a cornucopia by her left arm (see pl. XXVI in Dunand, *Le Culte d'Isis* II). She was, therefore, an Isis-Fortuna; on the date of this statue, see pp. 73–74 below. The second Isis with garland is a statuette: Oliverio (footnote 152 above, p. 27), pp. 166–167, pl. 23:9. This statuette could be from the late 3rd century after Christ in view of the geometric treatment of the figure and drapery; compare with Parthenope (Pl. 50) and Riemann, no. 46 (Pl. 51).

[165] See also **13**, p. 78 below. Of the two statues from Cyrene in this costume, one is a portrait of Faustina the Elder (Pl. 27; for the other see E. Rosenbaum, *A Catalogue of Cyrenaican Portrait Sculpture*, Oxford 1966, no. 175, pl. LXXVI); see footnote 78, p. 79 below. The statues have wreathed heads as well as the long garland over the dress of Isis (Pl. 27). A youth in tunic and mantle, possibly also from Cyrene, wears a similar garland; Rosenbaum (*op. cit.*, p. 134, pl. 107) considers this youth to be Hadrianic in date and a priest of Isis. This statue, also cited by Griffiths (*The Isis Book*, p. 132), need not belong to the cult of Isis. He holds the short cloth, a mantle often held by camilli in Roman state rites: see I. S. Ryberg, *Rites of the State Religion in Roman Art* (*Memoirs of the American Academy in Rome* XXII), 1955, pp. 18 and 40. He should be dated later than the reign of Hadrian, to the 50's of the 2nd century, considering the proportions and S-curved stance characteristic of sculpture and relief figures of this time. Compare his head to the portrait of a prince, Louvre MND 2087: *Das römische Weltreich*, T. Kraus, ed., Berlin 1967, p. 259, fig. 311.

[166] Boston, M.F.A. 1972.875 (C. Vermeule and M. Comstock, *Romans and Barbarians* [Museum of Fine Arts exhibition, December 17, 1976—February 27, 1977], Boston 1976, p. 27, no. 32) and Brooklyn 70.132, also from Behnassa. The Brooklyn relief has traces of red and green paint on the thick garland. It may be later than the Boston relief on account of the massive torso with drapery carved in bold curving sections cutting into the figure, possibly 4th century; see also footnote 2 above, p. 1.

[167] It is the earliest preserved example of a young woman with this long garland also holding the mammiform situla of the cult of Isis. Although this relief is non-Attic, there may have been similar contemporary monuments in Athens. The Eretria relief (see p. 67 below) is slightly earlier than the earliest Attic grave reliefs with women in the dress of Isis.

[168] *Metamorphoses* XI.9 (women wearing wreaths in the processions); XI.7 (priest with circlet); and XI.17 (greenery for the sanctuary of Isis). On the latter, see Griffiths, *The Isis Book*, p. 268.

The depiction of a few women wearing a garland and the dress of Isis on Attic grave reliefs may reflect their interest in the festive side of the cult.

CISTS

On a few Attic grave reliefs with women in the dress of Isis, cists are represented;[169] they usually occupy the center of the pediment. These cylindrical containers often have handles on the sides and a conical lid with knob on top. They occur on reliefs of the late 1st century B.C. through the early 4th century after Christ, including the earliest as well as one of the latest reliefs of this series.[170]

These cists may have been wicker baskets. Rounded ridges carved on five of them resemble coils of a basket,[171] while incised lines on a cist on the Aigina stele may represent the texture of the weave.[172] Several cists, less carefully carved, have been reduced to a flat rectangle with triangular lid.[173]

There are several mystery cults in addition to that of Isis which employed a *cista mystica* to contain the sacred objects of the cult.[174] Cists were part of the Eleusinian Mysteries and the cults of Dionysos, Cybele and Attis, and Mâ-Bellona.[175] Owing to the secrecy of the mystery cults, the contents and exact use of these *cistae mysticae* are unknown.[176]

The importance of the *cista mystica* is stressed by Roman authors,[177] but its origin is unknown.[178] One suggestion is that it came from the East, was first employed in the Orphic Sabazios mysteries, and then was used in the cult of Dionysos before its use spread to other

---

[169] See Conze, p. 107.

[170] The earliest is Athens, N.M. 3036 (Conze 1972, no. 23) of the last quarter of the 1st century B.C. (pp. 67–68); for one of the latest "Isis" reliefs, see **34** (Pl. 51). For those of the 1st century after Christ, see Riemann, no. 57 (Pl. 15) and the Aigina stele pediment (Pl. 14). For the 2nd century, Athens, N.M. 1308 (Pl. 24); and for the 3rd century, see **25** and four in the Epigraphical Museum, Athens (Conze 2139–2142; Pls. 36, 40, and footnote 116 below, p. 107).

[171] Athens, N.M. 1308 (Pl. 24) and Athens, Third Ephoria 1160 (Pl. 23), both late Hadrianic; Athens, E.M. 9730, early 3rd century after Christ (Pl. 36); see **25**, second decade of the 3rd century (Pl. 40); Athens, E.M. 2067, 40's of the 3rd century (Conze 2139; footnote 116 below, p. 107).

[172] Aigina Museum (Pl. 14), possibly Flavian in date.

[173] Athens, N.M. 3036 (Conze 1972, no. 23), pp. 67–68 and see also **1**; Riemann, no. 57 (Pl. 15); and Athens, E.M. 1036 (Conze 2141): see footnote 116 below, p. 107. The late example, **34** (Pl. 51), has no handles. The misshapen cist on an earlier relief (3rd century after Christ) is not on the pediment but on the entablature: Athens, E.M. 9706 (Conze 2140).

[174] Mau, *RE* III; Lenormant, DarSag I, ii; Griffiths, *The Isis Book*, pp. 222–226.

[175] *Ibid.*; G. Mylonas, *Eleusis and the Eleusinian Mysteries*, Princeton 1961, pp. 245 and 319; C. Kerényi, *Eleusis*, New York 1967, pp. 32, 75, and 77; R. Turcan, *Les Sarcophages romains à représentations dionysiaques*, Paris 1966, pp. 419, 485, 538; M. J. Vermaseren, *Corpus Cultus Cybelae Attidisque* III, Leiden 1977, p. 140, no. 426 and p. 152, no. 466; F. Cumont, *Les Religions orientales dans le paganisme romain*, Paris 1929, pl. II:2 for the cistophor of Mâ-Bellona; on the latter, see also Sichtermann, Helbig⁴ II, no. 1179.

[176] Mau, *RE* III and Lenormant, DarSag I, ii.

[177] Tibullus, 1.7.47; Plutarch, *Phokian*, 28; Apuleius, *Metamorphoses* XI.11; Clement of Alexandria, *Protrepticus*, 14. See also footnote 176 above.

[178] See footnote 176 above.

mystery cults.[179] The earliest preserved examples, however, are for Demeter of the Eleusinian Mysteries and date to the 4th century B.C., e.g., a terracotta pinax and votive reliefs
from Eleusis as well as representations in Attic red-figured vase painting.[180] The cist, then,
could have been prominent first in the Eleusinian Mysteries but may have been common
to all mystery cults at that time or earlier.[181] Either possibility could account for the surprising homogeneity of the cists among the various mystery cults.[182] Roughly contemporary
with the representations of the cist for the Eleusinian Mysteries is the cist for the cult of
Bakchis-Sabazios on coins from Macedonia, minted shortly after the death of Alexander the
Great,[183] while the first cist for the cult of Isis is found on coins from Ephesos of 83/2 B.C.[184]

The cists on Attic grave reliefs appear to have been specific to the cult of Isis.[185] They
mark the top of reliefs representing women in the dress of Isis or are accompanied by a
sistrum from the cult of Isis.[186] One of the largest and most three-dimensional cists (on **25**,
Pl. 40) was cut into and through the crowning ornament of the pediment, the center antefix.
This bold re-use emphasizes the importance of the cist to the cult of Isis.

In conclusion, there are several features that permit identification of 106 Attic grave
reliefs as "Isis" reliefs. The origin of many of them may be traced back to Egypt, but the
history of each is different. The *cista mystica* is the only one that appears to have been based
on Greek traditions concerning mystery cults, while the long locks worn by women in the
dress of Isis may be the result of a mixture of Greek and Egyptian traditions. The occasional
garland seems to belong to the general color and pomp of Isis processions.

The Egyptian dress with fringed mantle knotted at the chest may have been brought
with the cult of Isis as it spread into the Mediterranean, possibly as early as the late 4th

---

[179] *Ibid.* Mau made this suggestion but the evidence is inconclusive. M. S. H. G. Heerma van Voss ("The
Cista Mystica in the Cult and Mysteries of Isis," in *Studies in Hellenistic Religions* [*Études préliminaires aux
religions orientales dans l'empire romain* LXXVIII], M. J. Vermaseren, ed., Leiden 1979, pp. 23–29) does
not establish an Egyptian origin for the cist in the cult of Isis.

[180] H. Hörmann (*Die inneren Propyläen von Eleusis*, Berlin 1932, p. 46, note 6) cites Attic vases of the 6th
century B.C., but the earliest preserved representations are of the 4th century B.C.: see Mylonas (footnote 175
above, p. 29), p. 213 with fig. 88, p. 190, note 11 with fig. 63; Kerényi (footnote 175 above, p. 29), p. 151,
fig. 42; K. Schefold, *Untersuchungen zu den Kertscher Vasen*, Berlin/Leipzig 1934, p. 80, London 94,
pl. 26:2 and p. 117, Leningrad 368, pl. 35.

[181] Mau, *RE* III and Lenormant, DarSag I, ii. Mau considers the cist to have come from the East and
originated possibly with the Orphic Sabazios mysteries. The latter is referred to by Demosthenes, *de Corona*,
260, but the first representations, also in the 4th century B.C., are for the Eleusinian Mysteries: see footnote
180 above.

[182] See p. 29 above.

[183] Mau, *RE* III, col. 2591 and Lenormant, DarSag I, ii, p. 1205, fig. 1545.

[184] G. Hölbl, *Zeugnisse ägyptischer Religionsvorstellungen für Ephesus*, Leiden 1978, p. 70, pl. XII:a, b.
See also a grave relief from Eretria of the mid-1st century B.C. (see p. 67 below) where a young woman holds
the mammiform situla of the Isis cult and beside her feet is a cist; she also wears a long garland and a wreath
on her head. This is one of the few non-Attic "Isis" reliefs from the Mediterranean.

[185] Conze, p. 107.

[186] See the stele of Elate and Epigonos (Pl. 24) and the stele of Methe (Pl. 23).

century B.C.[187] It is, however, difficult to determine when and how often it was worn for the cult of Isis, as there are only three extant representations of individuals in this dress from the Hellenistic period in the Mediterranean, two from Smyrna and one from Rhodes.[188]

It is not known when this dress was first worn in Athens for the cult of Isis. A representation of the goddess Isis in this costume is barely preserved on a votive relief in Athens, which is dedicated to Isis of Justice, Δικαιοσύνη (Athens, E.M. 8426; Pl. 1), and should be dated early in the 1st century B.C. according to the officials named in the inscription.[189] The introduction of the cult of Isis into Athens or the environs must have occurred prior to the date of an inscription of 333/2 B.C.[190] Evidence for the dress is also lacking from the island of Delos, whose sanctuary of the Egyptian gods known as Sarapieion C was richly endowed both by the city of Athens and by many of her citizens after 166 B.C., while Delos was an Athenian possession.[191]

It was in Athens, possibly first under Roman rule, that this Egyptian garb was in fashion for the greatest duration. It was repeatedly worn by women in connection with the cult of Isis. The numerous grave reliefs from Athens with women in this dress span from the late 1st century B.C. to the early 4th century after Christ. Wearing this Egyptian costume was of great importance to these women, but they also chose to modify the arrangement and secure both ends in the knot at the chest.

The appearance of Attic "Isis" grave reliefs first in the reign of Augustus may seem surprising. In Rome he had prompted distrust of this foreign cult with its animal-headed gods to denigrate his competitor, Antony, and his Egyptian queen, Cleopatra VII.[192] As Dunand has pointed out, the cult of Isis in Athens appears to have been independent of Augustus' interference.[193]

The choice of this Egyptian costume for the cult of Isis in Athens could have been stimulated by a very recent and immediate model or be bound to a long-established and time-honored one. A vivid model could easily have been Cleopatra VII herself, who appeared,

[187] On the spread of the cult of Isis and the Egyptian gods into the Mediterranean, see Fraser, *OpusAth* 3, 1960, pp. 1–49, esp. p. 23 for evidence from Athens for an introduction of the cult sometime before 333/2 B.C. (*IG* II², 337); on the latter, see also Dow, *HThR* 30, 1937, p. 185; Vidman, *Sylloge*, no. 1.

[188] See pp. 53–54 below and Pl. 1.

[189] Athens, E.M. 8426 (*IG* II², 4702 = Vidman, *Sylloge*, no. 6) is dated by Dow (*HThR* 30, 1937, pp. 212–213, 226). Isis stands in a naos or temple façade, between columns or antae (the base of the one on the left is preserved). The tip of the mantle falling like a cape on the left indicates that she wears the knotted costume; see Figure 1 for the draping.

[190] See footnote 189 above. *IG* II², 337 (= Vidman, *Sylloge*, no. 1) is from Piraeus. The decree permitted Cypriotes to build a sanctuary for Aphrodite as had been done for Isis by Egyptians; see Dow, *HThR* 30, 1937, p. 185; Fraser, *OpusAth* 3, 1960, p. 23; Dunand, *Le Culte d'Isis* II, pp. 4–5.

[191] There are no "Isis" reliefs from Rheneia, the funerary island of Delos: see plates in Couilloud (footnote 91 above, p. 18); nor can any of the finds from Delos with its three sanctuaries for Egyptian gods be identified as depicting an individual in this Egyptian dress: see Roussel, *Cultes égyptiens* and Marcadé, *Délos*, pls. LVI, LVII.

[192] See Hornbostel, *Sarapis*, pp. 364–367 and Malaise, *Conditions*, p. 378.

[193] Dunand, *Le Culte d'Isis* II, p. 133.

according to Plutarch, in the dress of Isis on several occasions.[194] The practice of wearing the knotted fringed mantle for the cult of Isis in Athens, however, may have preceded Cleopatra VII. The model for this costume may instead have been an image of Isis in this costume; the only evidence for such at Athens thus far is the small figure of Isis Δικαιοσύναι (Pl. 1) belonging to the early 1st century B.C.[195]

[194] Plutarch, *Antonius*, 54; Dunand, *Le Culte d'Isis* I, pp. 42–43; Heyob, *Cult of Isis*, p. 20; and see also references in Fraser, *Ptolemaic Alexandria*, chap. 5, note 441.

[195] See footnote 189 above, p. 31.

II

ARCHAEOLOGICAL EVIDENCE AND
INTERPRETATION

We seek evidence which may serve to date and explain the importance of Attic grave reliefs depicting women in the dress of Isis. Much is lost to us, as many were moved from their original grave sites and records concerning the circumstances of their discovery are often minimal. The few whose findspot is known are promising. Careful observation of what is preserved, the original size, composition, and quality of the sculpture, and any special features on these grave stelai may help us assess the original importance of the "Isis" reliefs as funerary monuments and the significance of the cult.

Information from inscriptions on these reliefs, particularly possible references to individuals who are known in dated inscriptions, is very important. Although few names are known, this prosopographical data serves to confirm the chronology of the Attic "Isis" reliefs (and thereby that of other, contemporary grave reliefs), which is established principally on the basis of style.[1] Some of the vitality stemming from individual interest in the cult can be gleaned from specific monuments which were re-inscribed and used again as grave reliefs.

PROVENIENCE

Little is known concerning the original location of Attic grave reliefs of the Roman period. We might expect to find them in the Kerameikos, possibly the most important cemetery of Athens as early as the 8th century B.C.[2] Here along the broad road leading from the monumental Dipylon gate of Athens to the Academy, Pausanias in the 2nd century after Christ had seen, still standing, monuments of the prominent citizens of the 6th through 4th centuries B.C.[3] To the late 1970's, none of these monuments of famous men had been identified.[4]

---

[1] See Chapters III and IV. The article by Muehsam (*Berytus* 10, 1952, pp. 55–114) is the only study of a broad selection of Attic grave reliefs of Roman date. Her observations on some of the inscriptions and reliefs are informative, but the summaries are vague and those on style misleading. The article by Dow and Vermeule (*Hesperia* 34, 1965, pp. 273–297) is devoted to one grave relief of Roman date and its place in Attic sculpture (the Damaskenos, Conze 2038). Five grave reliefs in the Athens National Museum have been briefly discussed and dated by hairstyle in an article by A. Stauridis ('Αρχαιογνωσία 2, fasc. 2, 1981, pp. 277–282). A chronology has not been established; see footnote 1 below, p. 58.

[2] Wycherley (*Stones of Athens*, pp. 254–255) considers the Kerameikos an important cemetery from the 12th century B.C.; monumental vases first mark graves of the 8th century B.C. See also Travlos, *Pictorial Dictionary*, pp. 299–301; for the 12th–8th centuries B.C., see K. Kübler and W. Kraiker, *Kerameikos, I, Die Nekropolen des 12. bis 10. Jahrhunderts*, Berlin 1939; K. Kübler, *Kerameikos, IV, Neufunde aus der Nekropole des 11. und 10. Jahrhunderts*, Berlin 1943; *idem, Kerameikos, V, Die Nekropole des 10. bis 8. Jahrhunderts*, Berlin 1954; *idem, Kerameikos, VI, Die Nekropole des späten 8. bis frühen 6. Jahrhunderts*, Berlin 1959.

[3] Pausanias, I.29.2; Travlos, *Pictorial Dictionary*, p. 301; Wycherley, *Stones of Athens*, p. 257.

[4] Wycherley, *Stones of Athens*, p. 257. On the large monuments found here near the Dipylon gate, see Ohly, *AA* (*JdI* 80), 1965, pp. 314–330.

The adjacent roads could have been lined with tombs of Roman date. The Sacred Way led northwestward to the sanctuary of Demeter and Kore at Eleusis, the most important sanctuary in Attica in antiquity. Along this road went the procession to the sanctuary, in whose mysteries the most prominent Athenians participated and served as priests and officials from at least the 6th century B.C. on, to judge from the inscriptions preserved.[5] Further south the Street of the Tombs led to the Piraeus. These two roads were found by excavators to be flanked by terraced grave plots with monuments of prominent families of the 5th and 4th centuries B.C.[6]

Along the Sacred Way in particular, successive layers of fill allowed later monuments and graves to be placed in the same area, but the upper layers with graves of Hellenistic and Roman date have been partially destroyed by post-Classical water channels,[7] while the foundations of the Church of Hagia Triada cut through the cemetery north of the Sacred Way.[8] The Street of the Tombs was no longer in use in Roman times;[9] further excavation to the west and south may verify whether this change represents shrinkage of the cemetery at that time. Other cemeteries of Hellenistic and Roman date have not been the subject of such careful excavation and study.[10] We may hope that some are well preserved and will be explored.

The provenience of grave monuments of the Hellenistic and Roman periods if recorded is often too briefly stated. The context of a monument is rarely noted, nor has any assessment been made of accompanying finds and the stratigraphy of the site to determine its date and place in the history of the cemetery.[11] It is uncertain whether some of the monuments

[5] On Eleusis, see Mylonas, (footnote 175 above, p. 29), esp. pp. 243–252; on the processions, *ibid.*, pp. 245–247. On the inscriptions recording the Athenians of prominent families who participated in the cult, see Clinton, *TAPS* 64, pp. 5–47 and p. 63 below.

[6] On the cemetery along these roads, see Ohly, *AA* (*JdI* 80), 1965, pp. 327–359, with earlier literature; Travlos, *Pictorial Dictionary*, pp. 299–301; Wycherley, *Stones of Athens*, p. 259.

[7] Ohly (*AA* [*JdI* 80], 1965, pp. 350, 353, 355, fig. 36) describes the layers that covered Classical grave plots along the Street of the Tombs and (p. 359) later water channels; see B. Schlörb-Vierneisel and U. Knigge, "Eridanos-Nekropole," *AM* 81, 1966 (pp. 1–135), pp. 75–76, 122, for the strata of the 4th century B.C. in the area between the Sacred Way and the Street of the Tombs, and p. 123, for the poor remains of Hellenistic and Roman date.

[8] See the plan in Travlos, *Pictorial Dictionary*, p. 303, fig. 391. Many of the grave monuments of Classical to Roman times were found broken and re-used in the walls of the church: Riemann, p. v.

[9] Ohly, *AA* (*JdI* 80), 1965, p. 350.

[10] Brief mention of the Hellenistic cemeteries is made in Kurtz and Boardman, *Greek Burial Customs*, p. 162. On Roman grave sites, see the account by M. Collignon of those in northeast Athens, from Stadiou Street ("Inscriptions funéraires d'Athènes," *Revue archéologique*, n.s. 31, 1876, pp. 346–349); by T. D. Goodell on those further east between Akademias and Vasilissas Sophias (T. D. Goodell and T. W. Heermance, "Grave-Monuments from Athens," *Papers of the American School at Athens* VI, 1897, Part I, pp. 431–441); and by A. Keramopoullos south of the Olympieion, «Ἀθηνῶν εὑρήματα», Ἀρχ Ἐφ, 1911, pp. 257–261).

[11] See footnote 10 above. More detailed accounts omit stratigraphy and relationship of the graves: see the graves in the northwest along the Sacred Way east of Triptolemos Street (Kyparissis, Δελτ 10, Παράρ., pp. 54–85) and at Eleusis (Alexandri, Δελτ 22, Β′ 1, pp. 122–125).

reported from grave sites were found *in situ*, in their original place on the contemporary grave plot, or were discarded, possibly carefully buried to allow room for later monuments,[12] or were re-used as construction material, often as cover slabs for stone-lined graves.[13] If the stele was not *in situ*, the question arises whether the original grave plot was in this area or whether the monument had been moved.

There is one instance where the date of a grave provides a *terminus ante quem* for the stelai found in it. Built into a grave of the 3rd century after Christ, found in 1904 along the eastern edge of the Stadium, were three grave reliefs which should be dated to the early 3rd century by style, figure proportions, technique, and hairstyle of the women.[14] If the grave could have been dated more closely, one might have had an idea how long the stelai stood as grave monuments before being used in this stone-lined grave. The surprising homogeneity of the reliefs may indicate that the three stelai originally stood together, possibly not far from where they were found.[15] If they were from the same grave plot, they may be monuments of persons who were not related by family but rather shared in the ownership of the grave plot as a group, like the koinon in Rhodes of the 2nd and 1st centuries B.C.[16] and Roman funerary colleges.[17] Only one of the inscriptions on these three reliefs gives patronymic and demotic.[18] On the other two the profession of the deceased is emphasized, unusual for Attic grave reliefs but common on Roman funerary monuments of freedmen.[19]

Of the five "Isis" reliefs from grave sites, possibly one is from the original grave plot. The fully preserved stele of Sosibia (Pl. 30) was found with four grave monuments of Roman date and a plaque inscribed with the name Eunois.[20] They were found in 1875 along

[12] Ohly (*AA* [*JdI* 80] 1965, p. 359) cites examples of the early 4th century B.C.

[13] Grave reliefs lined post-Classical water channels (Ohly, *loc. cit.*) and cisterns of Roman date (Goodell [footnote 10 above, p. 34], p. 434). On cover slabs, see footnote 15 below.

[14] A. N. Skias, Νέος Ἑλληνομνήμων II, Athens 1905, p. 263: Hermione, Athens, N.M. 3396 (Conze 1914 and Bieber, *Ancient Copies*, pl. 191, fig. 717); Timokrates, Athens, N.M. 3316 (Pl. 36); Praxiteles (Pl. 36). See footnote 96 below, p. 104, and Walters, *AAA* 12, 1979, pp. 220–221 on the date.

[15] As grave stelai re-used in stone-lined graves usually are one meter high and one meter wide, transport is not a problem; chance may have governed the final provenience. For example, I have found a difference of at least 70 years between reliefs used as a cover for grave ζ west of Triptolemos Street along the Sacred Way: Gnome, Athens, N.M. Θησ. 142 (late Hadrianic; cf. Alexandra, pp. 75–76 below, Pl. 24) and a woman, Athens, N.M. Θησ. 143 (early 3rd century after Christ; cf. Hermione, Conze 1914: see Kyparissis, Δελτ 10, Παράρ. pp. 65–66, figs. 11 and 10). Seventy years or more seems rather long for the maintenance of a grave plot if these reliefs originally stood together. Few of the well-known Athenian families can be traced beyond three generations; see M. Woloch, *Roman Citizenship and the Athenian Elite*, Amsterdam 1973.

[16] Fraser, *Rhodian Funerary Monuments*, pp. 58–68.

[17] S. Dill, *Roman Society from Nero to Marcus Aurelius*, Oxford 1904, pp. 259–266.

[18] Praxiteles son of Sotos from Iphistiadai (*IG* II², 6299; Pl. 36. See footnote 96 below, p. 104).

[19] Muehsam, *Berytus* 10, 1952, p. 55 and note 1; Hermione (Conze 1914) was a midwife (*IG* II², 11329) and Timokrates a scribe (*IG* II², 12794; Pl. 36).

[20] Sosibia, Boston, M.F.A. 1971.209 was found with the following stelai: Dionysia and Synpherousa (Conze 1940), Hilara (Conze 1951), pediment of Claudius Klearchos (*IG* II², 10106), columnar monument of Nymphios (*IG* II², 9818), and plaque of Eunois (*IG* II², 11441): Collignon (footnote 10 above, p. 34), pp. 346–349.

Stadiou Street just north of Constitution Square in the excavation for foundations of a building. Although none of the inscriptions refer to the same names or demes, it may not be by chance that the three fully preserved stelai represent young women and belong to the first 60 years of the 2nd century after Christ.[21] If it seems odd to have three stelai of young women, probably unrelated, from the same grave plot, then why is one of these reliefs shared by unrelated persons, Dionysia daughter of Demosthenos of Paiania and Synpherousa daughter of Antiochos from Acharnai?[22]

The stele of Alexandra (Pl. 24), an impressive late Hadrianic "Isis" relief, according to Curtius came from grave A in the Kerameikos just west of the Church of Hagia Triada with four other funerary monuments.[23] It was not in its original condition or context. The stele preserving the figure of Alexandra was carefully trimmed, probably for use as construction material or to serve as the cover slab of a later grave. The latter seems likely because the right half of this stele is large enough to cover the length and width of a stone-lined grave.[24] If the date in the 1st century B.C. is correct for the columnar grave monument of Zopiros which was found marking grave A,[25] and if grave A was contemporary, then the stele of Alexandra was re-used in a later, possibly neighboring grave. The diversity of the grave monuments found here strongly suggests several periods of occupancy. The earliest is the beautiful relief of Mika and Dion, belonging to the late 5th century B.C.[26]

The third "Isis" relief (Pl. 14) from a cemetery was found in 1965–1966 in road maintenance work at Eleusis.[27] This Flavian relief lay in fill of undetermined origin, dated without reference to the 61 graves of Geometric to Roman date also found along Leophoros

[21] The relief of Sosibia should be dated to the 60's of the 2nd century (pp. 79–80 below); possibly contemporary is the relief of Dionysia and Synpherousa (Conze 1940; see footnote 22 below), while the stele of Hilara is Trajanic (cf. footnote 49 below, p. 74; Pl. 20). The difference of 40 to 50 years between them could permit the reliefs to be from the same plot.

[22] Although the names of Dionysia and Synpherousa (Conze 1940) might have been added at different times, Kirchner, who dated their inscription (*IG* II², 7042) to the 2nd century after Christ, noted no difference to separate them in time. This Neo-Classical relief with two nymphlike figures was thought to date in the 1st century B.C. by Hauser (footnote 91 above, p. 18) and Muehsam (*Berytus* 10, 1952, p. 83, note 4 and p. 108, note 3) but could belong to the 60's of the 2nd century after Christ if the drawing in Conze is correct, as the figure proportions, snug composition, and weighted fall of the drapery are characteristic of middle Antonine reliefs (pp. 79–80, Pls. 29, 30). Neo-Classical reliefs were produced longer than Hauser and Muehsam thought; a replica (Agora S 2698) should be dated to the 30's of the 3rd century after Christ (see footnote 112 below, p. 84; Pl. 42).

[23] Alexandra, Athens, N.M. 1193 (Conze 1969; pp. 75–76 below); with it were two columnar monuments (Zopiros, *IG* II², 6789; Lucius Cornelius, *IG* II², 11148) and two reliefs (Mika and Dion, Athens, N.M. 765, *IG* II², 12129; Hilara, *IG* II², 9681): C. Curtius, "Der attische Friedhof vor dem Dipylon," *Archäologische Zeitung* 29, 1872 (pp. 12–35), pp. 17–18.

[24] The stele of Alexandra (H. 1.69; W. 0.47 m.) could cover a grave like that found west of Triptolemos Street: interior measurements 1.70 × 0.40 m.; see Kyparissis, Δελτ 10, Παράρ., p. 65, fig. 8.

[25] Kirchner dates the monument of Zopiros to the 1st century B.C. (*IG* II², 6789). Curtius (footnote 23 above) records that it marked grave A which contained a gold bracelet with stamped owl decoration, gold earring, and leaves; possibly these grave goods could be dated, but they were only mentioned without illustration. Gold leaves from wreaths, common grave gifts, may escape dating: see Kurtz and Boardman, *Greek Burial Customs*, pp. 101, 163, and 165.

[26] Athens, N.M. 765 (Conze 157): K. Friis Johansen, *The Attic Grave-reliefs of the Classical Period*, Copenhagen 1951, p. 38, fig. 19.

[27] Alexandri, Δελτ 22, B′ 1, pp. 122–125, pl. 102:B.

Thebon.[28] As the top of the stele is cleanly sheared off, this "Isis" relief may also have been prepared for re-use as construction material.

The remaining two "Isis" reliefs from grave sites served as cover slabs for stone-lined graves. The "Isis" stele of Aphrodeisia (Pl. 6), Tiberian in date, was found with a second relief of two women that should be slightly later in the second quarter of the 1st century, capping grave η west of Triptolemos Street.[29] The later of the two reliefs should provide a *terminus post quem* for the grave. To judge from the other reliefs used as covers for graves of the same orientation in this area, the possible sequence could be grave η (after the 40's of the 1st century after Christ), grave π (after the 70's of the 2nd century), and grave ξ (after the beginning of the 3rd).[30] Of this group, grave λ is the deepest and possibly the latest; in it were found glass flasks of the 2nd century and an inscription of the early 4th century after Christ.[31]

South of the Olympieion was found the other "Isis" relief, Athens, N.M. 3256 (Pl. 46), that was used as a cover slab.[32] Unfortunately in this 1911 report nothing was noted concerning the grave or cemetery. The relief can be dated to the 40's of the 3rd century after Christ by style, figure proportions, and decorative pattern of the drapery.[33] How long the relief stood as a grave monument is unknown, nor do we know if this re-use was the first.

Attic grave reliefs showing women in the dress of Isis, as we have seen, were found as far as Eleusis, southwest of Athens. Others were found towards and at the harbor of Athens, the Piraeus, and one on the island of Salamis.[34] The one from farthest east was found in Laurion, while a pediment, part of the top of an "Isis" stele, in the Aigina museum probably came to the island as ballast before being built into a house at the main harbor.[35]

[28] For the date, see p. 72 below; for provenience, see Alexandri, Δελτ 22, Β' 1, pp. 122–125.

[29] Aphrodeisia, Athens, N.M. Θησ. 140 (p. 69 below). Athens, N.M. Θησ. 146: Kyparissis, Δελτ 10, Παράρ., pp. 69–70. The thick sheathlike drapery of the latter should be a forerunner to Claudian drapery (e.g. Athens, N.M. 1250, Pl. 9).

[30] From grave π is the late Antonine relief of Chloe, Athens, N.M. Θησ. 144 (cf. Stratonike, Conze 1906 and London, B.M. 630, p. 81 below, Pl. 32). From grave ζ are the following: mid-4th-century B.C. stele of Aristagora, Athens, N.M. Θησ. 145 (*IG* II², 10746); late Hadrianic relief of Gnome, Athens, N.M. Θησ. 142 (cf. Alexandra; pp. 75–76 below, Pl. 24); and an early 3rd-century relief, Athens, N.M. Θησ. 143 (cf. Hermione, Conze 1914 and **20**, Pl. 35): Kyparissis, Δελτ 10, Παράρ., pp. 65–67, figs. 20, 11, and 10 (respectively).

[31] Kyparissis, Δελτ 10, Παράρ., p. 67, figs. 16, 71, 72; these glass flasks should be contemporary with those from Köln of the 2nd century after Christ (F. Fremersdorf, *Das naturfarbene sogennante blaugrüne Glas in Köln*, Köln 1958, 43 N 616 b, pl. 89) and from Trier of the second half of the 2nd century (K. Goethert-Polaschek, *Katalog der römischen Gläser des Rheinischen Landesmuseums Trier*, Mainz am Rhein 1977, p. 298, nos. 639, 640, and 644, pl. 52). Kyparissis (*op. cit.*, p. 73) would date the inscription to the early 4th century after Christ.

[32] Athens, N.M. 3256 (Conze 1957a); Keramopoullos (footnote 10 above, p. 34), p. 257. Conze's report that it was found in the south city wall is incorrect, as is his inventory number (5256).

[33] See p. 85 and Pl. 46.

[34] Sempronius and Agathemeris, London, B.M. 630, late Antonine (p. 81 below, Pl. 32) was found in 1876 between Athens and Piraeus. Built into houses in Piraeus were the following: Flavian relief of Kallo and Synpheron (p. 72 below, Pl. 13); early Antonine Lamia Viboullia, Piraeus Mus. 1160 (p. 78 below, Pl. 27); and a middle Antonine fragment (p. 80 below, Pl. 32). The Salamis relief of Zosimos and Aphelia is from an early 3rd-century workshop in Athens (footnote 101 below, p. 83; Pl. 37).

[35] The Laurion relief of Sosipatros and Epiteugma is from an early Antonine workshop in Athens (p. 78 below, Pl. 29). The Aigina stele pediment is probably of the late 1st century after Christ (footnote 41 below, p. 72; Pl. 14); Kourouniotis, Ἀρχ Ἐφ, 1913, p. 97: 1st to 2nd century.

The majority of the well-preserved "Isis" reliefs have no known provenience. According to 19th-century records, they were stored in the Theseion,[36] Library of Hadrian,[37] Tower of the Winds,[38] and Varvakeion.[39] Each of these structures served as a museum prior to the construction of the National Museum in Athens in 1866; the final transferral of these collections to the main museum took place in 1891.[40] The reliefs could have been found in these vicinities or scattered throughout the city.

The fragmentary "Isis" reliefs from the Akropolis[41] were probably used as construction material like those found in the excavations in the Agora and Kerameikos.[42] The Agora fragments had been built into structures of Byzantine to modern date.[43] The re-use for construction material still occurs with whole "Isis" reliefs. For example, the relief of Kallo and Synpheron (Pl. 13), which Conze published in 1922 with a photograph showing it over a door of a house in Piraeus, turned up in Athens in 1966 and is badly battered.[44] It was found in the demolition of a house in Athens at 4 Polytechneion Street.

Several forms of re-use are documented by the "Isis" reliefs. Some continued to serve as funerary monuments but were taken over by and inscribed to other individuals.[45] Five "Isis" reliefs were carved into re-used columnar grave monuments,[46] the most numerous type of grave monument[47] and in their smallest size probably the least expensive.[48] These stumplike

---

[36] Sophia and Eukarpos, Athens, N.M. 1214, second decade of the 3rd century after Christ (p. 84 below, Pl. 37); Athens, N.M. Ἀπο. 54 + 231 (Pl. 37), early 3rd (p. 83 below).

[37] Conze refers to the Library of Hadrian as the Stoa of Hadrian; cf. T. H. Dyer, *Ancient Athens*, London 1872, pp. 251–252 and Travlos, *Pictorial Dictionary*, p. 244. Stored there were the following: Trajanic Mousaios and Amaryllis, Athens, N.M. 1233 (p. 74 below, Pl. 19); late Hadrianic Epigonos and Elate, Athens, N.M. 1308 (pp. 76–77 below, Pl. 24); late 3rd-century Parthenope, Athens, N.M. 1244 (p. 89 below, Pl. 50); fragments, early Antonine, Athens, N.M. Ἀπο. 237 and **13** (p. 78 below, both Pl. 28); late Antonine, Athens, N.M. Ἀπο. 235 (Conze 1972, no. 17; p. 81 below); and early 3rd century, Athens, N.M. Ἀπο. 232 (Conze 197, no. 8; footnotes 101, 102 below, p. 83).

[38] Early Antonine relief, Athens, N.M. 1249 (p. 78 below, Pl. 28); pediment of the 40's to 50's of the 3rd century, Athens, E.M. 2067 (see footnote 116 below, p. 107).

[39] Stele of the son of Soterion, Athens, N.M. 1223, second decade of the 3rd century after Christ (p. 84 below, Pl. 38); and fragments, Athens, N.M. Ἀπο. 233, Caligulan (footnote 22 below, p. 70); Athens, N.M. Ἀπο. 234, 20's of the 3rd century (footnote 104 below, p. 83).

[40] S. Karouzou, *National Archaeological Museum, Collection of Sculpture. A Catalogue*, Athens 1968, pp. viii–xii.

[41] Pediments: Athens, E.M. 1036 (Conze 2141), 40's of the 3rd century after Christ (see footnote 116 below, p. 107); Athens, E.M. 9706 (Conze 2140), 60's of the 3rd century (see footnote 116 below, p. 107); four fragments of torsos with garlands (Conze 1957 b–d) and Akropolis Mus. 3194, 40's of the 3rd century (p. 86 below, Pl. 44).

[42] See Appendix 1 and Riemann, p. v, on provenience, and nos. 57–59, 61, and 62.

[43] **32** was built into a Byzantine cistern; **5, 10**, and **34** came from Byzantine houses. Only four were from modern fill: **4, 6, 15**, and **29**. **9** was found in the demolition of the Church of Prophet Elias, while the rest were from modern houses.

[44] Kallo and Synpheron (Conze 2077) was not recognized as the same relief: Alexandri, Δελτ 22, B′ 1, p. 37, pl. 65:B.

[45] See pp. 50–52 below.

[46] **8, 13, 14, 28**, and **29**.

[47] There are over 2,000 columnar markers to judge from the inscriptions, *IG* II², 5229–13017. Numerous examples are in the Epigraphical Museum and Kerameikos in Athens; those published by Conze are Conze 1744–1830. A good selection from the Agora excavations is published by D. Bradeen (*Agora* XVII).

[48] Postlike monuments are the smallest, 0.15–0.20 m. in diameter, while the broadest are 0.40–0.54 m.

monuments were first made in the late 4th century B.C., as a result of the sumptuary laws of Demetrios of Phaleron (317–307 B.C.) restricting Attic grave monuments to plain markers, and continued to be made in a range of sizes throughout the Roman period.[49] Into the broadest size were carved five "Isis" reliefs, of which one is Trajanic,[50] two are early Antonine in date,[51] and two are from late in the 30's of the 3rd century after Christ.[52] The quality and execution of three of these reliefs show that, even in re-use, care could be and was taken if the commission merited it.[53]

Originally Attic grave monuments of the Roman period stood on plots outside the city walls along roads leading away from Athens.[54] It is known from Cicero, in the 1st century B.C., that the Athenians buried their dead outside the city walls, a custom which appears to go back at least to the 6th century.[55] Cemeteries of Roman date may well have been in the same areas as those which were in use in the Classical period and possibly earlier. The grave monuments of Roman date probably stood on higher ground owing to successive layers of accumulated fill and would have accommodated graves and later monuments of each intervening period.[56]

It may not be fortuitous that two of the most impressive grave reliefs of the Roman period, the "Isis" reliefs of Aphrodeisia (Pl. 6) and Alexandra (Pl. 24), were found not far from the Sacred Way.[57] These handsome reliefs would have been appropriate funerary monuments for this cemetery which would have been an important showcase for family and individual monuments.[58] In the case of the Tiberian "Isis" relief of Aphrodeisia, its place

[49] For Demetrios of Phaleron and funerary restrictions, see Conze, p. 29 and pp. 1–6 and 10 on columnar monuments; also Kurtz and Boardman, *Greek Burial Customs*, pp. 166–168. See also p. 58 below. The range in size, 0.15–0.54 m., occurs throughout their production; see examples from the Agora of the 3rd century B.C., nos. 241 (0.20 m. in diameter) and 398 (0.54 m.), and of the Roman period, nos. 516 (0.24 m.) and 111 (0.47 m.) in Bradeen, *Agora* XVII.

[50] **8** (p. 74 below, Pl. 20).

[51] **13** and **14** (p. 78 below, Pls. 28, 29).

[52] **28** and **29** (p. 85 below, Pl. 45).

[53] **8**, **14**, and **28** (Pls. 20, 29, 45). On quality and execution of the Attic "Isis" reliefs, see Chapter III.

[54] Graves of Roman date were found between Triptolemos and Hiera Streets, not far from the ancient Sacred Way: Kyparissis, Δελτ 10, Παράρ., pp. 65–66. The Sacred Way left the northwestern part of Athens by the Sacred Gate, and like the adjacent road to the Academy, in the Kerameikos it was lined with funerary monuments: Travlos, *Pictorial Dictionary*, p. 169, figs. 219 and 299; Wycherley, *Stones of Athens*, pp. 253–260.

In the northeast, Collignon ([footnote 10 above, p. 34], pp. 436–439) and Goodell ([footnote 10 above, p. 34], pp. 434–435) consider the grave monuments (and graves in the case of the latter) of Roman date to be just north of the ancient city walls; Goodell calls the circuit walls Hadrianic (A.D. 117–138), but these walls, now assigned to Valerian (A.D. 253–260), encompassed the expansion of the city under Hadrian: see Travlos, *Pictorial Dictionary*, p. 161.

In the south, Keramopoullos ([footnote 10 above, p. 34], pp. 257–261) reported graves at least of the 40's to 50's of the 3rd century (cf. p. 81) outside the city wall south of the Olympieion.

[55] Cicero, *ad familiares* IV.12.3; Travlos, *Pictorial Dictionary*, p. 299; Wycherley, *Stones of Athens*, pp. 253–260.

[56] On the Kerameikos, see pp. 34–35 above; in the northeast, Collignon ([footnote 10 above, p. 34], pp. 346–349) reported grave monuments of Roman date found not far from those of the late 5th century B.C.

[57] Aphrodeisia, Athens, N.M. Θησ. 140, Tiberian, p. 69 below. Alexandra, Athens, N.M. 1193, late Hadrianic, pp. 75–76 below, and provenience, p. 36 above.

[58] See p. 34 above.

along the Sacred Way seems all the more likely owing to its quality and to the fact that it is one of the few reliefs of the Roman period which bears the name of a man who may have been a magistrate in Athens, thesmothete at the beginning of the 1st century after Christ.[59]

Grave reliefs of Roman date, like those of the preceding periods, 6th century through Hellenistic, were freestanding. To judge from the treatment of the lower part of the stelai of the Roman period, the majority would also have been set into stone bases possibly secured by mortar or lead.[60] Many have a notched end or tenon to be set into a stone base.[61] Stelai with a shallow margin below the feet of the relief figures would also have stood upright if the fit with the slot in the base was snug,[62] while the few with thick, heavy ends could have been set directly into the soil.[63] Columnar monuments have been found set into stone bases as well as standing in the soil over a grave.[64]

The one instance that I have found of a relief of Roman date set into a niche of a funerary building may represent re-use, possibly in Christian times. In 1900 in the Kerameikos the small relief of Cornelia was found in a niche of a funerary building coarsely constructed of field stones, plastered and painted red.[65] Near it were found remnants of other such structures with painted decoration which were considered late Hellenistic or Roman by Delbrück and Brueckner.[66] Although there is no date for any of these structures, there are two features that suggest that the relief of Cornelia may have been re-used in a building of

[59] Athens, N.M. Θησ. 140 (p. 69 below, Pl. 6); for the inscription, see p. 48 below.

[60] See Adam, *Technique*, pp. 16–17 and 80–81 on monuments of Archaic to Classical date. In these periods either the stelai were placed across the grave plot or their bases were set into the enclosure walls of the plot, the top of the base level with the top of the wall: see Brueckner, *Eridanos*; Ohly, *AA (JdI* 80), 1965, p. 343, fig. 37; Schlörb-Vierneisel and Knigge (footnote 7 above, p. 34), p. 76. The view from the road and the proximity of the grave plot to major roads were important to one's family pride and social standing.

[61] Notched stelai: Claudian relief of Hilaros, Athens, N.M. 1250 (footnote 29 below, p. 71; Pl. 9); Trajanic relief of Neikon (Riemann, no. 56); late Severan "Isis" relief, Broom Hall (p. 84 below, Pl. 39). With tenons: fragmentary relief of Heliodoros, third quarter of the 1st century B.C. according to Riemann (p. 53, no. 51); late Hadrianic stele of Mousonis, Brussels, M.R.A.H. (Conze 1985; Guarducci, *Epigrafia greca* III, p. 167); late 3rd-century "Isis" relief of Parthenope, Athens, N.M. 1244 (p. 85 below, Pl. 50).

Many may have escaped notice because the ends are rarely described or shown in the photographs. The tenon of the stele of Parthenope is not shown in Conze but is seen in the photograph in Dunand, *Le Culte d'Isis* II, pl. II. The tenon of the stele of Mousonis shown in the drawing in Conze is not visible in the photograph in Guarducci as it is set into a base. Improper restoration has filled in the notches of the stele of Aphrodeisia alias Epilampsis, Cambridge, Fitzwilliam Museum GR 5.1919 (see p. 48 below); they are visible in Conze (Conze 1930) but not in L. Budde and R. Nicholls, *A Catalogue of the Greek and Roman Sculpture in the Fitzwilliam Museum*, Cambridge 1964, no. 133, pl. 44.

[62] Many examples of these stelai exist, e.g., a late Flavian relief of Titus Flavius, Athens, N.M. 3725 (p. 72 below, Pl. 17) and a middle Antonine relief of Neike, Athens, N.M. 1303 (footnote 79 below, p. 79; Pl. 32).

[63] **32** of the 60's of the 3rd century after Christ (p. 87 below, Pl. 49) and Smirna, Athens, N.M. 2700, of the 70's of the 2nd century after Christ: cf. Agathemeris, London B.M. 630 (p. 81 below, Pl. 32).

[64] See Conze 1749; three of the four columnar monuments stand in the base at the Kerameikos. Kirchner dates those of Zosime and Isidoros to the beginning and Philion to the middle of the 2nd century after Christ (*IG* II², 5484). The early 3rd-century B.C. marker of Philokrateia was found standing in soil over a grave: Schlörb-Vierneisel and Knigge (footnote 7 above, p. 34), p. 104, no. 189, pl. 5; *IG* II², 5447.

[65] R. Delbrück, "Über einige Grabhügel bei Agia Triada," *AM* 25, 1900 (pp. 292–305), pp. 300–301, figs. 6 and 7; Brueckner, *Eridanos*, p. 52, fig. 26. The stele of Cornelia is also published by Conze, without photograph or drawing (Conze 1843); *IG* II², 9734: "aetat. Rom."; H. 0.50 m.

[66] Delbrück (*op. cit.*), pp. 296–305; Brueckner, *Eridanos*, pp. 49–52.

the Christian period.[67] First, the niche in the building is too large for the relief. Second, a second inscription ΘΕΣ, thought to abbreviate Ἐπικουρίοις Σωτηρίοις (to the Epicurean gods Saviors), may well be the Christian Θεός (God) like the ΘΣ marking the forehead of a woman (Pl. 3) from an Augustan grave relief.[68] There are a few other instances of re-use of Attic grave reliefs of Roman date in Christian times.[69]

FORMS OF STELAI

Grave stelai of the Roman period were made from one block of stone, often thick with figures and framed in high relief recalling the deep naiskos-framed stelai of the 4th century B.C.[70] The late Classical examples, however, were made of four slabs: two for the sides, the back one for the relief, and one for the pediment.[71] A few of the large reliefs of Roman date have no frame, simply a clean margin.[72] This omission appears to be a classicizing feature for such large Attic grave reliefs.[73] The fairly low plinth at the bottom of many grave

[67] Brueckner, *Eridanos*, p. 52.

[68] Agora S 2443 (footnote 17 below, p. 69).

[69] A relief of a seated woman (Conze 1866) was re-carved, given decorative linear drapery similar to that found on figurines of the 4th century after Christ: see D. B. Thompson, *Miniature Sculpture from the Athenian Agora* (Excavations of the Athenian Agora Picture Book 3), Princeton 1959, ill. 70; on the contemporary figured lamps of Isis: C. Grandjouan, *The Athenian Agora*, VI, *Terracottas and Plastic Lamps of the Roman Period*, Princeton 1961, p. 34, no. 942. Built into the small Metropolitan Church is another grave relief of two women (Conze 1936) from the 40's to 50's of the 3rd century after Christ: compare with Athens, N.M. 3669 (footnote 128 below, p. 87; Pl. 48). The cross with inscription is a Christian elaboration of this monument; see photograph in Bieber, *Ancient Copies*, pl. 121, fig. 718.

[70] Grave reliefs of Roman date are usually of moderate size (H. 1.0, W. 0.75–0.47 m.) but are often thicker than the usual 0.10 m. of comparable Classical reliefs (e.g. Mika and Dion, Athens, N.M. 765, Conze 157). A good example of Roman date is the Trajanic "Isis" relief of Mousaios and Amaryllis, Athens, N.M. 1233 (Pl. 19); its thickness is 0.15 m. and relief height 0.08 m. See footnote 11 below, p. 59, for larger reliefs of Roman date.

[71] Large stelai of Roman date with figures five-sixths to life size have a thickness of 0.25–0.33 m. and a relief height of 0.17–0.24 m. The largest figure is the Damaskenos (Conze 2038): H. 1.925 m.; Hadrianic in date (footnote 56 below, p. 75; Dow and Vermeule, *Hesperia* 34, 1965, pp. 273–275). Next in height are the stele of Alexandra, Athens, N.M. 1193 (H. 1.69, p.W. 0.47, Th. 0.26 m.), which is late Hadrianic (pp. 75–76 below, Pl. 24), and the imposing but fragmentary stele of Philodamos, originally life size, Berlin R 104 (C. Blümel, *Staatliche Museen zu Berlin, Katalog der Sammlung antiker Skulpturen*, V, *Römische Bildnisse*, Berlin 1933, p. 43; Dow and Vermeule, *Hesperia* 34, 1965, p. 296, note 40) of the late 30's of the 3rd century after Christ (footnote 120 below, p. 86).

Fourth-century B.C. examples of this size or larger were made of four slabs: see Adam, *Technique*, pp. 17 and 117–120 concerning Athens, N.M. 870.

[72] Flavian relief, Athens, N.M. 2725 (Conze 2008): compare pose and inattention to anatomy with Olympia Titus (G. Daltrop *et al.*, *Die Flavier: Das römische Herrscherbild* II, i, Berlin 1966, pl. 22:d); early Hadrianic stele at Corinth (S 187 + 196; Johnson, *Corinth* IX, p. 122, no. 247; cf. Athens, E.M. 10040, pl. 23, dated to A.D. 120); late Hadrianic 10 (p. 77 below); middle Antonine 15 (p. 80 below, Pl. 29); Philodamos, Berlin R 104, of the late 30's of the 3rd century after Christ (Blümel, footnote 71 above). For these slabs of Roman date, there is no anathyrosis in preparation for a frame (see Adam, *Technique*, p. 80); a pin was once set in the edge of 10, also indicating that the stele was in its final form (see pp. 42–45 below).

[73] Some of the most impressive grave reliefs have no frame on the sides, such as the stele of the youth from Salamis (Athens, N.M. 715), last quarter of the 5th century B.C. (Karouzou [footnote 40 above, p. 38] p. 50, pl. 25).

stelai of Roman date, particularly the largest,[74] is a common feature of Classical grave reliefs, while stelai with a rudimentary tenon, where the lowermost corners are trimmed to allow the stele to be set into a base, seem to have appeared first in the Roman period;[75] those with tenons are common in the Hellenistic period.[76] The line of discoloration on the rudimentary tenon of the late Hadrianic "Isis" relief of Epigonos and Elate (Pl. 24) shows that either the stele stood for considerable time in a base without mortar or that the mortar had long been dissolved;[77] the discoloration is from water seeping into the base.

IRON PINS

A number of grave reliefs of Roman date have iron pins in the front and sides of the stele. It has been thought that the lower ones on the sides, placed one-third the length of the stele from the bottom, were to attach the stele to a curb around the grave plot or to a wall to keep the stele upright,[78] while the pins that often frame the relief figure's head and are also in the entablature or at this level in the sides of the stele are thought to have held garlands or wreaths.[79] If the lower pins were structural, then why are they found so infrequently? Their infrequency and the fact that they occur on stelai which have a tenon on the bottom to be set into bases argues against a structural use.[80]

Iron pins are not essential. Not only are they infrequent, varying in number and placement, but also they do not differ in size either according to the dimensions of the stele or the place on the stele. All are thick studs (0.02 to 0.025 m.).[81] Large circular lumps on several

[74] Dow and Vermeule (*Hesperia* 34, 1965, p. 276) consider the shallow bottom of the stele of the Damaskenos (Conze 2038) insufficient to keep the stele upright when set into a base, but such shallow plinths are often found on even the large reliefs of the late 4th century B.C., e.g. Athens, N.M. 870 (Adam, *Technique*, pp. 117–120).

[75] The earliest may be the Claudian relief of Hilaros, Athens, N.M. 1250 (Pl. 9); compare with a statue of Claudius at Olympia (Niemeyer, *Studien*, pl. 34:2).

[76] See the stelai from Rheneia, the funerary island of Delos, second half of the 2nd century B.C. to first half of the 1st century B.C. (Couilloud [footnote 91 above, p. 18]) and the contemporary stelai of Rhodes (Fraser, *Rhodian Funerary Monuments*, pp. 33–42).

[77] Athens, N.M. 1308 (Conze 1962), pp. 76–77.

[78] Dow and Vermeule, *Hesperia* 34, 1965, p. 277; Budde and Nicholls (footnote 61 above, p. 40), p. 82.

[79] Conze and Riemann consider the pins hooks for garlands or wreaths: see Conze 2066, 1971, 1969, and 2068; Riemann, pp. 58 and 60. Only the upper pins are considered hooks for wreaths by Budde and Nicholls (*loc. cit.*), as were pins framing the head of the Damaskenos (Conze 2038): see Dow and Vermeule, *Hesperia* 34, 1965, p. 277.

[80] Pins on stele with notched ends: late Hadrianic "Isis" relief of Epigonos and Elate, Athens, N.M. 1308 (Pl. 24); the middle Antonine relief of Aphrodeisia alias Epilampsis, Cambridge, Fitzwilliam Museum GR 5.1919 (Conze 1930; p. 48 below). The Trajanic relief of Melisia, Athens, N.M. 3724 (Pl. 21), carved into a columnar marker, was originally set in a base; compare her with Amaryllis (p. 74 below, Pl. 19) in stance, thick drapery, few folds, and snug composition. There are at least three other reliefs with lower pins (cited in footnote 84 below, p. 43), but I know of no instance where there are only lower pins.

[81] Early Antonine "Isis" relief of Lamia Viboullia, Piraeus Mus. 1160 (p. 78 below, Pl. 27: H. 1.55 m.); middle Antonine "Isis" relief of Sosibia, Boston, M.F.A. 1971.209 (pp. 79–80 below, Pl. 30: H. 0.90 m.); late Antonine "Isis" relief of Agathemeris and Sempronius, London, B.M. 630 (p. 81 below, Pl. 32: H. 1.69 m.). One pin is in the background on the stele of Artemidoros, Athens, N.M. 1192 (Conze 2052), middle Antonine like the Attic sarcophagus at Corinth (Johnson, *Corinth* IX, no. 241) and the votive relief, Athens, N.M. 1390, which repeats the hairstyle of Faustina the Younger of A.D. 160 (Wegner, *Die Herrscherbildnisse*,

stelai are the swollen, corroded end of the pins that originally jutted out from the stone.[82] Many iron pins were cut level with the surface of the stele or robbed out, often carefully removed leaving rectangular slots but also battered out, breaking the stele.[83] When this confiscation took place is unknown, but it may have been in times of duress or poor economy when iron was scarce.

Pins on the sides of stelai were set in pairs. If one is set in one side of a stele, a second pin at the same height is on the other side. Although this pairing could give the impression that these pins are structural, they are often set too close to the front edge of the stele and are too shallow in all instances to secure the stele to an upright surface.[84]

The purpose of the iron pins in stelai was probably to hold garlands or wreaths in honor of the deceased; the placement of the pins would permit these decorations to be applied without obscuring the relief figures.[85] It seems that the number and placement of the pins varied according to the dictates of the person or family who paid for the monument. Iron pins are found on stelai impressive in quality if not also in size.[86] That nearly half of the stelai with pins are "Isis" reliefs[87] emphasizes the importance of these reliefs.

---

pl. 38). Five pins are in the large, late Hadrianic "Isis" stele of Alexandra (Pl. 24); one is on the entablature, two frame the head, and two are in the side. Three are across the entablature of the contemporary relief of Methe, Third Ephoria 1160 (Pl. 23); each pin is rectangular and measures 0.03 m. in width.

[82] Corroded pins appear like dark lumps in the photographs of these stelai: two frame the head of Alexandra (Pl. 24; see Conze 1969 for the three in the entablature); at the level of Sosibia's inscription is a pair of pins, one in each side of entablature (Pl. 30:c); pins are between the heads of the women on the stele of Neike (Pl. 32).

[83] A single pin, clipped to the level of the background, is beside the head of Lamia Viboullia, while one at the level of her head and one at the level of her knee were robbed out of the sides (Pl. 27:c). Those in the upper corners of the background of the relief of Agathemeris and Sempronius (Pl. 32) were clipped while those in the sides were carefully removed, chiseled out like those of Lamia Viboullia and like the lower ones in the stele of Sosibia (Pl. 30). The upper break on **10** runs through the slot of an iron pin that was set into the side of this relief; another, clipped or broken, is in the background to left of the sistrum (Pl. 25). Pins have been battered out of the Eleusis "Isis" stele (Pl. 14).

[84] The large stele of Attikos (H. 1.27, W. 0.78, Th. 0.18 m.) has a pin in the side at the level of the entablature and one unusually low, 0.10 m. from the plinth (Pl. 22): they are 0.05 m. from the front edge. The stele of Agathemeris and Sempronius (H. 1.69, W. 0.90, Th. 0.26 m.) had a pin at the level of the heads and at the level of the knees of the figures, each set 0.03 m. from the front edge and at a depth of 0.025 m. Pins centered in the sides of the stelai of Lamia Viboullia (H. 1.55, W. 0.77, Th. 0.15 m.) and of Sosibia (H. 0.90, W. 0.48, Th. 0.10 m.) are also too shallow (set 0.02–0.025 m. into the stele) to secure these heavy slabs of stone; see Pls. 27 and 30. Only a large armature such as that used for the stele of Attikos in the Mantua Ducal Palace would hold these stelai upright (Pl. 22). The single pin barely set into the top of the largest preserved stele of Roman date, the Damaskenos, would not be sufficient to clamp the stele upright to a wall as suggested by Dow and Vermeule (*Hesperia* 34, 1965, pp. 276–277).

[85] If the wreaths were small circlets, 0.08–0.10 m. in diameter, or soft, deep loops, they would easily frame the head of the relief figure such as that of Lamia Viboullia (Pl. 27) or Amaryllis (Pl. 19); the pins are spaced farther apart on the stelai of Alexandra (Pl. 24) and Neike (Pl. 32) so that larger wreaths or thicker and deeper swags of garlands could have been suspended. The pins in the entablature or pediment as well as those on the sides could take wreaths or garlands.

[86] E.g., the statuesque figures of Tryphon in the Fitzwilliam, on loan from the British Museum (Pl. 11), and the contemporary Neronian "Isis" relief, Athens, N.M. 1270 (Pl. 10); Tryphon's stele is quite tall, 1.79 m. in height.

[87] Nineteen of 39 reliefs with iron pins are "Isis" reliefs: Conze 1954, 1955, 1958, 1960, 1962, 1963, 1968–1971, 2077; Riemann, no. 57; **10, 12, 15**; Eleusis relief (Pl. 14); Athens, Third Ephoria 1160 (Pl. 23). The

Iron pins in Attic grave reliefs appear to be a feature of the Roman period. An early example is the stele of Hilaros and Gaius (Pl. 9), Claudian in date.[88] Even earlier may be the stele of a young man with a siren (Pl. 3) in the Piraeus Museum, which should be dated early in the last third of the 1st century B.C., at the beginning of the Imperial period.[89] In the upper left break there appears to be a slot where a pin may have been robbed out.

A problem arises with a late Hellenistic relief of a youth with low draped mantle, also in the Piraeus Museum.[90] This stele, probably of the middle of the 1st century B.C.,[91] has pin holes framing the battered head of the youth. Are these pins contemporary with the relief, or are they later additions, made in the Roman times when the stele may have been re-used as a grave monument for someone else? The latter seems most likely since stelai with pins, with the exception of this relief, are of Roman date.

The custom of decorating Attic grave stelai with greenery is known at least since the late 5th century B.C. Scenes painted on white-ground lekythoi show wreaths laid on the stepped base of one stele, while sprigs are caught by fillets tied around the shaft of another.[92] So common was the use of wreaths and greenery to honor the dead that little mention of the practice is made by Greek authors.[93] The custom was widespread in the Hellenistic and Roman periods.[94] There are numerous inscriptions of Imperial date in Italy that mention annual offerings of wine and flowers as well as the establishment and maintenance of gardens at the grave site.[95]

Iron pins to hold wreaths or garlands in honor of the dead are known at least since the 4th century B.C. from a chamber tomb at Olynthos and one in Eretria.[96] In the latter a

---

others: Conze 1902, 1913, 1930, 1934, 1966, 2003, 2005, 2029, 2031, 2038, 2052, 2066, 2068, 2069, 2079, 2106, 2127; Riemann, nos. 46, 56; Athens, N.M. 3725 (Pl. 17), 3724 (Pl. 21).

[88] Athens, N.M. 1250 (Conze 2066), footnote 29 below, p. 71.

[89] Piraeus Mus. 223; proportions, stance, and bold sweep of the main contours compare well with the statue of Megiste of *ca.* 27 B.C. (Athens, N.M. 710): see P. Graindor, *Album d'inscriptions attiques d'époque impériale*, Paris 1924, p. 13, pl. 2. The Piraeus relief shares with the late Augustan grave relief Agora S 2443 (Pl. 3) a distinctive outlining of major parts of the face and figure, emphasizing the geometry of each part.

[90] Piraeus Mus. 388: J. Fink, *Die bildschöne Jungling*, Berlin 1963, p. 57, fig. 12 and H. Möbius, "Eigenartige attische Grabreliefs," *AM* 81, 1966, Beil. 88, pp. 158–160.

[91] Compare this figure to the men on the Attic relief, Berlin, Staat.Mus. 1462 (Conze, p. 8), dated by M. Bieber ("Ikonographische Miszellen," *RM* 32, 1917 [pp. 118–146], p. 132) to the 1st century B.C. and (p. 146), by the portrait of the man on the right, to the 40's of the 1st century. They have the same figure proportions and similar long sweeping curves of the decorative drapery. See the discussion of the Berlin relief, footnote 2 below, p. 67.

[92] Kurtz and Boardman, *Greek Burial Customs*, p. 104. See pl. 4:1 in J. D. Beazley, *Attic White Ground Lekythoi*, Oxford 1931.

[93] Kurtz and Boardman, *Greek Burial Customs*, p. 144.

[94] See references in W. von Sydow, "Eine Grabrotunde an der via Appia antica," *JdI* 92, 1977 (pp. 241–309), p. 301.

[95] Dill (footnote 17 above, p. 35), pp. 258–276; J. Toynbee, *Death and Burial in the Roman World*, Ithaca 1971, pp. 62–63.

[96] D. M. Robinson, *Excavations at Olynthus*, XI, *Necrolynthia*, Baltimore 1942, pp. 117–124, dated by Robinson to the first quarter of the 4th century B.C.; K. G. Vollmoeller, "Über zwei euböische Kammergräber mit Totenbetten," *AM* 26, 1901 (pp. 333–376), pp. 342–344; Kurtz and Boardman, *Greek Burial Customs*, p. 280. The Eretria tomb P. Auberson and K. Schefold (*Führer durch Eretria*, Bonn 1972, p. 149) would date to *ca.* 300 B.C.

painted wreath accompanied the pin.[97] In the vaulted tomb of Lyson and Kallikles at Leukadia early in the 2nd century B.C., a thick garland suspended from pins was represented in paint along the walls.[98] Bosses of stone on funerary altars from Rhodes of the second half of the 2nd and first half of the 1st century B.C. and possibly rims on columnar monuments in Attica may have served as collars to keep wreaths in place.[99] There is one Hellenistic grave stele on which a garland carved in relief is suspended from the upper corners of the relief panel.[100]

The use of iron pins to provide for the use of greenery to honor the dead, which seems to be a practice unique to Attic grave reliefs of the Roman period, may represent the taste or temperament of the little known, probably newly propertied, middle class who commissioned these stelai.[101]

INSCRIPTIONS

Attic grave reliefs of the Roman period are not readily dated by the accompanying inscriptions. Unlike the precise development that can be traced in earlier Attic inscriptions, letters are difficult to date after the middle of the 2nd century B.C.[102] Not only can letter forms vary within the same inscription but also there is a pronounced eclecticism, with letters of earlier periods carefully copied or varied.[103] Difficulties also arise from the fact that dated inscriptions may belong to different forms of monuments, each of which may have a certain style of letter and may not compare well with other types of monuments.[104] The range in letter forms and execution thus compounds the difficulties in dating inscriptions on Attic grave reliefs of the Roman period.[105]

There is one grave relief with an inscription that cites a historical event. This relief, the stele of Telesphoros (Pl. 32), can be assigned to the 70's of the 2nd century after Christ.[106] The inscription states that Telesphoros, 28 years old, fought in war and returned unwounded only to die, leaving his child an orphan, ten months old.[107] The war could be either that

---

[97] Vollmoeller, op. cit., p. 342.

[98] C. I. Makaronas and S. G. Miller, "The Tomb of Lyson and Kallikles," *Archaeology* 27, 1974, pp. 248–259.

[99] Fraser, *Rhodian Funerary Monuments*, pp. 17 on date and 22. Kurtz and Boardman, *Greek Burial Customs*, p. 166; Attic columnar grave monuments date from the late 4th century B.C. on: see p. 58 below.

[100] From Mylasa, early 2nd century B.C.: Pfuhl and Möbius, *Die ostgriechischen Grabreliefs* I, p. 263, no. 1075, pl. 161. It may be as late as the middle of the 1st century B.C. by close comparison with three statues of women of the family of L. Valerius Flaccus of Magnesia dated 63/2 B.C.: see A. Linfert, *Kunstzentren hellenistischer Zeit. Studien an weiblichen Gewandfiguren*, Wiesbaden 1976, p. 180, pl. 5, figs. 22–24.

[101] See pp. 56–57 below.

[102] This information is from conversations with Dr. Christian Habicht and Dr. Anthony Raubitschek. See the summary by A. G. Woodhead, *The Study of Greek Inscriptions*, Cambridge 1967, pp. 62–64.

[103] Follet, *Athènes*, pp. 12–14.

[104] *Ibid.*

[105] The summary by Muehsam (*Berytus* 10, 1952, pp. 55–65) is helpful, but more than one criterion must be available to date Attic grave reliefs of the Roman period.

[106] Athens, N.M. 1775, *IG* II², 9898; "*fin s.* II *p.*" according to Muehsam (*Berytus* 10, 1952, pp. 62 and 68), but it should be earlier (see discussion above). Follet (*Athènes*, p. 226) assigns it to A.D. 170/1–175/6.

[107] *IG* II², 9898: Τελεσφόρος Εὐκάρπου Μειλήσιος |ἐτῶν ΚϜ | ἐ<ξ>έφυγον πόλεμον δεινὸν καὶ ἦλθον ἄ|τρωτος μοῖραν δ᾽οὔκ εἴσχυσα φυγεῖν ἀλλ᾽ ἐν|θάδε κεῖμαι παῖδα λιπὼν μηνῶν δέκα ὀρ|φανόν οἴμμοι.

against the Costoboci in A.D. 170 or that against the Heruli in A.D. 267.[108] The early and unexpected death of Telesphoros could be from one of the plagues that raged through the Empire beginning in the 60's of the 2nd century.[109] The war against the Costoboci is probably the one intended since the stele of Telesphoros in figure proportions and snug composition compares well with an ephebic-decree relief of A.D. 192/3.[110] The cursive letters used for his epithet can occur in the 1st through 3rd centuries[111] and resemble those of the statutes of the Iobakchoi of A.D. 174/5 or 175/6.[112]

Prosopography

Little is known concerning the individuals named in the inscriptions on Attic grave reliefs of the Roman period. As summarized by Follet, the numerous funerary epithets have limited utility: they rarely offer intrinsic elements for dating, and as they often name only one individual, they contribute relatively little to the study of the prosopography.[113] A few stelai bear names of persons known from other inscriptions; these may or may not be the same individuals or be from the same family. It was common to name the eldest son after his paternal grandfather.[114] To which generation would the name on a grave stele belong? It is equally possible that the name on the stele may belong to a homonymous individual otherwise unknown. At most, a possible prosopographical reference may support a date for the stele based on style, execution, and any distinctive features such as a hairstyle worn in a certain period.[115]

The inscriptions state the name of an individual followed by the father's name and the name of the place from which they come or, for citizens of Attica, the deme to which they belong. Inscriptions from the second half of the 1st century B.C. to the beginning of the 2nd century after Christ are often lengthy, recording that the person is the daughter of a certain man and the wife of another.[116] Two-figure or three-figure reliefs may bear the name of one

[108] J. A. O. Larsen, "Roman Greece," in *An Economic Survey of Ancient Rome* IV, Baltimore 1938, pp. 494–495.

[109] *Ibid.*, pp. 494–496; J. F. Gilliam, "The Plague under Marcus Aurelius," *American Journal of Philology* 82, 1961, pp. 225–251 with earlier bibliography.

[110] Athens, N.M. 1470 (*IG* II², 2130); J. Kirchner, *Imagines inscriptionum atticarum*, Berlin 1935, p. 29, no. 140, pl. 50.

[111] See Athens, E.M. 8653 (*IG* II², 1990: A.D. 61/2): Kirchner, *op. cit.*, p. 27, no. 127, pl. 47; Athens, E.M. 8488 (*IG* II², 2124: A.D. 190–200): Graindor (footnote 89 above, p. 44), p. 54, no. 83, pl. 66; such letters are on the stele of Parthenope, late 3rd century (Pl. 50).

[112] Athens, E.M. 8187 (*IG* II², 1368): Kirchner, *op. cit.*, pp. 28–29, no. 137, pl. 50; Follet, *Athènes*, p. 141; Muehsam, *Berytus* 10, 1952, p. 62.

[113] Follet, *Athènes*, p. 8.

[114] Muehsam, *Berytus* 10, 1952, p. 66; Follet, *Athènes*, p. 14.

[115] The few examples of distinctive hairstyles include Boston, M.F.A. 1971.209 (Pl. 30), Athens, N.M. 1224 (Pl. 2), N.M. 2558 (p. 69 below, Pl. 6), N.M. 1233 (p. 74 below, Pl. 19), N.M. 1303 (footnote 79 below, p. 79; Pl. 32), N.M. 2014 (footnote 98 below, p. 82; Pl. 42), N.M. 1164 (see footnote 116 below), and Conze 2093 (Munich stele, Pl. 7), 2096 (Grenoble relief, Pl. 22), 1902, 1906, 1914 (p. 35 above with footnotes 14 and 15), 1921.

[116] Seconda Serulia (Conze 1863, *IG* II², 6367) may be the earliest of these reliefs, as the long-legged figures and emphatic gestures are characteristic of reliefs of the third quarter of the 1st century B.C.: see Kallo, with hairstyle of Livia (Athens, N.M. 1164, Conze 1857, *IG* II², 9721) on coins of Livia of 10 B.C. (pl. 3 in

individual,[117] but a family relationship is fairly common.[118] With the representations of a man and a woman, it may be implied that they were husband and wife. When the names are not related, the individuals may have had some other association such as a business arrangement or possibly the same patron.[119] On the stele of Zosas and Nostimos, there are two unrelated men.[120] Zosas who stands with a bull probably was a cattleman while Nostimos holding a vine stock would have kept a vineyard. They may have shared the same property, or Zosas, the taller of the two whose hairstyle and portrait recall that of Hadrian, may have been the landowner.

Only in one instance has it been suggested that persons represented on different grave reliefs are from the same family. From the stele of brothers Eukarpos and Philoxenos, Eukarpos is thought to be the father of Telesphoros named on the stele of the latter.[121] As the stelai are close in date,[122] the persons could be related but it is equally possible that they are not.

Certain names suggest a general period to which the stelai should belong.[123] The name Titus Flavius (Pl. 17) places his stele in the Flavian period, where it also belongs in style.[124] Lamia Viboullia (Pl. 27) would be a contemporary of the famous Vibullii of Marathon of the 1st and 2nd centuries after Christ and belongs to an unknown family of Sounion; stylistically this "Isis" stele belongs to 50's of the 2nd century.[125] The name Aurelius has an even broader span from the beginning of the 2nd century to late in the 3rd, if not longer.[126] The bearers of the unusual names of Bathyllos and Epilampsis on grave stelai may be contemporary with but are probably not related to the famous persons that they are named after. As the stele of Gaius Silios Bathyllos (Pl. 8) is Claudian in date by figure proportions, drapery, composition, and style, he is too late to be the son of the famous comic actor Bathyllos of the

W. Gross, *Iulia Augusta*, Göttingen 1962, pp. 22–23), and Asklepias (Conze 1837, *IG* II², 10890), dated by Riemann, p. 52. One of the latest may be the Trajanic relief of Hilara (footnote 49 below, p. 74; Pl. 20). These inscriptions continue the tradition of such Classical stelai as that of Proxenos (Conze 1570f, *IG* II², 7704) and are found on plain grave markers as well (e.g., Athens, E.M. 186, *IG* II², 6842).

[117] Titus Flavius (*IG* II², 12377), p. 72 below, Pl. 17; Hilara (*IG* II², 9683), footnote 49 below, p. 74, Pl. 20.

[118] Paramonos and son Alexandros (*IG* II², 6692), footnote 59 below, p. 64, Pl. 21; Sosipatros and wife Epiteugma (*IG* II², 12726), Pl. 29. Three-figure reliefs are usually family groups: Mousaios and sister Amaryllis (*IG* II², 5568), Pl. 19; Zosas' family (Conze 2120, *IG* II², 11546); Onasas (Conze 2119a, *IG* II², 12367).

[119] Gaios and Hilaros (*IG* II², 9687), Pl. 9; Zosas and Nostimos, Pl. 25; Dionysia and Synpherousa (p. 36 above). Grave monuments of freedmen in Italy in the late Republic and in Imperial times may include the patron: see Boston, M.F.A. 37.100 (Comstock and Vermeule, *Sculpture in Stone*, p. 200, no. 319); P. Zanker, "Grabreliefs römischer Freigelassener," *JdI* 90, 1975, pp. 267–315.

[120] Marathon Museum (*IG* II², 9631), late Hadrianic (p. 77 below, Pl. 25).

[121] Conze 2068 (*IG* II², 9599); see Muehsam, *Berytus* 10, 1952, p. 68.

[122] Eukarpos and Philoxenos, Athens, N.M. 1243 (Conze 2068, *IG* II², 9599) of the 60's of the 2nd century after Christ (footnote 86 below, p. 80; Pl. 32); Telesphoros, Athens, N.M. 1775 (*IG* II², 9898), dated by the inscription to the 70's of the 2nd century (pp. 45–46 above, Pl. 32). They were found built into houses in different parts of Athens, and they differ in style and execution so that they should be assigned to different workshops; neither fact supports or negates the suggested identification.

[123] Follet, *Athènes*, pp. 90–98.

[124] Athens, N.M. 3725 (*IG* II², 12377), p. 72 below.

[125] Piraeus Mus. 1160 (*IG* II², 7441; p. 78 below); on the Vibullii, see Woloch (footnote 15 above, p. 35), pp. 116–123.

[126] Follet, *Athènes*, pp. 90–98.

reign of Augustus.[127] The theater masks in the center of the relief suggest that Gaius, too, was an actor, possibly one who emulated the famous Bathyllos or was his successor in Athens.[128]

Follet suggested that "Aphrodeisia alias Epilampsis" on a stele in the Fitzwilliam was the mother of the famous Ailia Epilampsis, the priestess of Demeter and Kore towards the end of the 2nd century after Christ.[129] The woman on the relief, however, is too young, and she may have been a musician, as indicated by the accompanying lyre, rather than a member of Ailia Epilampsis' prominent family.[130] Stylistically this stele is of the 60's of the 2nd century.[131]

The majority of the identifications from the inscriptions on the Attic grave reliefs are tentative. Usually only one other reference is preserved, most often from an ephebic catalogue.[132] These catalogues are securely dated, but since membership in the ephebia comprised all Athenian young men at the age of eighteen, it is hard to be sure that in any given instance we have true identification.[133] Outside the ephebia, there are only three references, to officials, that may possibly be connected. First, a thesmothete at the beginning of the 1st century after Christ, Demetrios son of Alexandros of Sphettos, may be the father of Aphrodeisia on a Tiberian "Isis" relief (Pl. 6).[134] Second, a prytanis ca. 50–40 B.C., Diotimos of Azenia, may be the father of Demetria on an Augustan grave relief (Pl. 2).[135] Third, a presbis after 38/7 B.C., Diogenes of Eitea, may be the father of the husband of Pompeia Isias on a grave relief of the 30's of the 1st century B.C. (Pl. 2).[136]

The lack of information preserved in the inscriptions on the "Isis" reliefs indicates that these persons are members of the numerous, if little known, middle class in Athens who

---

[127] Stele of Gaius Silios Bathyllos, Verona, Mus.Lap. (*IG* II², 5302). On Bathyllos, see Gensel, *RE* III, 1899, col. 137; Conze and Muehsam (*Berytus* 10, 1952, p. 59) refer to the famous actor as a contemporary of the person on the Attic grave relief, while Woloch ([footnote 15 above, p. 35] p. 101) repeats Kirchner's suggestion that Gaius Silios was the son of the famous actor. The Claudian date of the stele would preclude a close family tie; for the date based on style, see footnote 29 below, p. 71.

[128] Conze (2113) notes the theater masks; Muehsam (*Berytus* 10, 1952, p. 59) regards Gaius Silios as having assumed the name of the famous actor. Such emulation could occur at any time, but the 1st century after Christ is likely.

[129] Aphrodeisia alias Epilampsis, Fitzwilliam GR 5.1919 (*IG* II², 6725); Follet, *Athènes*, pp. 195–196 on Ailia Epilampsis priestess of Demeter and Kore (*IG* II², 3687). The term of office of the latter Clinton (*TAPS* 64, p. 75, no. 16) places towards the end of the 2nd century after Christ.

[130] On the family of Ailia Epilampsis, Follet, *Athènes*, pp. 195–196 with stemma.

[131] Compare with Sosibia, Boston, M.F.A. 1971.209 (Pl. 30) for figure proportions, bold modeling of figure, and weighted fall of the drapery.

[132] See Muehsam, *Berytus* 10, 1952, pp. 66–69.

[133] Follet, *Athènes*, p. 14; on ephebes, see O. W. Reinmuth, "The Ephebate and Citizenship in Attica," *Transactions of the American Philological Association* 79, 1948, pp. 211–231.

[134] Stele of Aphrodeisia, Athens, N.M. Θησ. 140 (*IG* II², 7507); Demetrios son of Alexandros of Sphettos, thesmothete (*IG* II², 1729, line 3).

[135] Demetria (Conze 1838, *IG* II², 5304), Augustan in date (see p. 68 below). Diotimos of Azenia, prytanis (B. D. Meritt, "Greek Inscriptions," *Hesperia* 36, 1967 [pp. 225–241], p. 237, no. 47, line 17).

[136] Concerning Pompeia Isias, Athens, N.M. 1224 (*IG* II², 5540), the father of her husband may be Diogenes of Eitea, presbis after 38/7 B.C. (*IG* II², 1051, line 19; Muehsam, *Berytus* 10, 1952, p. 66); the stele can be dated to the 30's of the 1st century B.C. by hairstyle (see coins of Livia of ca. 10 B.C. in Gross [footnote 116 above, p. 46]).

could afford and chose to have grave reliefs. Although the fragmentary condition of the "Isis" reliefs has limited the number of names available to us, the proportion of stelai with prosopographical references to those with inscriptions preserved reflects that found in Muehsam's survey of Attic grave reliefs of the Roman period:[137] 7 of 26 "Isis" reliefs have possible prosopographical references.[138]

One identification from an "Isis" relief (**25**, Pl. 40) is all too tenuous: preserved on a pediment is part of a name, Stephepho-. Meritt would restore it to Stephephoros of Aixone, prytanis in A.D. 174/5.[139]

Four instances are questionable. The first concerns Kallo (Pl. 13) daughter of Achilleus of Eupyridon, whom Kirchner suggests may be related to Achilleus son of Euphorosynos, ephebe in A.D. 155/6, but the relief is early Flavian in style, 80 years earlier than the ephebe cited.[140] The second questionable identification is for an "Isis" relief in Mantua belonging to Attikos son of Zotikos of Phlya (Pl. 22). According to Follet, Patron, who was an ephebe in the middle of the 2nd century after Christ, could be the son of the same Zotikos, hence a brother of Attikos.[141] As the relief in Mantua belongs with Hadrianic reliefs and should be dated to the 20's of the 2nd century, the two men could not be brothers, nor is it easy to calculate an alternative generation to which Patron could belong. The "Isis" relief of Epigonos and Elate (Pl. 24), which should be dated to the 30's of the 2nd century after Christ, has a similar conflict.[142] Kirchner and Conze suggest that Menodoros son of Glykon of Bereneikidai, ephebe in A.D. 145/6, is related to Elate, daughter of Menodoros named on the "Isis" relief.[143] As the ephebe would have been a child when Elate died, what relation could he have been? The last of the four questionable identifications concerns Lamia Viboullia (Pl. 27). Muehsam would date this "Isis" relief to the end of the 2nd century as she considers Lamia Viboullia to be the sister of Eukarpos son of Philokratos, prytanis in A.D. 180.[144] Stylistically the relief can only be early Antonine, 50's of the 2nd century.

---

[137] Muehsam, *Berytus* 10, 1952, pp. 66–69. Two others are Demetria (see footnote 135 above, p. 48) and Theophilos (Athens, N.M. 1309; Conze 2003, *IG* II², 6797) who may be related to Dionysios of Marathon, ephebe in A.D. 111/2 or 112/3 (*IG* II², 2022, line 33); for the date see Follet, *Athènes*, p. 55. The latter should be early Antonine; compare Pl. 26.

[138] Seven are cited above; the rest are Conze 1972, no. 23 (*IG* II², 7467); Riemann, no. 57 (*IG* II², 5403); Conze 1969 (*IG* II², 6945); Conze 1956 (*IG* II², 9697); Conze 1967 (*IG* II², 12726); Conze 1955 (*IG* II², 6441); Conze 1963 (*IG* II², 6498); Conze 1959 (*IG* II², 10181); Conze 1958 (*IG* II², 6311); Conze 1961 (*IG* II², 12752); **22**; Conze 1966 (*IG* II², 10182); Conze 1954 (*IG* II², 12418); Conze 2142 (*IG* II², 7431); Conze 2141; Conze 2139 (*IG* III, 3647); Conze 2140 (*IG* II², 5909); Aigina Museum, pediment fragment (Kourouniotis, Ἀρχ᾽Ἐφ, 1913, p. 97); stele of Methe, Athens Third Ephoria 1160 (unpublished; see p. 50 below for the inscription).

[139] B. D. Meritt, "Greek Inscriptions," *Hesperia* 23, 1954 (pp. 233–283), p. 281, no. 171.

[140] Kallo and Syngheron (*IG* II², 6148), Flavian (p. 72 below); Achilleus, ephebe (*IG* II², 2068, line 40).

[141] Attikos, Mantua, Duc.Pal. 6677 (*IG* II², 7667), early Hadrianic (p. 75 below); Follet (*Athènes*, p. 223) refers to Patron as a relative of Attikos (*IG* II², 2069, line 29).

[142] Epigonos and Elate, Athens, N.M. 1308 (*IG* II², 6458), late Hadrianic (pp. 76–77 below); Muehsam (*Berytus* 10, 1952, p. 67) also notes this conflict between the stylistic data of the stele and the possible prosopographical reference.

[143] Kirchner (*IG* II², 6458) and Conze (1962) refer to Menodoros, ephebe (*IG* II², 2052, line 37).

[144] Lamia Viboullia, Piraeus Mus. 1160 (*IG* II², 7441), early Antonine (p. 78 below); Muehsam (*Berytus* 10, 1952, p. 67) refers to Eukarpos, prytanis (*IG* II², 1794, line 13), as does Kirchner (*IG* II², 7441).

Two "Isis" reliefs with prosopographical references merit consideration. The first is the Tiberian relief of Aphrodeisia (Pl. 6).[145] It is one of the most impressive Attic grave reliefs of the Roman period and would be an appropriate monument for a member of a prominent Athenian family. Aphrodeisia's father could have been Demetrios, son of Alexandros of Sphettos, who served as thesmothete at the beginning of the 1st century after Christ.[146] The second is the unusual three-figure relief of Mousaios and his sister Amaryllis (Pl. 19). The older man, Mousaios son of Antipatros of Alopeke, may be the father of Antipatros, ephebe in A.D. 110 or 120/1.[147] According to Oliver and Meritt, the career of Antipatros can be traced from ephebe to prytanis in A.D. 135/6 and agoranomos in the 40's or 50's of the 2nd century.[148] Stylistically the date of the grave relief of Mousaios is late Trajanic,[149] *ca.* A.D. 110–120, which is the decade assigned by Meritt to Mousaios as father of Antipatros. As the relief is outstanding in quality and execution and bears a striking portrait of Mousaios, it would not be surprising if he were the father of a man who held two public offices.

A handsome, fully preserved, late Hadrianic relief in the Third Ephoria of Athens (Pl. 23)[150] bears only the name of the woman who wears the dress of Isis.[151] "Methe (daughter or wife) of Herakleidos of Kephale" indicates that she is an Athenian citizen, but who is the man around whom she places her right arm? Such a gesture should indicate a family relationship.[152] Most important is the fact that only the woman in the dress of Isis is given a name, hence is the one most honored here.

CONTINUED USE AND RE-USE

From the inscriptions we also learn of continued use and re-use of grave reliefs as funerary monuments. As in the Classical period and later, not only could members of the same family add their names to the relief but also the relief could be re-used, inscribed to unrelated persons as their grave monument.[153] Names were simply added, or the original

---

[145] Aphrodeisia, Athens, N.M. Θησ. 140 (*IG* II², 7507), Tiberian (p. 69 below).

[146] *IG* II², 1729, line 3.

[147] Mousaios and Amaryllis, Athens, N.M. 1233 (*IG* II², 5568), late Trajanic (p. 74 below, Pl. 19); Antipatros is named as ephebe in *IG* II², 2020, line 26, which Follet (*Athènes*, p. 203) would date *ca.* A.D. 120/1. Prosopographical reference: Kirchner (*IG* II², 5568); Conze 1971; Muehsam, *Berytus* 10, 1952, p. 68; J. H. Oliver, "Greek Inscriptions," *Hesperia* 11, 1942 (pp. 29–90), pp. 40–43; B. D. Meritt, Prosopographical Index at the Institute for Advanced Study, Princeton.

[148] Oliver, *loc. cit.*; Meritt, *loc. cit.*

[149] On the date of the stele, see p. 74 below.

[150] Third Ephoria 1160, unpublished; brought to this storeroom in 1971 after the demolition of a house in this part of Athens.

[151] Late Hadrianic date of this relief, p. 76 below; the inscription: ϭ´ Μέθη ῾Ηρακλείδου Κεφαλληθέν

[152] Brief mention is made of gestures between man and wife by Muehsam (*Berytus* 10, 1952, pp. 89–90). This shoulder embrace is shown on the Attic relief in Paris (Conze 2098; Muehsam, *op. cit.*, pl. XVIII:3), probably man and wife, but the inscription (*IG* II², 9410) does not preserve the full names. On a three-figure relief, Athens, N.M. 1230 (Conze 2120), the woman also embraces the man on her right, and the inscription indicates that this is a family (*IG* II², 11546):

Ζωσᾶς Ζοίλου | Ζοίλος Τειχίππου | ᾿Ονησιφόρου

[153] Kurtz and Boardman, *Greek Burial Customs*, p. 136. There are three reliefs of Roman date with names added by family members: on the Trajanic relief of Paramonos and his son (Pl. 21), see the son's name Alexandros enlarged and rambling into the pediment (Piraeus Mus. 222; *IG* II², 6692; see footnote 118 above,

inscription was erased first. Although to add inscriptions is an easy and economical way to provide a grave monument, the re-used stelai of Roman date appear to have been chosen for iconography or quality.[154]

Six re-used "Isis" reliefs are preserved. Of the two cases that can be dated, one (Pl. 28) is as late as the early 4th century after Christ.

The carefully detailed "Isis" reliefs, often boldly carved, were the ones chosen for re-use. The late Hadrianic two-figure relief of Epigonos and Elate (Pl. 24) was subsequently given a second inscription of an unrelated woman Eision, carefully centered on the epistyle.[155] The stele is one of the few "Isis" reliefs to have a lotus-topped sistrum and a coiled basket for the cist.[156] The handsome early Hadrianic relief of Attikos in Mantua (Pl. 22) bears the name of an unrelated woman, which is coarsely inscribed in an erasure over the relief figure of a woman in the dress of Isis.[157] Similarly, the name squeezed over the woman in the dress of Isis would be a later addition to the small, yet boldly carved Broom Hall relief of two women of the middle Severan period (Pl. 39).[158]

Bold revision of one stele emphasized an Isis cist. A large and deep stele pediment (**25**, Pl. 40) in the Agora was taken over and re-inscribed to a man Stephepho- with the addition of a large cist cutting through the center akroterion.[159] These changes occurred in the 20's of the 3rd century after Christ, to judge from the shape, proportions, and three-dimensionality of the cist.[160] This man surely called attention to the cist and the importance of the Isis cult, if not also to his membership in the cult.

An inscription with relief was added to a small but carefully carved, early Antonine "Isis" relief (Pl. 28), Athens, N.M. 1249.[161] It has been thought that the inscription of the feminine name Eisias identified the "Isis" relief figure,[162] but the usual place for an inscription is in the area above the relief figure, which is broken away. The inscription of Eisias is above the lower relief and could name this figure, a woman in chiton and mantle with

---

p. 47 above); on the Flavian "Isis" relief of Agathostratos and his daughter (Pl. 15), see the squeezed name of the daughter "Ma" (Riemann, no. 57; *IG* II², 5403; footnote 39 below, p. 72); on the late Trajanic "Isis" relief of Mousaios and his sister Amaryllis (Pl. 19) a space is left for the name of the third figure (Athens, N.M. 1233; *IG* II², 5568; p. 74 below).

[154] The stele of Artemidoros resembles Attic sarcophagi; it is the only grave relief with a hunt scene in a landscape. It has three inscriptions of which the upper two are later additions for unrelated men (Athens, N.M. 1192; Conze 2052, *IG* II², 5895); Muehsam (*Berytus* 10, 1952, p. 68) thought that the three men were from the same family, but only the demotic is shared by the upper two inscriptions. On the middle Antonine date, see footnote 92 below, p. 81.

[155] Athens, N.M. 1308 (*IG* II², 6458; for the date of the stele, see pp. 76–77 below). Date of the added inscription unknown.

[156] See p. 20 above on the sistrum, p. 29 above on the cist.

[157] Mantua, Duc.Pal. 6677 (*IG* II², 7667); for the date of the stele, see p. 75 below. The letters preserved of her undated inscription indicate that she was from a different deme and that her father's or husband's name was not Attikos.

[158] Broom Hall (*IG* II², 10182); for the date of the stele, see p. 84 below.

[159] See p. 30 above.

[160] See **25**, p. 107 below.

[161] Athens, N.M. 1249 (Conze 1956, *IG* II², 9697; date of stele, p. 78 below).

[162] Dunand (*Le Culte d'Isis* II, p. 145, note 3) incorrectly considers the lower figure to be a man, hence the woman in the dress of Isis to be "Eisias".

mirror in the background.[163] Stylistically the lower relief belongs to the late 3rd or early 4th century after Christ.[164] It is understandable that the later relief was carved into the vacant area below the "Isis" relief, but why was the "Isis" relief not sheared away? Its retention reflects the interest in the cult by the individual who re-used the stele, the second person, whose name is based on Isis.[165]

The large and impressive "Isis" relief in Trieste (Pl. 43) may also have been re-used as a funerary monument, possibly as late as Christian times.[166] Stylistically it should belong late in the 30's of the 3rd century after Christ.[167] It may owe its good state of preservation to its dramatic and decorative appearance. Below the figure's left hand on the background is inscribed the name of the Muse Erato, popular particularly in the 3rd century and early Christian period for funerary monuments.[168]

INTERPRETATION OF THE ATTIC "ISIS" RELIEFS

None of the persons named on the Attic grave reliefs with women in the dress of Isis is known from the inscriptions preserved concerning the cult of Isis in Athens.[169] What was their role in the cult? The grave reliefs are strictly funerary in representation with figures standing side by side or with one seated. There is no narrative scene to show their role in the cult.[170]

Difficulties arise with the interpretation of women in the dress of Isis on Attic grave reliefs. As summarized by Dunand, there are three possibilities: the women could represent the goddess Isis, priestesses, or participants in the cult.[171] In literature a fine linen dress is

---

[163] See Pl. 28; Conze (1956) recognized the lower figure as a woman. Her dress of long chiton and mantle is only worn by women on Attic grave reliefs of the Roman period; the mirror hung on the wall is like that on the stele of Hieronis in Istanbul of Roman date (see Bieber, *Ancient Copies*, pl. 122, fig. 719).

[164] Cf. a prime example, the grave monument with similar, geometric figures of a man and a woman on a grave relief of this period from the Kerameikos (Riemann, no. 46; p. 88 below, esp. footnote 135; Pl. 51); see also **34** (Pl. 51) for the short hairstyle.

[165] See also the second inscription on the relief of Epigonos and Elate, p. 51 above. Dow (*HThR* 30, 1937, pp. 116–224) concludes that names based on the Egyptian gods may reflect the popularity of the name more than that of the cult, but in the case of the re-used "Isis" reliefs the name based on Isis may indeed imply interest in the cult.

[166] Trieste, Mus.Civ. 2214 (Conze 1972), pp. 85–86 below.

[167] *Ibid.*

[168] The decorative appearance of this figure would be appropriate for a Muse; for the popularity of the Muse Erato in the 3rd century after Christ and Christian period, see A. M. McCann, *Roman Sarcophagi in the Metropolitan Museum of Art*, New York 1978, pp. 47–48 and K. Weitzmann, *The Age of Spirituality, Late Antique and Early Christian Art, Third to Seventh Century* (Metropolitan Museum of Art exhibition, Nov. 9, 1977–February 12, 1978), New York 1979, p. 204. Conze (1972) and Muehsam (*Berytus* 10, 1952, p. 58) consider the letter forms of the name of Erato to be without parallel, probably modern, but they may be compared with Attic inscriptions of the early Christian period: see J. S. Creaghan and A. E. Raubitschek, "Early Christian Epitaphs from Athens," *Hesperia* 16, 1947, pp. 1–54.

[169] See Vidman, *Sylloge*, pp. 3–18, nos. 1–33b and Koumanoudes, Δελτ 25, 1970, p. 68, no. 24.

[170] See p. 55 below.

[171] Dunand, *Le Culte d'Isis* II, pp. 148–149.

worn by Isis, priests and priestesses, and initiates in the cult.[172] Similarly the sistrum and situla may be held by all three.[173]

Attic grave reliefs consistently show women with the fringed mantle drawn over both shoulders and knotted at the chest.[174] This arrangement is Athenian, probably the way in which the dress of Isis was worn by women in Athens who belonged to the cult. It appears on Attic grave reliefs at least as early as the reign of Augustus,[175] is found on a few statues of Isis, the empress as Isis, and portrait statues by Athenian sculptors.[176] By the 2nd century after Christ it is found in decorative adaptations by local sculptors in Tunis (Pl. 52), Palmyra, and Israel.[177]

On the few comparable, contemporary funerary monuments in Italy a variety of dress and hairstyle is worn by women either holding or framed by sistrum and situla,[178] while a few Hellenistic grave monuments show women in the fringed mantle, usually with one end caught and knotted at the chest.[179] None of these monuments in representation or inscription clarifies the role of these women in the cult of Isis. On the earliest, a grave stele from Smyrna of the beginning of the 2nd century B.C., a young woman, Isias (Pl. 1), in the knotted fringed mantle holds sistrum and situla and stands beside a tree, a setting which belongs

---

[172] Plutarch, de Is. et Os., 3 and 4; Apuleius, Metamorphoses XI.3–4, 9–10, and 23. See Griffiths, De Iside, p. 270 and The Isis Book, p. 192.

[173] Sistrum: Apuleius, Metamorphoses XI.4 (Isis), 12 (priest), and 10 (initiates). Situla: Apuleius, Metamorphoses XI.4 (Isis) and 10 (priest). See Griffiths, The Isis Book, pp. 187, 269, 273, and 275. See also pp. 20–25 above.

[174] See pp. 6–7, 18, 30–31 above; Fig. 1.

[175] Pp. 67–69 below.

[176] Herakleion Mus. 314 (Pl. 12); Rome, Mus.Cap. 744 (Pl. 31); from Zagreb, Arch.Mus. 34 (Pl. 44). Empress as Isis: Vatican, Mus.Greg.Eg. 83 (Pl. 41). From Cyrene there are two portrait statues in this dress of Isis, one of which represents the empress Faustina the Elder (Pl. 27); see footnote 78, p. 79 below.

[177] Tunis, Bardo Museum: D.A.I., Rome neg. 61.580; Askelon, Israel (Encyclopedia of Archaeological Excavations in the Holy Land, A–D, London 1975, p. 127); probably from Palmyra, Hamburg Museum 1968.38 (H. Hoffman et al., "Erwerbungsbericht des Museums für Kunst und Gewerbe Hamburg 1963–1969," AA [JdI 84], 1969 [pp. 318–377], p. 323, fig. 5:a–c; compare with figs. 72, 74 in M. R. R. Colledge, The Art of Palmyra, London 1976).

[178] Funerary altar of Balullia Varilla, Naples, M.N. 2929 (Corpus inscriptionum latinarum VI, 13454; Vidman, Sylloge, p. 215, no. 446; Pl. 51) with Flavian-Trajanic hairstyle and plain mantle folded and pinned on right shoulder (see Witt, Isis, fig. 32). Late Hadrianic funerary altar of Fabia Stratonice, Karlsruhe, Badisches Landesmuseum 64/134; she wears chiton and plain mantle (Grenier, L'Autel funéraire isiaque, p. 5, pls. I–III). Early Antonine relief of Galatea, Vatican, Loggia Scoperta (Pl. 51).

[179] From Smyrna (Pl. 1), stele of Isias, London, B.M. 639 (see below) and stele of Demetrios and Sarapias, Oxford Museum (Pfuhl and Möbius, Die ostgriechischen Grabreliefs I, pp. 227–228, no. 878: ca. 100 B.C.; Pl. 1); funerary altar, Rhodes, Arch.Mus. (ibid., p. 131, no. 377, pl. 62; dated to mid-2nd century B.C. by Fraser, Rhodian Funerary Monuments, p. 11; Pl. 1); from Eretria, stele of Euphrosyne of mid-1st century B.C. with figure in chiton and plain mantle (see p. 67 below). The Rhodian figure holds a broad, shallow basket on her head and may be a kanephoros. The latter is known from a few Isis inscriptions from Athens and Delos: Vidman, Sylloge, nos. 8, 9, and 20 from Athens; Roussel, Cultes égyptiens, nos. 112 bis, 135, 141, and 156. Possibly like kanephoroi in other cults (Mittelhaus, RE X, 1919, cols. 1862–1866: ten other cults) the kanephoros on the Rhodes funerary altar may have served cult processions, an honorary rather than a priestly role; see Malaise, Conditions, p. 136, note 6.

to the general iconography of Hellenistic grave reliefs.[180] The inscription identifies her as Isias daughter of Metrodoros of Laodikea and states that the Demos gave the relief in her honor, perhaps out of gratitude to her or her family for some gift to the town's cult of Isis.[181]

The interpretation that women in the dress of Isis with sistrum and situla on these grave monuments represent the goddess can be dismissed.[182] None have the necessary emblem of Isis worn on the head except the early Antonine relief of Galatea (Pl. 51) in Rome.[183] Like statues of the empress as Isis, Galatea has been assimilated to the goddess.[184] On this grave relief a bearded man on the right adds incense to a burning thymiaterion, the focus of the composition, lit in honor of the deceased.[185]

The funerary monuments with women in the dress of Isis might represent priestesses of Isis.[186] Vidman and Heyob propose that the women on Attic grave reliefs are priestesses for life,[187] but the stelai are too numerous to support this suggestion.[188] Little is known concerning the cult of Isis. The hierarchy, role of the priestesses, length of service, and number

[180] London, B.M. 639 (Isias): Horn (footnote 60 above, p. 14), p. 40; Thompson, *Ptolemaic Oinochoai*, p. 113; Pfuhl and Möbius, *Die ostgriechischen Grabreliefs* I, p. 130, no. 376. For trees see a stele from Tarsus, Athens, N.M. 1158 (Horn, *op. cit.*, pl. 15:1) and one from Rheneia (Couilloud [footnote 91 above, p. 18], pl. 13, no. 58).

[181] A good parallel is the statue of Titiana of Sinope of the 2nd century after Christ set up in the temple of Sarapis by the town council in thanks to her father: Dunand, *Le Culte d'Isis* III, pp. 114–115 and 114, note 5.

[182] Dunand (*Le Culte d'Isis* II, p. 148) refers to Attic grave reliefs, but the same argument applies to the other monuments cited above.

[183] On the emblem of Isis, see p. 12 above; it is a crescent with a lotus on Galatea, Vatican, Loggia Scoperta (Pl. 51); W. Amelung, *Die Sculpturen des Vaticanischen Museums* I–II, Berlin 1903–1908, pp. 738–740, no. 19; W. Altmann, *Die römischen Grabaltäre der Kaiserzeit*, Berlin 1905, p. 237; M. Malaise, *Inventaire préliminaire des documents égyptiens découverts en Italie*, Leiden 1972, p. 143, Rome, no. 107. The braided hairstyle can be worn in Trajanic, Hadrianic, or Antonine periods (E. B. Harrison, "The Constantinian Portrait," *Dumbarton Oaks Papers* 21, 1967 [pp. 81–96], p. 88), but the portrait of the man, drilled pupils, and compact composition suggest an early Antonine date (Amelung, *op. cit.*, p. 738; Zanker [footnote 119 above, p. 47], p. 271, note 12); compare with relief figures from the Hadrianeum, Rome of A.D. 145: J. M. C. Toynbee, *The Hadrianic School*, Cambridge 1934, pp. 152–159, pls. 34:5 and 36:3.

[184] Julia Maesa as Isis, Vatican, Mus.Greg.Eg. 83 (Pl. 41), and possibly an idealized portrait of Faustina the Younger as Isis, Rome, Mus.Cap. 744 (Pl. 31). For literature on empresses as goddesses, see H. von Heintze, Helbig[4] IV, p. 73, no. 3082; for private persons and empresses as goddesses, see H. Wrede, "Das Mausoleum der Claudia Semne und die burgerliche Plastik der Kaiserzeit," *RM* 78, 1971, pp. 124–166. On imperial epiklesis, see Fraser, *Ptolemaic Alexandria*, p. 244, note 440. A good example of the representation of a private person as Aphrodite is a grave relief in the British Museum (Toynbee [footnote 95 above, p. 44], fig. 79) and one in Ostia (R. Brilliant, *Gesture and Rank in Roman Art*, New Haven 1963, p. 136, fig. 3:80).

[185] See Toynbee (footnote 95 above, p. 44), pp. 279–280, on thymiateria as tomb furnishings, and pl. 9, examples on the relief from the tomb of the Haterii, Rome.

[186] W. Drexler in W. H. Roscher, *Ausführliches Lexikon der griechischen und römischen Mythologie* II, i, Leipzig 1897, p. 386; G. Roeder, *RE* IX, 1916, col. 2131. Undecided: Lafaye, DarSag III, i, p. 584; Conze, p. 54; and Tran Tam Tinh, *Essai*, p. 96, note 4 and *Campanie*, p. 30, note 3.

[187] Vidman, *Isis und Sarapis*, pp. 48–49; Heyob, *Cult of Isis*, pp. 90–92. Their conclusions are based on four Attic grave stelai (Vidman, *Sylloge*, nos. 13, 18, 23, 24).

[188] Of the 106 (p. 1 above), I have dated 25 to the 2nd century after Christ and 29 to the first 60 years of the 3rd (see Appendix 3). These far outnumber the few individuals who served as priest for life in the Eleusinian Mysteries: see Clinton, *TAPS* 64, pp. 10–47 (hierophants), 44 (term of office), and 117–119 (list of priests and priestesses).

of priestesses are unknown.[189] No priestess of Isis is known before Imperial times.[190] One inscription from Athens specifies the length of office: a priestess in the 3rd century held office for one year;[191] was there possibly an annual change of office? The 28 Attic "Isis" reliefs assigned to the first 60 years of the 3rd century[192] are too few to account for an annual change in office even with a large margin allowed for poor preservation. If there was an annual change of office, the person who held this office may have had a titular role.[193]

Dunand regards two Attic "Isis" reliefs as representing a priestess of Isis participating in the cult: the upper small figure (Pl. 28) on the stele inscribed to Eisias in Athens and the large figure of Lamia Viboullia (Pl. 27) on a relief in Piraeus, also early Antonine in date.[194] On the former the young woman in the dress of Isis stands to the left of a small cylindrical altar, a cult altar according to Dunand, but the young woman cannot officiate at the altar as she does not hold the necessary patera.[195] The altar is probably a funerary altar accompanying the deceased and burning in her honor like the thymiaterion on the contemporary relief of Galatea (Pl. 51) in Rome.[196] Dunand considers the little girl on the left of Lamia Viboullia to be an acolyte assisting the priestess Lamia, but the girl holds an open jewel box and belongs to the traditional iconography of Attic grave reliefs.[197] Dunand has also suggested that Eukarpos accompanying Sophia in the dress of Isis (Athens, N.M. 1214; Pl. 37) had two priestly roles as zakore and hagiaphore in this cult.[198] The latter are known from inscriptions dating to A.D. 127/8, much too early to refer to the same man as on the stele of Sophia and Eukarpos which should date to the 220's after Christ.[199]

---

[189] Dunand, *Le Culte d'Isis* III, pp. 193–196; Heyob, *Cult of Isis*, pp. 93 and 101. Dunand discusses at length the possible hierarchy of the cult in Greece in Hellenistic and Roman times, but it must be remembered that Apuleius, *Metamorphoses* XI (2nd century after Christ) gives the one lengthy description of the cult and by no means defines the hierarchy, role, or importance of priests and officials known from the inscriptions or the rituals and mysteries of the cult.

[190] Vidman, *Isis und Sarapis*, pp. 48–49; Heyob, *Cult of Isis*, p. 90.

[191] Athens, E.M. 8159 and 8160 (*IG* II², 1950: after the middle of the 3rd century after Christ): Vidman, *Sylloge*, p. 16, no. 30 and *Isis und Sarapis*, pp. 49–50; Heyob, *Cult of Isis*, p. 92.

[192] See Appendix 3.

[193] See the discussion of the cult association of the Sarapiastai (*IG* II², 1292; Vidman, *Sylloge*, no. 2) of 215/4 B.C. headed by a woman: Dow, *HThR* 30, 1937, pp. 194–197. Nominal headship may also have been true for women who held the office of priestess in several cults simultaneously, such as Regilla, the wife of Herodes Atticus, who was the most important and wealthy Athenian in the 2nd century after Christ (see P. Graindor, *Un Milliardaire antique: Hérode Atticus et sa Famille*, Cairo 1930); Regilla was priestess of Demeter at Olympia and of Tyche in Piraeus (*ibid.*, pp. 84 and 87).

[194] Dunand, *Le Culte d'Isis* II, p. 149; Athens, N.M. 1249 and Piraeus Mus. 1160.

[195] On paterae, see Ryberg (footnote 165 above, p. 28), pp. 41, 57, and 58–59, pl. XVI, fig. 29; see also the votive relief to Demeter Karpophoros of Roman date in Athens: J. N. Svoronos, *Das Athener National Museum* I–II, Athens 1908–1911, pl. 72 and p. 439, no. 1438.

[196] See p. 54 above. Dunand (*Le Culte d'Isis* II, p. 149) mistakes the flames for fruit offerings; see description (Conze 1956) and Pl. 28; the blazing incense burner beside Galatea (Pl. 51) serves like the small altar on the Athens stele as a receptacle and brazier to consume gifts in honor of the dead (see footnote 185 above, p. 54).

[197] See Diepolder, *Die attischen Grabreliefs*, pls. 19, 20, 26.

[198] Dunand, *Le Culte d'Isis* II, p. 164, note 3.

[199] Two inscriptions (Vidman, *Sylloge*, nos. 16, 17) belonging to the Isis cult in Athens mention "Eukarpos", but no father's name or place is given in *IG* II², 4771 of A.D. 127/8 where Eukarpos is zakore and hagiaphore;

If the women on the Attic "Isis" reliefs are neither Isis nor her priestesses, they can only represent initiates in the cult. The large number of the reliefs and the range in size and quality of contemporary examples are indicative of a large, competitive, non-stratified social group such as the initiates in the cult of Isis.[200] Their coveted position and costly costume are well known.[201] Apuleius (*Metamorphoses* XI.9–10) vividly describes the popularity of the cult, the pomp of the procession, and the impressiveness of the throng of initiates, men and women who precede the small group of priests and carry sistra of bronze, silver, and gold. In fashion similar to Apuleius' description, the emphasis in the reliefs is on the linen dress and the hand-held attributes of sistrum and situla. The linen dress as we learn from Apuleius is synonymous with the costliness and prestige of initiation.[202]

A final argument against a priestly role for women in the dress of Isis on Attic grave reliefs is the fact that four reliefs show men with the same attributes, one of these in the same costume as the woman. Syntheron (Pl. 13) in tunic and plain mantle holds a sistrum with his raised right hand,[203] another man holds a situla from his lowered left hand,[204] while Sosipatros (Pl. 29) holds both items and wears the knotted fringed mantle.[205] The latest example preserved is a relief on the island of Paros (Pl. 37), probably carved by an Athenian.[206] On this relief, the man Kleitomenes holds sistrum and situla and also wears the fringed mantle drawn over both shoulders and knotted at the chest.

From these grave reliefs we learn that members of the prosperous middle class in Athens in the Roman period chose to be represented in the costume of their costly initiation into the cult of Isis. Dunand suggests that women in this dress on Attic stelai may have been consecrated to Isis at an early age,[207] but such dedications, like those of the hearth initiates in the Eleusinian Mysteries, were made by a few prominent and very wealthy families.[208]

---

this Eukarpos has been thought to be the same as Eukarpos son of Dionysios of Phyle in *IG* II², 4772, possibly dating to A.D. 120 (cf. footnote 25 below, p. 60; see also Clinton, *TAPS* 64, pp. 96–97). Concerning the Severan date of the "Isis" relief of Sophia and Eukarpos, son of Euporos of Miletos (*IG* II², 6311; Athens, N.M. 1214), see p. 83 below with footnote 104.

[200] Dunand, *Le Culte d'Isis* II, pp. 148–149 and *Religion populaire*, p. 21, note 42. Five to six reliefs can be dated to each 20-year span in the 2nd century after Christ and to each decade in the 3rd (see Appendix 3), too numerous and varied to represent priestesses (see p. 54 above). For the range in size and execution see the early Antonine "Isis" reliefs: **11–14** and the small relief, Athens, N.M. 1249, as well as the large and less carefully carved Lamia Viboullia, Piraeus Mus. 1160 (Pls. 26–29). This variety corresponds to that found in funerary monuments of freedmen in Rome, showing fluidity and rivalry within this society: see Zanker (footnote 119 above, p. 47), pp. 277–279.

[201] Plutarch, *de Is. et Os.*, 3; Apuleius, *Metamorphoses* XI.9–10, 23, 24, 28, 29; Griffiths, *De Iside*, p. 121 and *The Isis Book*, pp. 97, 99, 105; Vidman, *Isis und Sarapis*, pp. 66, 89; Heyob, *Cult of Isis*, pp. 105, 108–109.

[202] Apuleius, *Metamophoses* XI.9–10, 23, 24, 28, 29; Griffiths, *The Isis Book*, pp. 97, 99, and 105.

[203] Early Flavian relief of Kallo and Syntheron (Pl. 13); in his left hand is a round object, possibly a container for incense.

[204] Late Antonine, Athens, N.M. Ἀπο. 235 (Conze 1972, no. 17; footnote 90 below, p. 81).

[205] Early Antonine Sosipatros and wife, Laurion (Conze 1967; Dunand, *Le Culte d'Isis* II, p. 147). He wears the fringed mantle without the long undergarment, a chiton always worn by women on these reliefs (see p. 6 above).

[206] Early 3rd-century relief on Paros (see footnote 101 below, p. 83); he also does not wear the long undergarment.

[207] Dunand, *Le Culte d'Isis* II, p. 140.

[208] On hearth initiates, see Clinton, *TAPS* 64, p. 113; see footnotes 209, 210 below, p. 57 for comparable "Isis" dedications.

Among the few inscriptions preserved, concerning the cult of Isis in Athens, two dedicate daughters of important families to Isis in the 2nd century after Christ.[209] It is possible that the small statue of Noummia Kleo showed her in the knotted fringed dress.[210]

Since initiation was costly and prestigious, it may have become an important mark of social status. The inscription on the sarcophagus of Fabia Aconia Paulina in Ravenna late in the 3rd century after Christ states that she was initiated into three mystery cults, including that of Isis, by her husband.[211] The wealthy member of a family who provided a statue of a young woman in the knotted fringed costume in Tauromenium, Sicily was more important than the young woman, whose name was omitted from the inscription.[212] Even the empresses Faustina the Elder and Faustina the Younger may have been represented in Cyrene as initiates.[213]

Attic "Isis" reliefs represent initiates in the cult of Isis on their individual and competitive funerary monuments once set up along the roads leading from Athens. On one of the last Attic grave reliefs, Parthenope (Pl. 50) in the dress of Isis is not only honored on one of the few stelai signed by the sculptor, her proud husband,[214] but also the only relief figure to have held sistrum and situla of bronze.[215] The man who was buried in the northeastern part of Athens with silver sistrum, situla, incense box and myrrh, and copper coin of Constantine II (A.D. 337–340) may have been one of the last of these ostentatious initiates.[216]

[209] Claudia is dedicated to Isis by her mother, Athens, E.M. 396 (*IG* II², 4068; Vidman, *Sylloge*, no. 21) and Noummia Kleo by her parents, Athens, E.M. 8299 (*IG* II², 4070; Vidman, *Sylloge*, no. 22). On their families, see Woloch (footnote 15 above, p. 35), pp. 79–84 for Nummii, pp. 160–161 for Claudii, and p. 205 for this daughter Claudia.

[210] Athens, E.M. 8299 is a statue base (H. 0.17, W. 0.35, Th. 0.29 m.); the rough-picked hollow on top (0.19 × 0.15 m.) once took a marble statue (H. *ca.* 0.80 m.) under life size if a child or half life size if an adult. For a similar dedication of a statue of a young woman in the knotted fringed mantle, see Palermo, M.N. 704 (see footnote 212 below).

[211] Vidman, *Sylloge*, no. 586; Witt, *Isis*, p. 67; Heyob, *Cult of Isis*, p. 139.

[212] Vidman, *Sylloge*, no. 514: "Serapi, Isis sacrum |Ennius Secundus |votum a(nimo) p(io)." The statue (Palermo, M.N. 704) is published without reference to the inscription by N. Bonacasa, *Ritratti greci e romani della Sicilia*, Palermo 1964, p. 100, no. 128; late Antonine in date: compare to statue in Ostia identified by H. von Heintze (Helbig⁴ IV, p. 57, no. 3057) as Crispina (see Bieber, *Ancient Copies*, pl. 119, figs. 702, 703).

[213] See the portrait statues of Faustina the Elder (Pl. 27) and possibly Faustina the Younger in the fringed mantle drawn over both shoulders and knotted at the chest, the Athenian arrangement, from Cyrene. They wear a long garland and a wreath on their heads but do not have the emblem of Isis on top of the head, which would have designated them as Isis: see p. 12 above.

[214] Parthenope, Athens, N.M. 1244 (Conze 1954) late 3rd century after Christ (p. 89), *IG* II², 12418: Στήλλην Παρθ<ε>νόπης ἴδιος γαμέτης |ἐπόησεν <λ>αίνης ἀλοχ<ῳ> τοῦτο χαρί|ζομενος. (N.B. The accent should be χαριζόμενος.) See also E. Löwy, *Inschriften griechischer Bildhauer*, Leipzig 1885, p. 302, no. 452. Muehsam (*Berytus* 10, 1952, p. 58) cites Parthenope with other stelai that are signed; the other three are Conze 2022, 2070, and 2096. All appear to be from different periods with Parthenope the latest.

[215] See p. 24 above.

[216] The grave was found in clearance for the Royal Palace, now the House of Parliament: L. Ross, "Originalbeiträge über seine Ausgräbungen auf der Akropolis," *Kunstblatt* 56, 14 July 1836, pp. 233–234; Drexler (footnote 186 above, p. 54), p. 386; A. Rusch, *De Serapide et Iside in Grecia cultis*, Berlin 1906, p. 14; G. Roeder, *RE* IX, 1916, col. 2113; Dunand, *Le Culte d'Isis* II, p. 144. Roeder and Dunand consider him a priest of Isis, but an initiate seems more likely in view of the vivid description by Apuleius, *Metamorphoses* XI and the competitiveness of the Attic "Isis" reliefs. When the cult of Isis in Athens ended is unknown; there is no evidence later than the middle of the 4th century: see summary by Dunand, *Le Culte d'Isis* II, pp. 132–155.

III

PRODUCTION

The "Isis" reliefs are a part of the post-Demetrian production of grave reliefs for Athens; they are 106 in number and constitute about one third of those now published.[1] The sumptuary laws of Demetrios of Phaleron (317–306 B.C.) apparently were enacted against the costly and often very dramatic funerary monuments of the 4th century B.C.[2] These laws limited Attic grave monuments to plain stelai, rectangular tablelike slabs, stone basins, and columnar markers.[3] It seems that it was not until the first half of the 2nd century B.C. that grave stelai with figured decoration were again made.[4]

THE PRODUCTION OF ATTIC FIGURED GRAVE RELIEFS

Although identification of Attic grave reliefs belonging to the 2nd and 1st centuries B.C. is thus far limited to a few modest stelai with small figures in relief,[5] there appears to have been a resurgence in the production of large grave reliefs by the early 1st century B.C., to judge from fragmentary relief figures of life size found in the Agora and Kerameikos.[6] This resurgence may have occurred earlier, in the third quarter of the 2nd century B.C., if the monumental relief of horse and groom, found near Larissa rail station in Athens, is not unique.[7]

When more Attic grave monuments of the Hellenistic period, 3rd through 1st centuries B.C., have been identified, we may be able to confirm or more precisely date when figured grave monuments were again made in Athens. We would also have a better idea of the type and number of monuments produced and whether or not there was any period of

[1] The 106 "Isis" reliefs: Conze 1868, 1954–1972, 2077, 2139–2142; Athens, N.M. Θησ. 140 (Kyparissis, Δελτ 10, Παράρ., pp. 69–70, fig. 12); Aigina stele pediment (Kourouniotis, Ἀρχ Ἐφ 1913, p. 97, fig. 20); Eleusis (Alexandri, Δελτ 22, Β′ 1, p. 127, pl. 102); Riemann, nos. 57–59, 61, 62; 34 from the Agora Excavations (only the two with inscriptions, **22** and **25**, have been published; see Appendix 1); with permission of Dr. Alexandri, the unpublished relief, Athens Third Ephoria 1160. Attic grave reliefs of Roman date: Conze 1836–2142; Riemann, nos. 43–76; Kyparissis, Δελτ 10, Παράρ., pp. 54–85; V. Theophanides, Δελτ 11, 1927–1928 (1930), Παράρτημα, pp. 7–12; *idem*, Ἀρχ Ἐφ, 1939–1941, pp. 9–12; Stauridis (footnote 1 above, p. 33); *eadem*, «Ῥωμαϊκὰ γλυπτὰ ἀπὸ τὸ Ἐθνικὸ Μουσεῖο», Ἀρχ Ἐφ, 1984 (1986), pp. 161–190.

[2] Diepolder, *Die attischen Grabreliefs*, pp. 46–55, pls. 43–53.

[3] Kurtz and Boardman, *Greek Burial Customs*, pp. 161, 169; Conze, p. 29.

[4] H. Möbius, *Die Ornamente der griechischen Grabstelen klassischer und nachklassischer Zeit*, Berlin 1929, p. 46; J. Kirchner, "Attische Grabstelen des dritten und zweiten Jahrhunderts v. Chr.," Ἀρχ Ἐφ, 1937, Α′, pp. 338–340; *idem*, "Das Gesetz des Demetrios von Phaleron zur Einschränkung des Gräberluxus," *Die Antike* 15, 1939, pp. 93–97; Kurtz and Boardman, *Greek Burial Customs*, p. 169; Bradeen, *Agora* XVII, p. 1.

[5] Möbius, *op. cit.*, p. 46; Kirchner, Ἀρχ Ἐφ (footnote 4 above), pp. 339–340 and *Die Antike* (footnote 4 above), pp. 93–97; Riemann, pp. 51–53 and 55–57; Muehsam, *Berytus* 10, 1952, pp. 52, 82–83; see Conze 1870, 1989, 1990, and 1995 for the 2nd century B.C. and 1869, 1887, 1888, and 2092 for the 1st century B.C.

[6] Harrison, *Agora* I, pp. 16–18, nos. 5, 6; Riemann, pp. 56–57, no. 53.

[7] W. H. Schuchhardt, "Relief mit Pferd und Negerknaben im Nationalmuseum in Athen, N.M. 4464," *Antike Plastik* 17, 1978, pp. 75–98.

decline as a result of the sack of Athens by Sulla in 86 B.C. Continuity has been found by Riemann and Muehsam among stelai of the 1st centuries before and after Christ which have small relief figures, either inset in rectangular panels or in equally small architectural frames.[8] This continuity lends support to Conze's view that the post-Demetrian production of Attic grave reliefs continued into the Roman period.[9]

The earliest "Isis" reliefs, Augustan in date,[10] indicate that an increase in the production of Attic grave reliefs in the Roman period, as suggested by Conze, had begun at least by the last quarter of the 1st century B.C. They are not only impressive in quality and execution but also in size. The fragment **1** (Pl. 4), in addition to several other unusual features, is from a figure of life size, rare among Attic grave reliefs after the late 4th century B.C. and the largest size for figures on grave stelai of Roman date.[11]

The three centuries of post-Demetrian production, to which the "Isis" reliefs belong, do merit comparison with the flourishing period of Classical grave reliefs, the late 5th through 4th centuries B.C. The "Isis" reliefs in particular continued to be impressive in quality and include some of the largest grave stelai. They document that this later period of heightened production of Attic grave reliefs was sustained to the 60's of the 3rd century after Christ.[12]

Four "Isis" reliefs are among the latest known Attic grave reliefs, dated to the last third of the 3rd century;[13] two could be as late as the early 4th century.[14] It is clear from these monuments that the production of Attic grave reliefs did not end with the destruction of Athens by the Herulians in A.D. 267.[15] On the contrary, grave reliefs continued to be made, if in reduced number and, as always, changing in style.

THE PRODUCTION OF ATTIC "ISIS" RELIEFS

It has been thought that Attic grave reliefs with women in the dress of Isis were a homogeneous, uninteresting group.[16] Although Graindor recognized that the "Isis" reliefs

---

[8] Riemann, pp. 54–55; Muehsam, *Berytus* 10, 1952, pp. 82–83.

[9] Conze, p. 29.

[10] **1** and Athens, N.M. 3036 (Conze 1972, no. 23), but see pp. 67–68 below.

[11] Figures of life size include the following "Isis" reliefs: **1, 6, 7,** and possibly **17,** and Akropolis Mus. 3194 (p. 86, Pl. 44); other grave reliefs: youth, Corinth S 187 + 196 (Johnson, *Corinth* IX, p. 122, no. 247); the Damaskenos (Conze 2038); three heads from the same relief Athens, N.M. 3085–3087 (A. Hekler, "Studien zur römischen Porträtkunst," *Jahreshefte des Österreichischen archäologischen Institutes in Wien* 21–22, 1922–1924 [pp. 172–202], p. 201, figs. 69–71; A. Stauridis, Ρωμαϊκά πορτραιτά στό Εθνικό Αρχαιολογικό Μουσείο της Αθήνας, Athens 1985, pp. 52–53, 55–56, pls. 56, 59–61).

[12] See Appendix 3.

[13] Riemann, no. 61 below, **33, 34,** and Parthenope, Athens, N.M. 1244; see pp. 87–89.

[14] **34** and Parthenope: see pp. 88–89 below.

[15] The reliefs that Riemann (pp. 48–50) dated after A.D. 267 have not been given due consideration. For the traditional view that Attic grave reliefs and sarcophagi were no longer made after that date, see Muehsam, *Berytus* 10, 1952, pp. 78, 110; H. A. Thompson, "Athenian Twilight A.D. 267–600," *The Journal of Roman Studies* 49, 1959, pp. 61–72; A. Giuliano, *La Cultura artistica delle provincie della Grecia in età romana*, Rome 1965, p. 80; Harrison (footnote 183 above, p. 54), p. 87.

[16] Muehsam, *Berytus* 10, 1952, p. 90; Dunand, *Le Culte d'Isis* II, p. 145, cited by Grenier, *L'Autel funéraire isiaque*, p. 11, note 24.

are one of the richest series of grave reliefs of Roman date in Athens,[17] recent studies have given them no more than summary treatment.[18] Concerning a chronology for these monuments, only one scholar has questioned Graindor's view that the majority of the "Isis" reliefs were made in the 2nd century, if not specifically during the reign of Hadrian (A.D. 117–138) when the cult may have been particularly popular owing to this emperor's interest in Egypt and patronage of Athens.[19]

From the present study of the Attic "Isis" reliefs, it is clear that there was no isolated period in which they flourished. The idea that the cult of Isis in Athens was fostered by Hadrian or any emperor is not supported. The "Isis" reliefs gradually increased in number over three centuries, from the last quarter of the 1st century B.C. to the 60's of the 3rd century after Christ.[20] The known examples occur in clusters of three to five reliefs for each quarter of the 1st century after Christ,[21] four to five for every 20 years in the 2nd century,[22] and three to six for each decade of the first 60 years of the 3rd century.[23] The small number of "Isis" reliefs from the first half of the 1st century after Christ may be due to poor preservation.

THE SIGNIFICANCE OF THE "ISIS" RELIEFS FOR THE CULT

With regard to the cult of Isis in Athens, what is the meaning and importance of Attic grave reliefs with women in the dress of Isis? In Chapter II, these individuals were identified as initiates, the most esteemed participants in the cult of Isis.[24] The grave reliefs not only serve to document continuous participation in the cult by this group, but also indicate that these individuals belonged to the prosperous middle class.[25] Their participation spans

[17] Graindor, *Athènes sous Hadrien*, p. 283.

[18] Graindor, *loc. cit.* Nine are discussed and given dates by Muehsam: see her index for Conze 1954, 1955, 1961–1963, 1969, 1971 in *Berytus* 10, 1952. Eight of 22 listed in a chart are dated by Dunand: *Le Culte d'Isis* II, pp. 145–148. Four of the "Isis" reliefs with inscriptions preserved (Conze 1958, 1969, 1956, 1954) are included in Vidman, *Sylloge* (nos. 13, 18, 23, 24). From these four, Vidman (*Isis und Sarapis*, pp. 48–49) and Heyob (*Cult of Isis*, pp. 92–93) would interpret all the Attic "Isis" reliefs; consequently they misinterpret the role of these women in the cult (see p. 54 above) and its popularity.

[19] Graindor, *loc. cit.*; Muehsam, *Berytus* 10, 1952, pp. 57, 61, note 12; Heyob, *Cult of Isis*, pp. 92–93. Although Dunand (*Le Culte d'Isis* II, p. 149) accepts Graindor's view that the "Isis" reliefs were made mainly in the 2nd century, she questions (p. 151) his conclusion that the cult of Isis was particularly popular in that century owing to Hadrian's favor because inscriptions relating to the cult are just as numerous in the 3rd century after Christ as in the 2nd.

[20] See Appendix 3.

[21] Pp. 67–72 below.

[22] Pp. 73–82 below.

[23] Pp. 82–87 below.

[24] See pp. 52–57 above.

[25] See pp. 48–49 above; few of the individuals named on the "Isis" reliefs are known from other inscriptions (see p. 48 above). None are found among the inscriptions relating to the cult of Isis in Athens: see Vidman, *Sylloge*, nos. 9–12, 14–17, 19–22, 25–33 a–c, and Koumanoudes, Δελτ 25, 1970, p. 68, no. 24. Dunand (*Le Culte d'Isis* II, p. 146, note 3) took Eukarpos son of Euporos of Miletos, represented on the "Isis" relief Athens, N.M. 1214 (*IG* II², 6311), to be the same as the zakore and hagiaphore of the dedication of the refurbishment of the Isieion in A.D. 128 (*IG* II², 4771, Vidman, *Sylloge*, no. 16; see also p. 63 below), but the full name of this zakore is known from a second and contemporary dedication, Eukarpos son of Dionysios of Phyle

from the last quarter of the 1st century B.C. to the early 4th century after Christ; the gradual increase in number of the "Isis" reliefs indicates sustained growth in membership until the 60's of the 3rd century.[26]

The inscriptions relating to the cult of Isis in Athens also confirm the Roman period as one of heightened participation.[27] They indicate that membership in the cult may have begun as early as the last third of the 4th century B.C. and continued to the second half of the 3rd century after Christ.[28] An increase in the number and variety of inscriptions and dedications seems to have occurred under Roman rule.[29]

The cult of Isis, which spread throughout the Mediterranean in the Hellenistic period, was known in Athens during or before the last third of the 4th century but was not officially recognized until early in the 2nd century B.C.[30] To judge from the little evidence during the 2nd and 1st centuries B.C., it appears to have held a modest place among the cults in Athens at that time.[31]

In contrast to the limited evidence for the cult of Isis in Athens during the Hellenistic period, there is a wealth of inscriptions and monuments for this Egyptian cult on the island of Delos, an Athenian possession from 166 B.C. on.[32] Not only did Athenians of the best families serve as priests and other officials in the cult on Delos, often making costly gifts, but also the city of Athens provided the sanctuary on Delos with new buildings and other major dedications.[33] Delos served as a showcase for Athenian participation in the cult of Isis from the second half of the 2nd century to the 80's of the 1st century B.C., a period of prosperity and flourishing trade for Delos, a free port.[34]

Abandonment of the island of Delos and its cults with the exception of the time-honored cult of Apollo may have occurred after the Mithridatic War of 88 B.C., after the sack by pirates in 69 B.C., or upon the total eclipse of its trade by Corinth when the latter was established as a Roman colony in 44 B.C.[35] The cult of Isis in Athens appears to have grown in

---

(*IG* II², 4772, Vidman, *Sylloge*, no. 17). The "Isis" relief (Athens, N.M. 1214) should be later, dated to the early 3rd century after Christ: p. 55 above (for inscription) and p. 84 below.

[26] See above.

[27] Dow, *HThR* 30, 1937, p. 214; Dunand, *Le Culte d'Isis* II, pp. 15, 132–153. Twenty-three of 31 inscriptions are of Roman date: Vidman, *Sylloge*, nos. 7–12, 14–17, 19–22, 25–33b, and Koumanoudes, Δελτ 25, 1970, p. 68, no. 24.

[28] Vidman, *Sylloge*, nos. 1–33b; Guarducci, *Epigrafia greca* IV, p. 206, fig. 59; and Koumanoudes, *loc. cit.* The latest, *IG* II², 1950 (Vidman, *Sylloge*, no. 30), is dated after the middle of the 3rd century but Dunand (*Le Culte d'Isis* II, p. 141) considers it to belong to the end.

[29] See Vidman, *Sylloge*, nos. 7–12, 14–17, 19–22, 25–33b, and Koumanoudes, *loc. cit.*

[30] Dow, *HThR* 30, 1937, pp. 198–201 and 229; Fraser, *OpusAth* 3, 1960, p. 23; Dunand, *Le Culte d'Isis* II, p. 132. Fraser's study (*op. cit.*, pp. 1–49) shows that the cult spread through the Mediterranean on private initiative.

[31] See the evaluation by Dow, *HThR* 30, 1937, pp. 183–232; for the few inscriptions, see Vidman, *Sylloge*, nos. 4–6 and Guarducci, *Epigrafia greca* IV, p. 206.

[32] Roussel, *Cultes égyptiens*; Dow, *HThR* 30, 1937, pp. 202–207; Dunand, *Le Culte d'Isis* II, pp. 83–115.

[33] Roussel, *Cultes égyptiens*, pp. 261–272; Dow, *loc. cit.*

[34] Dow, *loc. cit.*; Fraser, *OpusAth* 3, 1960, p. 23.

[35] Roussel, *Cultes égyptiens*, p. 272; M. Rostovtzeff, *The Social and Economic History of the Hellenistic World*, Oxford 1941, p. 1024.

importance by the middle of the 1st century B.C., to judge from the inscriptions and especially from the masterly portrait of a priest of Isis found in the Agora.[36] A shift in attention from the cult of Isis on Delos to that in Athens may have occurred at that time. The inscriptions and monuments related to the cult in Athens may also indicate that Athens had begun to recover from the economic decline following the sack by Sulla in 86 B.C.[37]

What was the importance of the cult of Isis in Athens in the Roman period? Much remains unknown to us. We have no information concerning the status of the priests of Isis in relation to those of other cults, the extent of participation by members of the upper and lower classes, and the end of the cult in Athens.

Where was the sanctuary mentioned by Pausanias in the 2nd century after Christ? It is thought that this sanctuary, the Sarapieion, was near the present Metropolitan Church, where several inscriptions relating to the cult of Isis were found.[38] Dow considered the cult of Isis to be of minor importance in Athens, because none of the thrones in the first two rows of the Theater of Dionysos, which were inscribed to the Emperor, prominent officials, and priests, is inscribed to a priest of Isis, but in fact, we may never know whether or not the priest of Isis occupied one of these seats of honor, because sections of the first row are missing.[39]

Equally tantalizing and inconclusive is the fragmentary inscription of a list of priests in different cults, dated after the middle of the 3rd century after Christ.[40] A priestess of Isis Taposiris is included. We have no information concerning the significance of her priesthood, in comparison with other possible priests or priestesses of Isis, or why she was at the end of this list.

The evidence from sculpture and the inscribed gifts and dedications indicate that the cult of Isis in Athens was more significant than Dow and Dunand have thought.[41] Although the cult did not command the wealth and fame of the Iseum Campense in Rome, the most important sanctuary of the Egyptian gods in the Roman Empire,[42] nor the wealth of the sanctuary of these gods on Delos in the Hellenistic period,[43] there were costly dedications of exceptional quality belonging to the cult of Isis in Athens from the middle of the 1st

---

[36] Vidman, *Sylloge*, nos. 7–10; Dow, *HThR* 30, 1937, p. 214. The portrait is Agora S 333 (Harrison, *Agora* I, no. 3, pp. 12–13, pl. 3). A. Adriani ("Ritratti dell'Egitto greco-romano," *RM* 77, 1970 [pp. 72–109], pp. 78–79, pl. 37:2) would date it to the first half of the 1st century B.C., but the arguments and comparisons offered by Harrison in support of a mid-1st-century date are convincing.

[37] On the economy of Athens, see Graindor, *Athènes sous Auguste*, Cairo 1927, p. 11; J. Day, *An Economic History of Athens under Roman Domination*, New York 1942; Rostovtzeff (footnote 35 above, p. 61), pp. 744–745; G. Bowersock, *Augustus and the Greek World*, Oxford 1965, p. 85.

[38] Pausanias, I.18.4; Vidman, *Sylloge*, nos. 5, 11, 12, 20, 21. On the suggested location, see Dow, *HThR* 30, 1937, p. 187; R. E. Wycherley, "Pausanias at Athens, II," *Greek, Roman and Byzantine Studies* 4, 1963 (pp. 157–175), pp. 161–163 and *Stones of Athens*, p. 85; Dunand, *Le Culte d'Isis* II, p. 134.

[39] Dow, *HThR* 30, 1937, p. 232. On the inscribed seats, see E. Fiechter, *Das Dionysos-Theater in Athen* I, Stuttgart 1934, pp. 62–75; Guarducci, *Epigrafia greca* II, pp. 564–567; see also M. Maass, *Die Prohedrie des Dionysostheaters in Athen*, Munich 1972.

[40] Vidman, *Sylloge*, no. 30 = *IG* II², 1950.

[41] Dow, *HThR* 30, 1937, p. 232; Dunand, *Le Culte d'Isis* II, p. 132.

[42] Roullet, *Monuments*, pp. 23–30.

[43] Roussel, *Cultes égyptiens*; Dow, *HThR* 30, 1937, pp. 202–207; Dunand, *Le Culte d'Isis* II, pp. 83–115.

century B.C. to at least the 20's of the 2nd century after Christ. The first of these exceptional works is the portrait of a priest of Isis found in the Agora.[44] The second is the colossal statue of Isis in dark Eleusinian limestone, which was found on the south slope of the Akropolis and should be dated to the 40's of the 1st century after Christ.[45] If this exquisite statue, surprisingly rich in fine ornamental patterns in hair and drapery, shallowly yet masterfully carved, occupied the small Isieion on the south slope of the Akropolis, it would have been handsomely displayed.[46] The architectural refurbishment of this Isieion in A.D. 128 was the donation of a wealthy woman, whose name is not preserved, who served as lampbearer and dream interpreter in the cult of Isis.[47] Her gift made this temple ornate, if not more impressive than the comparable Isieion on Delos given by the city of Athens in 135 B.C.[48]

In addition to these major dedications, there is evidence from inscriptions that members of prominent Athenian families served in the cult of Isis in the 2nd and 3rd centuries after Christ. The priest during whose office the Isieion was refurbished was Dionysios of Marathon, who was cosmete in A.D. 126/7; he was the only iakchagogos in the all-important Eleusinian Mysteries and was honored with an inscribed throne in the Theater of Dionysos.[49] In A.D. 196/7–205/6, the Eponymous Archon, the most eminent magistrate in Athens, was Claudius Phokas of Marathon who was neokore in the cult of Isis.[50] There were also statues of daughters of two prominent families that were dedicated to Isis in the second half of the 2nd century after Christ.[51]

If the cult of Isis was secondary to other cults in Athens during the Roman period, these monuments confirm that it was highly esteemed. The importance of the cult of Isis among members of the prosperous middle class is evident from the grave reliefs of its initiates, which not only form the most numerous class among the published Attic grave reliefs of Roman date but also are often the best in quality.[52]

Judging from terracotta figurines and lamps,[53] the cult of Isis was popular in Athens to

---

[44] Agora S 333 of the mid-1st century B.C.: see footnote 36 above, p. 62.

[45] Meliades (footnote 72 above, p. 16); Walker, *BSA* 74, 1979, pp. 252–253. This statue merits full publication; for the date, see p. 70 below.

[46] Walker (*op. cit.*, p. 252) suggests that this statue was the cult image in this Isieion.

[47] Vidman, *Sylloge*, no. 16 (= *IG* II², 4771); Dunand, *Le Culte d'Isis*, pp. 134–135, 146, note 3; S. Walker, "Corinthian Capitals with Ringed Voids: the Work of Athenian Craftsmen in the Second Century A.D.," *AA* (*JdI* 94), 1979 (pp. 103–129), p. 110; Walker, *BSA* 74, 1979, pp. 243–257; Follet, *Athènes*, p. 111.

[48] The temple on Delos built and dedicated between 150 and 135/4 B.C.: Roussel, *Cultes égyptiens*, pp. 56–62, 129–130, no. 76. Its colossal statue of Isis (no. 86) was dedicated in 128/7 B.C.: Dow, *HThR* 30, 1937, pp. 202–203. Dunand (*Le Culte d'Isis* II, p. 94) would date the Isieion on Delos to 135/4 B.C.

[49] Vidman, *Sylloge*, no. 16 (= *IG* II², 4771); cosmete (*IG* II², 3733); in Theater of Dionysos (*IG* II², 5044); iakchagogos, see Clinton, *TAPS* 64, pp. 96–97; Walker, *BSA* 74, 1979, p. 254.

[50] Vidman, *Sylloge*, no. 29 (= *IG* II², 3681); D. J. Geagan, *Hesperia*, Suppl. XII, *The Athenian Constitution after Sulla*, Princeton 1967, p. 10; Follet, *Athènes*, pp. 372–374.

[51] Vidman, *Sylloge*, nos. 21 (= *IG* II², 4068) and 22 (= *IG* II², 4070). On these families, see M. Woloch, "Four Leading Families in Roman Athens," *Historia* 18, 1969, pp. 502–510; *idem* (footnote 15 above, p. 35): Nummius, no. 9 and Claudius, no. 100. The Nummii served as priests in the Eleusinian Mysteries: Clinton, *TAPS* 64, p. 109, no. 33 and pp. 78–79.

[52] For one of the latest of these ostentatious initiates, see p. 57 above.

[53] Dow, *HThR* 30, 1937, pp. 214–216, 225–232; Dunand, *Le Culte d'Isis* II, pp. 142–144; Grandjouan

the middle of the 4th century, but it may have lasted longer.[54] The cult of Isis at Kenchreai, east of Corinth, is known as late as the third quarter of the 4th century.[55] In Rome, where it persisted after the edict of Theodosius of A.D. 391, members of aristocratic families are known to have served as priests as late as A.D. 394.[56]

WORKSHOPS

Attic grave reliefs of Roman date belong to the conservative Classical tradition. Several have figures of life size, but compositions are limited, usually one to three figures standing within a naïskos frame. Although they are not the dramatic, often over life-sized figures of the late 4th century B.C., the bold relief recalls late Classical grave stelai.[57]

Attic grave reliefs of Roman date have been considered poor in quality and coarse in execution.[58] The majority are the work of competent sculptors, if eclectic in style and varied in execution. Unusual combinations are found, as figures and drapery were taken from models of different periods of Greek art, and odd juxtapositions result from selective treatment of parts of the figure and drapery.[59] Although unevenness in execution and extensive use of the rasp and deep drill betray most of the reliefs as works of Roman date, some are as carefully and evenly executed as fine grave reliefs of the late 5th century B.C.[60] A few grave reliefs of Roman date have been mistaken for Classical stelai.[61]

(footnote 69 above, p. 41), nos. 942, 1010–1011; see Perlzweig (footnote 57 above, p. 13), nos. 780, 805, pl. 23:j for boat lamps from the Kerameikos.

[54] On the long life of pagan cults in Athens, see A. Frantz, "From Paganism to Christianity in the Temples of Athens," *Dumbarton Oaks Papers* 19, 1965, pp. 187–205.

[55] R. Scranton, *Kenchreai*, I, *Topography and Architecture*, Leiden 1978, pp. 53–55, 70–71, and conclusion on p. 77.

[56] Malaise, *Conditions*, pp. 452–453; Heyob, *Cult of Isis*, p. 35.

[57] See Diepolder, *Die attischen Grabreliefs*, pp. 46–53, pls. 43–53.

[58] Muehsam, *Berytus* 10, 1952, pp. 83–85, 110; Giuliano (footnote 15 above, p. 59), p. 79.

[59] See the Trajanic stele of Paramonos and his son Alexandros, Piraeus Mus. 222 (Pl. 21); the lightly carved bearded head of Paramonos is like those on Classical grave reliefs such as that of Ktesilaos (Diepolder, *Die attischen Grabreliefs*, pl. 22), while the son with sharply drawn eyes, sagging cheeks, and hair combed forward bears a striking resemblance to the portrait of Trajan in the same museum (Piraeus Mus. 276: W. H. Gross, *Bildnisse Traians, Das römische Herrscherbild* II, ii, Berlin 1940, pl. 27); the son's figure and low-draped mantle recall Hellenistic examples (e.g., Poseidon of Melos: Karouzou [footnote 40 above, p. 38], pl. 66). Drapery on one figure may also have unusual contrasts, such as that of the joining early Antonine "Isis" relief fragments, Athens, N.M. Ἀπο. 237 and **13** (both Pl. 28).

[60] Fine examples include Bathyllos in Verona (Pl. 8) and the middle Antonine "Isis" relief of Sosibia, Boston, M.F.A. 1971.209 (Pl. 30). See also early 3rd-century "Isis" reliefs: Athens, N.M. Ἀπο. 54 + 231 (Pl. 37); Sophia and Eukarpos, Athens, N.M. 1214 (Pl. 37); and son of Soterion, Athens, N.M. 1223 (Pl. 38).

[61] Stele of a dancer, Athens, N.M. 1896 (Karouzou [footnote 40 above, p. 38], p. 116; on display in the second room of the 4th-century B.C. grave reliefs) should be Claudian in date; this stele has an unusual contrast between the small, well-proportioned figure and the dancer who is elongated, seems to vanish into the background although she is the larger figure on this stele, and has a bulbous, jutting head. Her sheer drapery with very shallowly carved, ribbonlike folds tends to dematerialize this figure as the fabric falls in sheaths loose over the legs. She compares well in figure proportions, drapery, and doll-like classicism with the figures on the stele of Bathyllos, Claudian in date (footnote 29 below, p. 71; Pl. 8). Also displayed with reliefs of the Classical period is a head of an old woman, Athens, N.M. 3552 (Pl. 21) that should be Trajanic; compare to the youth Athens, N.M. 1663 (Conze 2023) and Agora S 1118 (Pl. 21) where a youth wears a Flavian-Trajanic drilled-curl coiffure. All three are contemporary with, if not from the same workshop as, a Trajanic bust of a youth in Pentelic marble, Boston M.F.A. 88.348 (Comstock and Vermeule, *Sculpture in Stone*, p. 222, no. 352).

The "Isis" reliefs not only are representative of the variety of Attic grave markers of Roman date but also are often the best in quality. Many of them can be assigned to workshops and several to master sculptors who merited important commissions and made fine portraits.[62] A few can be assigned to workshops that also made sarcophagi; they should be dated at the earliest to the end of the 2nd century after Christ.[63] There is evidence among these reliefs for influence east and west, an exchange in style between Athens and Rome which seems to have extended to Asia Minor from the late 2nd century on.[64]

Rarely is an "Isis" relief from a workshop that may have specialized in statues of Isis.[65] They are usually from those that made a variety of grave reliefs and statues. Some are from workshops that made dry, academic copies.[66] A few are the work of fine sculptors who may have participated in carving historical reliefs comparable to official monuments in Rome.[67]

It is true that at the present we know very little about workshops for sculpture in Athens. The number of sculptors, length of apprenticeship, number and type of commissions, possible division of labor between sculptors, and frequency or duration of travel if they worked in other cities are all unknown. Areas of marble working and one possible workshop of Roman date have been found in the Agora, but there is little evidence of the kind of work produced.[68]

Because of the quality and number of the "Isis" reliefs many can be assigned to workshops. The full range of work produced in these workshops, however, lies beyond the stylistic evidence of this series. The lack of continuity in style between "Isis" reliefs of consecutive periods indicates a lack of specialization by sculptors or workshops. There is only one

[62] Augustan relief **1** (Pl. 4); early Flavian Kallo and Syntheron (Pl. 13); late Flavian **4** and Riemann, no. 57 (Pls. 16, 15); Trajanic Mousaios and Amaryllis, Athens, N.M. 1233 (Pl. 19).

[63] Late Antonine: **19** (Pl. 35); early 3rd century: Athens, N.M. Ἀπο. 54 + 231 (Pl. 37); 240's: **30** (Pl. 45) and Riemann, no. 59 (Pl. 46), Akropolis Mus. 3194 (Pl. 44); 250's: **31** (Pl. 47), Athens, E.M. 2067 (Conze 2139).

[64] See Alexandra, Athens, N.M. 1193 (Pl. 24), which is an excellent example of late Hadrianic classicism as known in Rome and found among statues from Hadrian's villa at Tivoli. The close resemblance of late Antonine **19** (Pl. 35) to the contemporary statues of Isis popular in Asia Minor and in North Africa indicates influence from the east (see pp. 77–78 below: e.g. statue of Isis from Laodicea). In the 40's of the 3rd century (Pls. 45, 46) and even more so in the 60's (Pl. 49), relief figures from Rome, Athens, and Asia Minor have much in common, indicating that an intense exchange in style and technique may have occurred in those times.

[65] See the Trajanic workshop of **6** and **7** (pp. 73–74 below, Pl. 18) and the middle Antonine workshop whose products included Sosibia, Boston, M.F.A. 1971.209 (pp. 79–80 below, Pl. 30).

[66] See the late Antonine stele of Agathemeris and Sempronius, London, B.M. 630 (Pl. 32) and its peers, **17** and **18** (Pl. 33). Possibly from academic workshops: Trajanic **8** (Pl. 20) and early Antonine **11** (Pl. 26).

[67] See the discussion of **1** (pp. 67–69 below, Pl. 4), Augustan; and stele of Attikos, Mantua, Duc.Pal. 6677 (p. 75 below, Pl. 22), early Hadrianic.

[68] See the summary by H. A. Thompson, *The Athenian Agora: Guide*, 3rd ed., Athens 1976, pp. 162, 176, 132–133 on the workshop. The latter was found in the southernmost of the western rooms that flank the doorway of the Library of Pantainos. According to the excavators, the *terminus ante quem* of the workshop is A.D. 280, the date of completion of the Late Fortification Wall that runs parallel to the western wall of the workshop: T. L. Shear, "The Sculpture found in 1933," *Hesperia* 4, 1935 (pp. 371–420), pp. 393–395; G. P. Stevens, "A Doorsill from the Library of Pantainos," *Hesperia* 18, 1949, pp. 269–274. Found in deposits with coins of the 2nd and 3rd centuries after Christ were statuettes and one unfinished portrait; the latter is late Antonine, Agora S 362 (Harrison, *Agora* I, pp. 46–49, no. 36). Which were made here, the statuettes or the portrait? If all were made here, the workshop was in operation for over a hundred years. Was the unfinished portrait a keepsake or here for re-use, to be carved into another statuette?

identifiable workshop in the 3rd century after Christ that may have been in production for as long as 40 years.[69] Two pairs of grave reliefs are so close that their sculptors not only must belong to the same workshop but also may have been related as brothers or as father and son.[70]

If more than one sculptor was responsible for the large figures on grave reliefs of Roman date as proposed by Dow and Vermeule,[71] the sculptors worked so closely on any one of the "Isis" reliefs that individual work is not discernible. It is more likely that each of these reliefs, small and large, was carved by a single sculptor. The large figure of Alexandra (Pl. 24), head and body, is crisply rendered and as unified in appearance as the two, well-modeled figures on the stele of Attikos (Pl. 22) and the less impressive Lamia Viboullia (Pl. 27), whose lightly carved drapery is as barely noticeable as the simple oval head.[72] There is only one example of Roman date where the head was worked separately and set into the draped body as was common for many statues of this period.[73] It is well known that sculptors traveled and worked in cities other than that of their origin.[74] According to Ward Perkins, Attic sarcophagi in partially finished form were sent with sculptors to be completed at the final destination or in a secondary workshop elsewhere in the provinces.[75] Several statues of Isis, empress as Isis, and empress as initiate in the cult of Isis, found in Rome, Crete, Cyrene, and Dalmatia, are the work of sculptors who made "Isis" reliefs.[76] The careful rendering of these statues may indicate that these works were sculptured by Athenians at the final destination and not exported in finished form from Athens. On the island of Paros the grave relief of Kleitomenes (Pl. 37) so closely resembles two Attic "Isis" reliefs of the early 3rd century after Christ that it should be the work of a sculptor from the same workshop in Athens; the relief of Kleitomenes, one of several reliefs of Roman date carved into the wall of a Hellenistic tomb,[77] must have been carved *in situ*.

[69] See the early Severan relief **20** and late Severan **26** which should be from the same workshop: Appendix 1 below, Pls. 35, 41.

[70] See the discussion of early Severan stelai, Sophia and Eukarpos, Athens, N.M. 1214 and soldier, Athens, N.M. 1247, as the work of one sculptor, and son of Soterion, Athens, N.M. 1223 and soldier, Athens, N.M. 1266, as the work of a second sculptor closely related to the first: p. 84 below, Pls. 37, 38.

[71] Dow and Vermeule, *Hesperia* 34, 1965, p. 289; they regard the Damaskenos (Conze 2038) as the work of two or more sculptors, but the differences in rendering head and body are slight, appropriate to the part represented, and could very well be the work of one sculptor.

[72] Alexandra, Athens, N.M. 1193; Attikos, Mantua, Duc.Pal. 6677; Lamia Viboullia, Piraeus Mus. 1160.

[73] See Pl. 9; Riemann, p. 66, no. 70. The cavity for the head could be the result of re-use.

[74] Richter (footnote 53 above, p. 13); J. M. C. Toynbee, *Some Notes on Artists in the Roman World* (*Collection Latomus* 6), Brussels 1951.

[75] J. B. Ward Perkins, "The Hippolytus Sarcophagus from Trinquetaille," *Journal of Roman Studies* 46, 1956 (pp. 10–16), pp. 14–16.

[76] Munich, Glyp. 250 from Rome (p. 70; Pl. 7); Herakleion Mus. 314 (p. 72; Pl. 12); Herakleion Mus. 260 (Pl. 19) and Isis in the Prytaneion at Gortyna (pp. 73–74 below; Dunand, II, pl. XXVI); two statues from Cyrene are nearly identical in the "Isis" dress, and one has been identified as a portrait of the empress Faustina the Elder (Pl. 27; see footnote 78, p. 79 below); Rome, Mus.Cap. 744 (p. 80 below); Vatican, Mus.Greg.Eg. 83 (pp. 84–85 below, Pl. 41); from Dalmatia, Zagreb, Arch.Mus. 34 (p. 85 below, Pl. 44).

[77] See footnote 101 below, p. 83.

IV

STYLE AND CHRONOLOGY

It is possible that Attic grave reliefs with women in the dress of Isis were first made about the middle of the 1st century B.C., concomitant with the growth in importance of the cult of Isis in Athens.[1] An "Isis" relief from Eretria may have been contemporary with the earliest Attic examples[2] but did not serve as the prototype, nor does it show influence from Attic reliefs. The differences in dress and omission of the sistrum on the Eretria relief, which may reflect separate customs for the cult in these two cities, could also be evidence of the newness of Athenian interest in depicting cult members in the knotted, fringed costume on grave reliefs. Although this exotic dress of Isis was known in Athens early in the 1st century B.C.,[3] the first preserved Attic "Isis" reliefs belong to the last third of that century.

First Century after Christ

Augustan

The earliest "Isis" reliefs, Augustan in date, are Agora relief **1** (Pl. 4) and the stele inscribed to Onesiphoron (Athens, N.M. 3036).[4] Although fragmentary, they are exceptional in execution, and the figures were also impressive in size. They are the only reliefs to show the hand-held attributes, sistrum and situla, in motion.[5] This unusual representation

---

[1] See discussion of cult of Isis by Dunand, *Le Culte d'Isis* II, pp. 132–153.

[2] The Eretria stele, which bears two inscriptions, was used twice as a grave stele. The "Isis" relief of a young woman belongs with the lower inscription which names Euphrosyne. They are later additions to the stele and should be dated after the early 1st century B.C., the date of the ornament (compare to an Attic stele: Möbius [footnote 4 above, p. 58], p. 48, pl. 35:b) and of the upper inscription which names a man (B. Petrakos, «Ἐπιγραφαὶ Ἐρετρίας», Δελτ 23, 1968, Α' [pp. 97–116], p. 109, no. 65, pl. 49). A mid-1st-century date for the swaying "Isis" figure on the Eretria stele is likely in view of the close comparison with figures on the Attic relief of a philosopher in Berlin, Staat.Mus. 1462 (Conze, p. 8); the latter is dated by Bieber (*op. cit.* [footnote 91 above, p. 44], p. 132) to the 1st century B.C. and (p. 146) to the 40's of that century by the portrait of the man on the right. Compare the young woman on the Berlin relief to statues of the family of L. Valerius Flaccus in Magnesia of 63/2 B.C.: Linfert (footnote 100 above, p. 45), pp. 30, 178–180, pl. 5, figs. 22–24.

[3] See p. 31 above.

[4] **1**, life size; Onesiphoron (Conze 1972, no. 23; *IG* II², 7467) five-sixths life size. The latter is published by Conze without photograph. Preserved are the pediment with cist incised and in high relief, a frontal female head, right sleeved forearm, and hand with sistrum.

[5] See **1**. The relief of Onesiphoron is less successful: although the sistrum is tilted towards the figure and folds of the sleeve on the arm holding the sistrum fall in response to the tilt, the sistrum is simply outlined in a lump of marble and would have to be painted to be seen. All other sistra are carved in relief.

There is no evidence for the use of paint, but color was used on Attic grave reliefs: see Adam, *Technique*, p. 113. If the background was given a solid color, the texture of the linen dress of Isis would not be lost. **8** (Pl. 20), carved in gray Hymettian marble, is carefully textured, a treatment which could be accentuated if lightly coated with white paint. Leaving the majority of the relief figures unpainted would permit the dress to

of sistrum and situla suggests that sculptors were experimenting, and it is possible that these reliefs are at the beginning of the series. The portrayal of such subtle motion is so rare that its occurrence on these first "Isis" reliefs makes it probable that they are contemporary, if not from the same workshop.[6]

The Augustan date for Onesiphoron is based on the close comparison with a late Augustan head in Naples (M.N. 6289; Pl. 2).[7] This idealized head and late Augustan hairstyle is repeated in profile on the small, well-carved stele of Demetria (Pl. 2), whose father may have served as prytanis *ca.* 50 to 40 B.C.[8] The stele of Demetria, possibly a third work from the same workshop, also shows the figure seated, correctly foreshortened; like the Agora relief **1**, it is one of the few Attic grave reliefs of Roman date to do so.[9]

1 (Pl. 4) is the work of a master sculptor. His summary but deft execution has imparted motion as well as the illusion of depth. The life-sized figure, one of the few at this scale, holds a small situla, uniquely depicted swinging from its handle.[10] The simple cuplike vase and ribbonlike handle may well represent a situla of glass.[11] The sculptor of **1** could have worked closely with, or may have been the same as, the master of the portrait of Agrippa in Boston (M.F.A. 99.347; Pl. 4), the only extant historical relief of early Imperial date from Athens.[12] This well-modeled head shares with the Agora relief the distinctive and very select use of a sharply driven, narrow chisel to enhance the illusion of depth and the immediacy of the figure. The volume of each of these relief figures is deftly conveyed by a single sharp contour, slightly undercutting the thumb of the Agora hand and the profile of Agrippa.[13] The unusually narrow chisel deeply scores the upper eyelid of Agrippa to draw attention to his slight upward turn of head and his brooding, deep-set brow and glance, while in the Agora relief, the fine chisel also conveys motion: inward turn of the hand by a deep contour on the left and by a fine, shallow line on the right to trace faintly the farthest

be the white of the marble. A white linen dress was worn by initiates to the cult of Isis, according to Apuleius (*Metamorphoses* XI.10 and 23).

[6] On Attic grave reliefs of Roman date, there is one other person shown playing a musical instrument: Serapias playing a cithara, Athens, N.M. 1319 (Conze 1844; *IG* II², 9324). Muehsam (*Berytus* 10, 1952, p. 70, pl. 8:1) considers it one of the earliest stelai of Roman date. An Augustan date is likely; compare with Isidotos (Conze 1973) dated by Riemann (p. 52) to the third quarter of the 1st century B.C. and compare both to the inscription and compact figure of Megiste, Athens, N.M. 710, a statue dedicated to Aphrodite in 27 B.C. (Graindor [footnote 89 above, p. 44], no. 3, pl. 2; *IG* II², 4714).

[7] Onesiphoron: O. Elia, "Testa isiaca e ritratti ellenistico-romani da Pompei," *Rivista dell'Istituto Nazionale d'Archeologia e Storia dell'Arte* 8, 1941 (pp. 89–106), pp. 95–96, figs. 5, 6; dated by Polaschek, *TrZ* 35, 1972, p. 158.

[8] Demetria, said to be in Athens: Conze 1838; *IG* II², 5304; see p. 48 above.

[9] One other correctly foreshortened seated figure is shown on the Claudian "Isis" relief, Athens, N.M. 1296 (Conze 1868; pp. 70–71 below, Pl. 8).

[10] See p. 23 above.

[11] See pp. 21–25 above on situlae, esp. pp. 23–24 for glass examples.

[12] Boston, M.F.A. 99.347, life size: Comstock and Vermeule, *Sculpture in Stone*, p. 209, no. 330; J. M. C. Toynbee, *Roman Historical Portraits*, Ithaca 1978, p. 63.

[13] See **1** and Pl. 4. A distinctive and most unusual use is made of a very narrow chisel to undercut slightly and draw attention to one contour, while carving a very shallow contour on the other side, as if the figure is enveloped in atmosphere and turns slightly back in space.

finger.[14] The portrait is impressive but less idealized than that of Agrippa on the Ara Pacis in Rome (13 to 9 B.C.), the official monument celebrating the Augustan peace and dynasty.[15]

Julio-Claudian

The next two "Isis" reliefs, from the first 40 years of the 1st century after Christ, are academic works that emphasize the pattern of the folds of the snug drapery and show little interest in the anatomy of the figure. For example, the Isis dress on tall Aphrodeisia (Athens, N.M. Θησ. 140; Pl. 6)[16] is covered by numerous narrow folds creating a crisp linear net over the figure that draws attention to its height and sway, as well as to the elegant gestures of the long arms. The soft surface of the folds and careful, even carving of the draped figure are barely noticeable.

Aphrodeisia's stele is from a Tiberian workshop that made elegant figures on reliefs of fairly modest size. An earlier work is the stele of Neike (Athens, N.M. 2558; Pl. 6), whose hairstyle is one of the few representations of a coiffure popular in Rome, the late Augustan–early Tiberian *nodus* coiffure.[17] The difference in rendering for the various types of figures on the stelai from this workshop is of interest. The youth Diodotos (Pl. 7) again has the pronounced sway, but the snug mantle has few folds, and his round abdomen is noticeable, while the seated figure of Ammia (Athens, N.M. 1163; Pl. 6) based on a Hellenistic Muse, also has few, flat folds and a more decorative appearance, although rounded in relief.[18]

Two statues of Isis that belong to this period are somewhat later than the stele of Aphrodeisia. On these statues, the pattern of folds, emphasis on the breadth of the figure, and fine narrow folds covering the costume are a development from that on the Tiberian

[14] The undercutting along the thumb on the hand of **1** and along the profile of Agrippa on the Boston relief clearly draws attention to the volume and slight turn of each. With the fine line faintly tracing the farthest finger, the hand seems to reach further back. A very fine line marks the back of Agrippa's head as if it was enveloped in space. The sharply drawn fine chisel line draws attention not only to his profile but also to his brooding expression and heavy brow (the brow and upper eyelid are sharply undercut).

[15] For the Ara Pacis, see Andreae, *The Art of Rome*, pp. 114–121, fig. 271; E. Simon, Helbig[4] II, no. 1937; G. Moretti, *The Ara Pacis Augustae*, Rome 1975, fig. 37. An excellent discussion of the portraits of Agrippa is given by Toynbee (footnote 12 above, p. 68), pp. 63–67; an additional portrait has been found at Nikopolis (D. Papastamos, «Εἰκονικστικὴ κεφαλὴ ἐκ Νικοπόλεως», *AAA* 4, 1971, pp. 430–432). It may be early, possibly just after the founding of Nikopolis following the Battle of Actium in 31 B.C. It is a replica of the Butrinto head, which C. Vermeule (*Roman Imperial Art in Greece and Asia Minor*, Cambridge 1963, p. 175) considers an Attic work exported to that city. The heads from Nikopolis and Butrinto could be from the same workshop, different from and somewhat earlier than the Boston Agrippa.

[16] Aphrodeisia: *IG* II², 7507. Her father may have been a thesmothete at the beginning of the 1st century after Christ (*IG* II², 1729, line 3); see p. 48 above and for provenience, p. 39 above.

[17] Neike: Conze 1929; *IG* II², 9803. For the hairstyle, see Polaschek, *TrZ* 35, 1972, p. 159 and Muehsam, *Berytus* 10, 1952, p. 70. A late Augustan example from an Attic grave relief is Agora S 2443 (Pl. 3; p.H. 0.15, p.W. 0.11, p.Th. 0.122 m.); it has the proportions of the female herm heads (S 553, S 554) from the Odeion of Agrippa, dated between 23 and 13 B.C.: H. A. Thompson, "The Odeion in the Athenian Agora," *Hesperia* 19, 1950, pp. 30–141; E. Harrison, *The Athenian Agora*, XI, *Archaic and Archaistic Sculpture*, Princeton 1965, nos. 220 and 219, pl. 59.

[18] Diodotos: Riemann, no. 52; Ammia: Conze 1836. On Muses, see Bieber, *Ancient Copies*, p. 123.

relief. On the colossal statue from the south slope of the Akropolis,[19] the rich pattern of narrow folds is subtly varied and serves to emphasize the massive figure, while on the statue of Isis with Harpokrates, of nearly the same size, from Rome but now in Munich (Glyp. 250; Pl. 7), the narrow folds fill panels that expand the breadth of the figure.[20] Although these two masterly works escape attribution, they do show that two fine Athenian sculptors were responsible for colossal statues of Isis, one in Athens and one in Rome during the reign of Caligula when the cult of Isis in Rome is known to have been given imperial favor.[21]

A less competent sculptor was responsible for the somewhat stumpy figure in half life size on a contemporary "Isis" relief (Athens, N.M. Ἀπο. 233).[22] Although weathered and worn, this "Isis" figure compares well in proportions and simplicity of drapery with that on a stele in Munich (Pl. 7).[23] Such stout, classicizing figures should be Caligulan in date, having much in common with the massive statue of Livia from the theater temple at Lepcis Magna, A.D. 35–36,[24] while the simple yet ornamental quality of their idealized heads compares well with a portrait of Caligula from Gortyna (Herakleion Mus. 64).[25]

Of greater interest and merit is the Claudian "Isis" relief (Athens, N.M. 1296; Pl. 8),[26] one of the few to show the dress loosely draped, recalling the pyramidal fashion popular in the Hellenistic period.[27] This small stele with slender figures, correctly foreshortened and

[19] Meliades (footnote 72 above, p. 16), p. 49; Walker, *BSA* 74, 1979, pp. 252–253; see also p. 63 above. It has not been published with photograph; p.H. 0.47 m., but originally over 3 m. tall.

[20] Isis with Harpokrates (p.H. 2.31 m.): A. Furtwängler, *Beschreibung der Glyptothek*, Munich 1910, p. 259. Name of dedicant on plinth: *Corpus inscriptionum latinarum* VI, iv, 3031 and 30916. It is cited by U. Kron ("Eine Pandion-Statue in Rom," *JdI* 92, 1977 [pp. 139–168], p. 151) as being most likely from the Iseum Campense in Rome, which is also suggested by Furtwängler. On the Iseum Campense, see Roullet, *Monuments*, pp. 23–30.

[21] The two statues have much in common but are distinct from one another in execution and treatment of the narrow folds. The Munich statue is a majestic and individual variation of the South Slope Isis; it should be the work of a sculptor familiar with the latter and a part of stylistic development in Athens, hence another contemporary Athenian sculptor, if not a competitor.

On the cult of Isis in Rome under Caligula, see Malaise, *Conditions*, pp. 395–400 and *idem* (footnote 183 above, p. 54), p. 213, attributing to Caligula the building of the Iseum Campense, the most important sanctuary of Isis in the Roman Empire.

[22] Athens, N.M. Ἀπο. 233: Conze 1972, no. 13, published without photograph.

[23] The Athens fragment shares with the Munich stele (Conze 2093) the stout proportions and thick drapery in few folds as well as the more decorative, cottonlike hair framing a round, low-crowned head, with fat curls pierced by a fine drill.

[24] Statue of Livia as Ceres from the theater temple at Lepcis Magna, A.D. 35–36: Ceres according to R. Bianchi Bandinelli, E. V. Caffarelli, and G. Caputo, *Leptis Magna*, New York 1966, fig. 14 and Livia as identified by H. von Heintze, review of W. H. Gross, *Iulia Augusta. Untersuchungen zur Grundlegung einer Livia-Ikonographie*, *AJA* 68, 1964 (pp. 318–320), p. 319.

[25] Head of Caligula from Gortyna: L. Fabbrini, "Caligola. Il ritratto dell'adolescenza e il ritratto dell'apoteosi," *RM* 73–74, 1966–1967 (pp. 134–146), p. 141, pl. 45.

[26] Athens, N.M. 1296: Conze 1868.

[27] The earliest is on the grave relief of Isias from Smyrna (pp. 53–54 above, Pl. 1) at the beginning of the 2nd century B.C.; in addition, there are a few relief figures of queens on Ptolemaic oinochoai (pp. 8, 9 above) and, also of the 2nd century B.C. and later, several representations of Isis (p. 14 above). In Athens the votive relief of Isis Dikaiosyne (footnote 189 above, p. 31, Pl. 1) also appears to have shown this loosely draped costume.

evenly carved in very low relief, is comparable to fine Classical grave reliefs,[28] but characteristic of Claudian drapery in Rome and found on several contemporary monuments in Greece are the numerous parallel folds that fall in sheets barely touching the figure and without regard for the anatomy.[29]

Neronian–Flavian

For the second half of the 1st century, more "Isis" reliefs have been preserved; they form two groups. The four earlier reliefs (Pls. 10, 11) are Neronian to early Flavian in style and appear to be from a workshop that specialized in statues with sheer, clinging drapery.[30] The five reliefs that belong to the later group, mostly late Flavian, may be from two or three workshops that differ in the degree to which the drapery served as a decorative adjunct to the head.[31] Together these reliefs show a development that resulted in the use of drapery as an elegant frame for tall, stately figures much like the Vestals and togati on the Cancelleria relief in Rome, an official monument of Domitian late in his reign.[32]

On the "Isis" relief Athens, N.M. 1270 (Pl. 10), the drapery is very sheer and chiffon-like and reveals the most feminine figure represented on these reliefs.[33] The sculptor displays such a mastery of sheer drapery that he may well have made fine, draped statues such as the mantled woman of Pentelic marble from Rome, now in Boston (M.F.A. 01.8191; Pl. 9).[34] A date early in the reign of Nero is likely because of the close comparison of this

[28] See the stele of Philostrate of the 420's B.C.: Diepolder, *Die attischen Grabreliefs*, p. 19, pl. 13:2.

[29] On Claudian drapery, see F. W. Goethert, "Studien zur Kopienforschung," *RM* 54, 1939, pp. 197–206. Examples in Greece include the statue of Augustus (Corinth S 1116 a–e) from the Julian Basilica at Corinth (C. de Grazia, *Corinth: The Roman Portrait Sculpture*, diss. Columbia University, 1973, pp. 17–18, 90–92, no. 10; Johnson, *Corinth* IX, no. 134); Claudius as Zeus at Olympia (Niemeyer, *Studien*, p. 107, no. 96, pl. 34:2); and on the Attic grave reliefs of Gaios and Hilaros, Athens, N.M. 1250 (Conze 2066; Pl. 9) and Bathyllos (in Verona, Conze 2113; Pl. 8). The "Isis" relief Athens, N.M. 1296 should be late Claudian as the figures are more slender and have narrow heads like Agrippina the Younger at Olympia (G. Treu, *Olympia*, III, *Die Bildwerke von Olympia in Stein und Thon*, Berlin 1897, pl. 63) and not the squat round head of the woman on the earlier stele of Bathyllos (Pl. 8) and of the statue of Livia from Lepcis Magna of A.D. 45/6 (Heintze [footnote 24, p. 70 above], p. 319, pl. 96).

[30] Athens, N.M. 1270; Riemann, no. 58; **2** and **3**. The life-sized statue of Isis, Herakleion Mus. 314 (Pl. 12) is unpublished and was merely cited by Dunand (*Le Culte d'Isis* II, p. 83, fig. 3, a rough sketch). The drapery is not so sheer as that on Athens, N.M. 1270 (Pl. 10), but as on the Kerameikos relief, thick folds frame the torso; the variety of folds and rich, ornamental effect of the drapery on each figure (Pls. 11 and 12) are characteristic of the most innovative Flavian draped sculpture, such as the statue of Titus from the Palatine, Rome (see footnote 37 below, p. 72).

[31] Kallo and Synpheron relief; Riemann, no. 57 (Pl. 15); Eleusis relief; **4** and **5**. See p. 72 below.

[32] J. M. C. Toynbee, *The Flavian Reliefs*, London 1957; E. Simon, "Zu den flavischen Reliefs von der Cancelleria," *JdI* 75, 1960, pp. 134–156 and 151 for date of A.D. 93–96; D. E. Strong (review of Daltrop, Hausmann, and Wagner, *Die Flavier*, Gnomon 40, 1968, p. 216) cites Simon's date, which also supports the views of Toynbee.

[33] Athens, N.M. 1270: Conze 1968.

[34] Each fold on Athens, N.M. 1270 is varied and puckers slightly as it clings to the figure; it falls over the legs in rippling arcs. See the description of **2** (Appendix 1; Pl. 10) which is a second and slightly larger work by this sculptor. The draped statue Boston, M.F.A. 01.8191 is Neronian according to G. H. Chase (*Greek and Roman Antiquities; A Guide to the Classical Collection*, Cambridge 1950, p. 147, fig. 190) and Claudian according to Comstock and Vermeule (*Sculpture in Stone*, p. 213, no. 337). They cite the spiral locks at the neck as a dating criterion, but such locks are found on hairstyles as late as the Flavian period: see L. Furnée

"Isis" figure with that of Tryphon in Cambridge (Pl. 11), especially in respect to their long-legged proportions and pronounced three-dimensional pose.[35] A second sculptor from this workshop was responsible for two "Isis" reliefs (Riemann, no. 58 and **3**; Pl. 11), and a life-sized statue of Isis in Crete (Herakleion Mus. 314; Pl. 12).[36] The thicker folds at the waist and on the statue, also flaring from the sides, frame the figure and create a decorative tension with the figure's stride, characteristic of early Flavian draped statues in Rome.[37]

The heads of the figures are emphasized on the majority of the late Flavian "Isis" reliefs and are often so carefully and distinctively carved that they could well be the work of fine portrait sculptors, possibly those responsible for portraits of the Flavian emperors in Athens. The man named Synpheron on one of these reliefs (Pl. 13) resembles the fine portrait of the emperor Vespasian from Rome, now in Copenhagen,[38] while the head on **4** (Pl. 16) has many of the subtle features particular to the portrait of Domitian in Athens (N.M. 345; Pl. 16).[39] Even the less carefully carved relief at Eleusis (Pl. 14) has its closest parallel with the portrait of the last Flavian emperor, Domitian, at Corinth.[40] The last of the Flavian "Isis" reliefs, **5** (Pl. 17), is a dry, academic work; it belongs with the large stele of Titus Flavius Onesiphoros (Pl. 17) whose draped figures are bold in relief, but the drapery is treated like a curtain with odd-shaped folds barely recording the pose of the figures.[41]

---

van Zwet, "Fashion in Women's Hairdress in the First Century of the Roman Empire," *Bulletin Antieke Beschaving* 31, 1956, pp. 1–22. More helpful and, to me, conclusive of a Neronian date are the long-legged figure proportions, deep-knee pose, and the emphasis on the sensuous qualities of the torso as revealed and augmented by the drapery; compare with the relief of Tryphon (Conze 2005) and statue of Nero from Gabii (see footnote 35 below).

[35] Tryphon, on loan to the Fitzwilliam Museum (Conze 2005), is very close to the statue of Nero from Gabii in the Louvre (inv. no. 1221; Niemeyer, *Studien*, pl. 3:2) and the head of Nero at Corinth, S 1088 (De Grazia [footnote 29 above, p. 71], pp. 19, 108–121, no. 13; Johnson, *Corinth* IX, no. 137, p. 77, figs. 1–3).

[36] Herakleion Mus. 314, unpublished. Riemann would date the Kerameikos reliefs nos. 57 and 58 to the Trajanic period with the stele of Mousaios and Amaryllis (Pl. 19), but these reliefs are earlier; no. 58 has the same dimplelike puckering folds as the Isis statue in Crete and similar flaring ornamental folds; their dramatic emphasis on the figure is found in the abrupt three-quarter turn and boldly modeled, bulbous hand of **3**. The latter is an exaggeration of Athens, N.M. 1270 (Pl. 10) and could well be from the same workshop but not carved by the same master.

[37] Statue of Titus as togatus and a companion statue: Vatican, Braccio Nuovo 2282 and 417 (H. v. Heintze, *Helbig*[4] I, nos. 417 and 447; Daltrop *et al.* [footnote 72 above, p. 41], pl. 22:c; H. v. Heintze, *Roman Art*, New York 1972, fig. 149).

[38] Kallo and Synpheron relief: Conze 2077. Synpheron resembles portraits of Vespasian from Rome (e.g. Copenhagen, Ny Carlsberg Glyp. 2585: Daltrop *et al.*, *op. cit.*, p. 10, pl. 3). Kallo is one of the few with Flavian hairstyles on Attic grave reliefs, like *Julia Titi* (*ibid.*, pl. 42). Synpheron's apparent role as initiate in the cult of Isis (p. 56 above) contributes to the interpretation of these "Isis" reliefs. For the present battered condition of this stele, see p. 34 above and Pl. 13.

[39] From another workshop, **4** is very close to the portrait of Domitian, Athens, N.M. 345, in the subtle rendering of the flesh, massive structure, and expression; the companion of **4** in the Kerameikos (Riemann, no. 57; Pl. 15) resembles the more idealized portrait of Titus, Athens, N.M. 4915 (Pl. 15): A. Stavrides, "Zwei Porträts des Kaisers Titus im Nationalmuseum zu Athen," *RM* 85, 1978, p. 478; a bust in the Agora (S 1319; Pl. 15) may be a second work by the sculptor of the latter: Harrison, *Agora* I, no. 14.

[40] Eleusis relief: Alexandri, Δελτ 22, B′ 1, pp. 122–125, pl. 102:b; these heads have the same stylized features and simple rendering as Domitian in Corinth, S 2272 (see De Grazia [footnote 29 above, p. 71], no. 15).

[41] Stele of Titus Flavius Onesiphoros, Athens, N.M. 3725: Theophanides, Ἀρχ Ἐφ (footnote 1 above, p. 58), p. 12, fig. 16; on the inscription, see p. 47 above. Proportions and ornamental drapery are like those on

Second Century after Christ

Several "Isis" reliefs can be dated to each 20 years of the 2nd century after Christ: Trajanic, Hadrianic, and early, middle, and late Antonine. There are some changes in figure proportions and much variation in the treatment of the drapery. There is a surprising lack of direct development from the preceding "Isis" reliefs of the Flavian period to their immediate successors in the early 2nd century.[42] The only continuous development is found between the middle and late Antonine works.[43] The drapery of the latter is an exaggeration of the dense folds of the former.

Trajanic

The Trajanic "Isis" reliefs, A.D. 98–117, are from a workshop that may have specialized in statues of Isis. From the Agora there are remnants of two "Isis" relief figures of life size, **6** and **7** (Pl. 18). It is rare to have two contemporary stelai with figures of this largest size. They are so strikingly similar that they are probably the works of the same sculptor who also made two statues found at Gortyna, Crete.[44] The reliefs and the statues share in the arrangement of the drapery into broad panels of shallow folds, which, across the chest, seem to measure and stress the width of the figure. They have the same exceptionally long fringe that also serves as a screen to encase the figure in rich banded patterns. They also share in the distinctive, rich mat surface on the drapery and the even execution that defines all the folds and contours of the costume with a broad, shallow drill.

The statue from the Isieion in Gortyna served as a cult image, while the second Isis, an Isis-Fortuna, was found in the Prytaneion.[45] The companion statue of Sarapis (Pl. 19) from the Isieion is very close in style and execution and should be a third work of this sculptor. His snug, almost foldless drapery is a good contrast to the rich drapery of the goddess.[46] The

---

late Flavian monuments in Rome, such as Domitian's Cancelleria relief (see p. 71 above) and the frieze of the Forum Transitorum, dedicated in A.D. 98: C. F. Leon, *Die Bauornamentik des Trajansforums und ihre Stellung in der früh- und mittelkaiserzeitlichen Architekturdekoration Roms*, Vienna 1971, p. 90; Andreae, *Art of Rome*, figs. 391–394. The pediment of another Attic "Isis" relief, in Aigina (Pl. 14), may also be late Flavian in view of its low pitch and linear decoration; for its provenience, see p. 37 above; Kourouniotis, 'Αρχ'Εφ, 1913, p. 97, fig. 20; Dunand, *Le Culte d'Isis* II, p. 214, pl. 40.

[42] Note especially the lack of continuity to the Trajanic "Isis" reliefs (Pls. 18–20) from their immediate predecessors, the late Flavian "Isis" reliefs (Pls. 13, 14).

[43] Compare the late Antonine stele, London B.M. 630 (p. 73 below and Pl. 32), with the middle Antonine stele, Boston, M.F.A. 1971.209 (pp. 79–80 below and Pl. 30).

[44] Isis, Herakleion Mus. 260 (Pl. 19) and Isis-Fortuna in the Prytaneion at Gortyna: Dunand, *Le Culte d'Isis* II, pp. 205–206.

[45] On the Isieion, see R. Salditt-Trappmann, *Tempel der ägyptischen Götter in Griechenland und an der Westküste Kleinasiens*, Leiden 1970, pp. 56–61.

[46] Sarapis, Herakleion Mus. 259 (Pl. 19) is strikingly similar to the Isis, Herakleion Mus. 260, in style and execution; they should be from the same workshop, possibly by the same sculptor. The Antonine date suggested by Hornbostel (*Sarapis*, p. 189, note 1) is not correct. Not only is the Trajanic date based on the correspondence of important features in drapery and proportions, style, and execution with those of the Agora reliefs, **6** and **7**, but also the basic structure of the figures from Gortyna and their clear, yet ornamental drapery have much in common with the majestic gods on Trajan's arch at Beneventum: cf. the southwest attic relief of the Capitoline gods (Andreae, *Art of Rome*, fig. 416). Most representations of Sarapis like this one are simply draped; hence the difference of figure type also contributes to the contrast between these contemporary statues from the Isieion.

increase in deeply drilled folds across the legs of the Isis-Fortuna may be the result of a development in technique. Similar folds riddle the costume of the Isis from the Isieion in Thessaloniki, which is the last of these three Isis statues shown wearing a peplos and may be the last work by this sculptor.[47]

Closely related to the Gortyna statues and the Agora "Isis" reliefs **6** and **7** are two other "Isis" reliefs, carved by two different sculptors from this workshop. The first is the stele of Mousaios and Amaryllis (Athens, N.M. 1233; Pl. 19). Attention is given to the well-modeled heads, suggesting that it is the work of a sculptor who made idealized portraits.[48] The drapery is boldly simplified, in particular reducing the dress of Isis to a few thick folds, while increasing the length of the fringe and emphasizing the large knot. At first glance, the second "Isis" relief, **8** (Pl. 20), is a coarse work, betraying a sculptor who made cursory yet accurate copies.[49] The heavy rasp quickly creates the appropriate texture of this linen costume, which was omitted in the other three "Isis" reliefs from this workshop.

A Trajanic date for these four "Isis" reliefs and the two Gortyna Isis statues is provided by the dated parallels for the well-preserved stele of Mousaios and Amaryllis.[50] The snug composition and squat figures compare well with those on the ephebic-decree relief Athens, N.M. 1469 of A.D. 115/6, and Mousaios resembles the portrait of cosmete Heliodoros, also of this decade.[51] The drilled-curl hairstyle, worn by the third figure on the Mousaios relief, was fashionable in Rome for women in the Flavian and Trajanic periods, late 1st and early 2nd centuries.[52] A late Trajanic date is likely for the other two works by the sculptor of Mousaios: a bust of a young man found at Phlious and an unusual relief of a youth with drilled curls from Eleusis, both of which show his familiarity with contemporary metropolitan art in Rome.[53]

---

[47] Isis, Thessaloniki, Arch.Mus. 843: Salditt-Trappmann (footnote 45 above, p. 73), p. 50, pls. 23, 44; and Dunand, *Le Culte d'Isis* II, p. 54, pl. 16:1. A late Hadrianic date is likely owing to the figure proportions and the very broad shoulders that seem to be suspended over the legs as in the figure of Alexandra, pp. 75–76 below, Pl. 24.

[48] Mousaios and Amaryllis: Conze 1971. For the inscription, see p. 50 above; on the unusual situla, see p. 24 above. This stele and **8** (Pl. 20) should be from the same workshop as **6** and **7**; they have the same drapery arrangement, very long fringe, and proportions, as well as even, careful rendering of the folds and fine surface texture. The stele of Mousaios and Amaryllis, however, should not be the work of the same sculptor as that of **8** since the emphasis is on the heads and thick-limbed figures; the folds are fewer and thicker.

[49] **8** is a cursory copy of the figure of Amaryllis. Shallow parallel folds also cover the figures on the stele of Hilara (Conze 1951; Pl. 20), whose heads are simplified versions of Amaryllis; this stele and two other relief heads in the Agora (S 880, S 584; Harrison, *Agora* I, nos. 21 and 22) could also be works by the sculptor of **8**.

[50] The stele of Mousaios and Amaryllis has long been considered Trajanic: Conze 1971; Muehsam, *Berytus* 10, 1952, pp. 57, 68, 71; Riemann, p. 60. For dated parallels, see footnotes 51–53 below.

[51] Compare the composition and figure proportions with Athens, N.M. 1469 (*IG* II², 2017): Lattanzi, *Cosmeti*, p. 80, pl. 35:b; Follet (*Athènes*, p. 56) suggests a date of A.D. 102/3 to 110. Mousaios resembles the cosmete Heliodoros of A.D. 100 to 110: Lattanzi, p. 34, no. 2, pl. 2; and Follet (pp. 202–203) dates him to A.D. 113/4–124/5.

[52] Concerning the Flavian-Trajanic spongelike hairstyle, see Harrison, *Agora* I, p. 27.

[53] Bust of a young man found at Phlious, Athens, N.M. 420 (Pl. 20): Hekler (footnote 11 above, p. 59), p. 175, fig. 58; R. West, *Römische Porträt-Plastik* II, Rome 1941, pp. 86–87, pl. 24. Bust length and hairstyle are late Trajanic: see G. Daltrop, *Die stadtrömischen männlichen Privatbildnisse trajanischer und hadrianischer Zeit*, Berlin 1958, figs. 28, 24. The unusual relief at Eleusis (Pl. 19) has a very similar idealized head of a youth with high cheek bones, prominent jaw and chin, and ornamental eyes, mouth, and nose recalling that

Hadrianic

The Hadrianic "Isis" reliefs are quite different from the preceding ones, retaining only the compact composition with figures tight to the frame. There is no evidence of continuity in style or execution. The majority of them are classicizing works, readily assigned to two different workshops. The long-legged figures have snug drapery with symmetrically arranged looping folds that recall Ptolemaic-Egyptian statues in this costume.[54]

Earliest in this group are two closely related reliefs that should be from the same workshop: the handsome two-figure stele of Attikos in Mantua (Duc.Pal. 6677; Pl. 22) and **9** (Pl. 22).[55] The Agora relief, although preserving only part of the torso, is clearly a crisp copy of the woman on the stele of Attikos. The latter is the work of a master sculptor who not only preferred soft rounded folds and cottony fringe but also excelled in the illusion of depth and the portrayal of the properties of different types of drapery and objects.

The two-figure stele of Attikos is remarkable in several respects. Most natural and unusual is the way the woman holds and plays the sistrum, turned three-quarters with the prongs loose and slipping. The subtle rendering of the capelike section of her fringed mantle in very low relief gives it the illusion of transparency. The optical adjustments of the figures, the head and upper torso enlarged to minimize distortion when viewed from below, suggest that the sculptor of the stele of Attikos studied or worked with the sculptor of such major commissions as the reliefs on the Philopappos Monument, A.D. 114–116 (Pl. 22), one of the few monuments known to us in Athens comparable to official historical reliefs in Rome.[56]

The stele of Attikos and Agora fragment **9** should be dated to the 20's of the 2nd century after Christ. They share in the slender proportions, long tapered limbs, and angular jutting hip found on the figure of the ephebic-decree relief Athens, E.M. 10040, dated to A.D. 120 (Pl. 23).[57] The Agora relief in particular prefigures the crisply carved and majestic figure of Alexandra (Pl. 24), which is the best known "Isis" relief.[58] A smaller version of Alexandra

---

of Amaryllis; the drilled coiffure which Conze (2133) also noted is like that of the camilli on the Arch of Trajan at Beneventum, A.D. 114: see M. Rotili, *L'Arco di Traiano a Benevento*, Rome 1970, pls. 28, 31; on the date, see F. J. Hassel, *Der Trajansbogen in Benevent*, Mainz am Rhein 1966.

[54] See pp. 8–11 above.

[55] Attikos: Conze 1960; for the inscription, see pp. 49 and 51 above; P. Graindor, *Athènes de Tibère à Trajan*, Cairo 1931, p. 203 (pre-Hadrianic as Attikos is beardless); Muehsam, *Berytus* 10, 1952, p. 96, note 6 (columnar antae like those of the Hadrianic stele of Alexandra); Budischovsky, *Diffusion*, p. 92 (1st century B.C.).

[56] Philopappos Monument on Mouseion hill: M. Santangelo, "Il monumento di C. Julius Antiochos Philopappos in Atene," *Annuario della Scuola Archeologica di Atene* n.s. 3–5, 1939–1941, pp. 153–253 and date, 197–198; Brilliant (footnote 184 above, p. 54), p. 128; Vermeule (footnote 15 above, p. 69), pp. 80–83; D. E. E. Kleiner, *The Monument of Philopappos in Athens*, Rome 1983. Muehsam (*Berytus* 10, 1952, pp. 81–82, 84–86) regards Attic grave reliefs of Roman date as poor works not to be compared to official art, while Dow and Vermeule (*Hesperia* 34, 1965, pp. 291–292) assign the relief figure of the Damaskenos (Conze 2038) to one of the sculptors of the draped figures on the reliefs of the Philopappos Monument. A closer comparison with the latter is the Attic stele in Grenoble (Pl. 22).

[57] Ephebic-decree relief of A.D. 120 (*IG* II², 2018), dated by Follet, *Athènes*, p. 204.

[58] Alexandra, Athens, N.M. 1193 (Conze 1969); Muehsam, *Berytus* 10, 1952, pp. 61, 79; most recently, see Parlasca (footnote 96 above, p. 19), p. 201. **9** and the woman on the stele of Attikos have the same drapery arrangement, short fringe, and small knot as Alexandra, but each is by a different sculptor. Although **9** is the closest, it lacks the refinements of Alexandra.

is found in the fully preserved "Isis" stele of Methe (Athens, Third Ephoria 1160; Pl. 23).[59] These two reliefs, Alexandra and Methe, are slightly later works from the same workshop as Attikos and **9**. A date in the 30's of the 2nd century is certain as Alexandra has been recognized as a prime example of late Hadrianic classicism.[60] Alexandra is related to the crisply carved copies of the Erechtheion caryatids at the villa of Hadrian at Tivoli,[61] but a more individual artist sculptured Alexandra. He drew attention to the small, austere head as well as the monumental appearance of her figure. He covered the taut folds with a rich, banded surface and used the deep drill only to mark major contours, while giving the hair and fringe a decorative appearance. The life-sized statue of Isis found in the Isieion at Sabratha (Pl. 24)[62] could be another work by this sculptor, possibly earlier owing to the slender proportions and interest in movement.

The Attic grave relief of Methe (Pl. 23) is very helpful not only for reconstructing Alexandra's pose and suggesting that her stele was a similar two-figure relief but also for demonstrating again her importance. The features that suggest that the relief of Methe is the work of a different sculptor are the more limited use of the drill on Methe's relief, the awkward placement of long locks of hair on her shoulders like large "pony-tails", and the different facial features. The incised irises and pupils of Methe are rare on Attic grave reliefs, and the earliest examples known to me are early Antonine in date.[63] Such detail in sculpture, marking the glance of the eyes, seems to have occurred in Athens first in late Hadrianic portraiture.[64] Methe's stele may be one of the few reliefs of late Hadrianic date to have this new feature.

A second "Isis" relief from Athens, modeled after Alexandra's stele, belongs to Epigonos and Elate (Athens, N.M. 1308; Pl. 24).[65] Owing to its coarse execution and stocky figures,

[59] The stele of Methe, wife or daughter of Herakleidos of Kephale, is unpublished; it was brought to the Third Ephoria in 1971 after being found in the clearance of a house; on the inscription, see p. 50 above. The figure of Methe and her unnamed husband(?) are half life size, half the size of Alexandra; Methe's relief: H. 1.17, W. 0.87, Th. 0.08 m. Description and illustration of this relief are made through the generosity of Dr. Olga Alexandri.

[60] See footnote 58 above, p. 75.

[61] On the dry copies of the Erechtheion caryatids at Tivoli made by Athenians, see P. Zanker, Helbig[4] II, pp. 155–158, no. 3194; E. Schmidt, "Die Kopien der Erechtheionkoren," *Antike Plastik* 13, 1973, p. 27, pls. 6, 11, 20, 26. The sculptor of Alexandra may have studied with the Tivoli sculptors in Athens because they share in proportions, crisp drapery defined by limited use of the deep drill, and similar idealized head. The sculptor of Alexandra is superior in imparting a richer surface and glow in the marble. He uses the flat chisel to carve the main features as well as the taut folds and the deep drill to draw attention selectively to hair and drapery.

[62] G. Pesce, *Il Tempio d'Iside in Sabratha*, Rome 1953, pp. 49–50, fig. 28; strikingly similar are the banded folds and decorative precision in execution. The very slender, long legs indicate an early Hadrianic date.

[63] The few examples include an early Antonine grave relief, Agora S 258 (Harrison, *Agora* I, no. 32) and Euphrosyne, Athens, N.M. 1232 (Conze 1902). For the latter, the inscription (*IG* II[2], 7349: mid-2nd century) may refer to her son or younger brother Phileros, an ephebe in A.D. 165 (*IG* II[2], 2086, line 12); an early Antonine date, also offered by Muehsam (*Berytus* 10, 1952, pp. 76, 78, pl. XVII:3), seems likely owing to close comparisons with statues from Herodes Atticus' nymphaeum at Olympia, e.g. Faustina the Elder (R. Bol, *Olympische Forschungen*, XV, *Das Statuenprogramm des Herodes-Atticus-Nymphaeums*, Berlin 1984, pls. 36, 37).

[64] See the discussion of the portrait of Sabina, wife of Hadrian, Athens, N.M. 449: M. Wegner, *Hadrian, Plotina, Marciana, Matidia, Sabina: Das römische Herrscherbild* II, iii, Berlin 1956, pp. 87–88, pl. 43:a; A. Carandini, *Vibia Sabina*, Florence 1969, pp. 161–166, figs. 111, 112.

[65] Epigonos and Elate (Conze 1962); for the inscription, see pp. 49 and 51 above; figures are half life size.

this work could well be from another contemporary workshop. **10** (Pl. 25) is from a large "Isis" stele possibly by the same sculptor as that of Elate. Although much is omitted in the coarse figure of Elate with her thick limbs, large knuckled hands, and squashed head, surprising detail is recorded on this heavily rasped stele and on its companion, the stele of Zosas and Nostimos in Marathon (Pl. 25).[66] The resemblance of Zosas to portraits of Hadrian as well as the stocky proportions and ponderous stance may suggest that the sculptor of these heavily rasped stelai also worked on the cuirassed statues of that emperor, which were made in great number.[67]

A mixture of Trajanic and Hadrianic features is found on a grave relief from the southern necropolis at Oropos, inscribed to Neikias son of Neikias from Oropos and to Aristo Euphra (Pl. 25).[68] Although this is not an Attic grave relief (it was not found in Athens or the region of Attica), the figures and portraits bear such a close resemblance to Attic grave reliefs that the Oropos relief could be the work of an Athenian.[69] The care in defining the dress of Isis worn by Aristo would place this relief among the better "Isis" reliefs from Athens. The compact figures and the soft, waved hairstyle recall the Trajanic relief of Mousaios and Amaryllis (Pl. 19), but the portraits resemble later ones of the mid-2nd century.[70] The "Isis" figure, Aristo, presents a mixture: the taut folds in broad bands are like the late Trajanic relief **8** (Pl. 20) and the snug position of the limbs like that of Amaryllis, while the arrangement of the fringe and swelling left hip of Aristo resembles late Hadrianic figures.[71] A date towards the middle of the 2nd century, early Antonine, is likely for the relief from Oropos. Its combination of features also suggests that the artist was not trained in one of the

---

[66] Zosas and Nostimos, now in the Marathon Museum (Conze 2069); on the inscription, p. 47 above. Hadrianic for the features cited above: Muehsam, *Berytus* 10, 1952, pp. 75, 87, 89. It is very close to the stele of Epigonos and Elate in style and technique. Unusual details are found on each: the lotus-topped sistrum of Elate (see p. 20 above) and coiled-basket cist (see p. 29 above); the tall, laced boots of Zosas and Nostimos and the carefully textured hair and beard of Zosas.

[67] Zosas' serious, frowning face, hair, and beard are like the portraits of Hadrian: see the head of the cuirassed statue from Diktynnaion, Crete (Andreae, *Art of Rome*, fig. 86). For a good comparison for the rasped technique see the cuirassed statue of Hadrian in the Agora (S 166; Harrison, *Agora* I, no. 56); closer in pose and proportions to the relief figures is the statue of Hadrian on Thasos (K. Stemmer, *Untersuchungen zur Typologie, Chronologie und Ikonographie der Panzerstatuen*, Berlin 1978, p. 86, no. VII 21). On the numerous statues of Hadrian, see pls. 22, 27–29, 31:3 and 4, 60, 74 of Stemmer and discussion by Harrison.

[68] The relief from Oropos was found in the 1982 excavation of the eastern necropolis between the modern streets of Koimeseos Theotokos and Agios Georgios.

Νεικίας (Νεικίου) Ὠρώπιος | Ἀριστ<ὡ> Εὐφρᾶ

I am grateful to Dr. Petrakos for this information, the photograph, and permission to publish this recent find.

[69] Cf. a Paris relief (Conze 2098; *IG* II², 9410). Muehsam (*Berytus* 10, 1952, p. 72) would date this relief to the 160's according to the hairstyle, but there are closer comparisons such as an early Antonine head from a grave relief, Agora S 258 (Harrison, *Agora* I, no. 32). The man's portrait compares well with the portrait of Hadrian from Diktynnaion, Crete in the serious expression, facial proportions, and short cropped beard which became fashionable under Hadrian; see the references in footnote 67 above. The small, oval face of the woman Aristo, with little modeling of bone structure, resembles Agora S 258.

[70] E.g. Agora S 258 (Harrison, *Agora* I, no. 32). The small, oval face of Aristo has none of Amaryllis' prominent bone structure or boldly modeled features; for the Trajanic date of the latter, see p. 74 above.

[71] Compare with the Hadrianic stelai: Methe (Pl. 23) from Athens, Third Ephoria 1160 and Elate, Athens, N.M. 1308 (Pl. 24). Aristo shares with these women in the dress of Isis not only the characteristic jutting hip but also the higher placement of the knot; the breasts are not hidden by long fringe.

workshops in which Attic "Isis" reliefs were made but rather that this Athenian drew freely from Trajanic and Hadrianic models.

Early Antonine

For the early Antonine period, the 40's and 50's of the 2nd century, the "Isis" reliefs differ so greatly in style, execution, and rich detail that it seems unlikely that many are from the same workshop.[72] They do share in the loosely draped costume of Isis recalling the pyramidal arrangement popular in the Hellenistic period.[73] An increase in thick, drooping folds seems to have occurred in the 150's, as seen in Agora fragment **14** (Pl. 29), the small upper figure on the stele of Eisias (Athens, N.M. 1249; Pl. 28), and the Laurion relief of Sosipatros and Epiteugma (Pl. 29).[74]

The first of the early Antonine "Isis" reliefs include **11** (Pl. 26) and two large stelai, Athens, N.M. Ἀπο. 237 + **13** (Pl. 28) and Lamia Viboullia (Piraeus Mus. 1160; Pl. 27). Although the sculptors of these three stelai carved the figures in high relief, the heavily rasped surface of figure and costume detracts from the modeling and seems to dissolve the three-dimensionality of figure and drapery. The most peculiar treatment is evident on Athens, N.M. Ἀπο. 237 (Pl. 28) where the breast is illogically sunk while the framing folds and knot are thickest. The modest relief **11** also overemphasizes the thick folds of the mantle and incises folds into the breast. The lightly carved figure and drapery of Lamia Viboullia make her seem to disappear.[75]

The early Antonine date for these three reliefs is evident from the swaying pose and loose-limbed, lanky figures like the center figure on the ephebic relief, Athens, N.M. 1483, A.D. 143/4,[76] and the statue of Regilla from the nymphaeum of Herodes Atticus at Olympia, A.D. 150–153.[77] Closely related to these "Isis" reliefs are two statues from Cyrene,

[72] See **11–14** (Pls. 26, 28, 29), the Laurion stele of Sosipatros and Epiteugma (Pl. 29), and the upper relief on Athens, N.M. 1249 (Pl. 28).

[73] See pp. 14, 53–54 above and Pl. 1.

[74] **14** and the stele of Eisias should be contemporary with the Laurion stele (Conze 1967), but the draped figures on the latter are so brusquely carved that it should be assigned to another workshop, that of the stele of Eukarpos, Athens, N.M. 1195 (Conze 2078). The stele of Eisias has recently been published by A. Stauridis [(footnote 1 above, p. 33), p. 172], but a Severan date such as she proposed is unlikely owing to the striking resemblance to the figure of Lamia Viboullia (Pl. 27), early Antonine in date (see below).

[75] **13** and Lamia Viboullia: (Conze 1957); on the inscription of the latter, see pp. 47, 49 above. They are so different in execution and treatment of the drapery and garland that they should be from different workshops. Barely visible, shallow folds evenly carved cover the figure of Lamia and obscure the boldness of the relief, and the garland is plain and ropelike, while draped figure **13** has soft, thick folds that thin to mere scratches and a more carefully carved floral garland.

[76] Athens, N.M. 1483 (*IG* II², 2050): Lattanzi, *Cosmeti*, p. 82, pl. 36; on the date, see Follet, *Athènes*, p. 174.

[77] Regilla: Treu (footnote 29 above, p. 71), pl. 3:5; on the date of the sculpture from the nymphaeum, see Graindor (footnote 193 above, p. 55), p. 87, and Wegner, *Die Herrscherbildnisse*, p. 52. Although they proposed a date of A.D. 147–149, the inscription permits a later date, A.D. 153–157: Follet, *Athènes*, p. 176; the architecture, according to Walker (*AA* [footnote 47 above, p. 63], p. 119, note 50), supports a date of A.D. 150–153. According to the most recent research, by Bol ([footnote 63 above, p. 76], p. 14, note 50 and p. 21), a date early in the 50's of the 2nd century is presented. Bol argues, however (pp. 26–27, no. 41), that this statue should be identified as a daughter of Herodes Atticus, not as his wife, Regilla. Although Bol's reconstruction

nearly identical in drapery and pose. These statues are important as they were found in the Isieion at Cyrene, are over life size, and include a portrait of the empress Faustina the Elder (Pl. 27).[78] A third Athenian sculptor, a dry academician, should be responsible for these statues and may be from the same workshop as the carver of the larger "Isis" relief figure from the Agora, **13** (Pl. 28).

Middle Antonine

For sculpture in the round or in relief of the middle Antonine period in Athens (160's and 170's), the emphasis is on the immediacy of figure and portrait. The best works are boldly modeled and have prominent bone structure and well-knit bodies displayed by the drapery.[79] Among these fine works are several "Isis" reliefs.

The small relief of Sosibia (Boston, M.F.A. 1971.209; Pl. 30) masterfully shows her in a bold, three-quarter turn, while her drapery has numerous thick folds that fall in response to and reveal the striding pose.[80] That she belongs to the middle Antonine period is also evident from her compact, square-jawed face like the portrait bust of Melitine (Louvre MA 3068) from Piraeus, A.D. 164,[81] and from her hairstyle similar to that of members of the imperial family, Lucilla and Crispina.[82] There is much space, particularly to the left of

---

and identification of the draped statues may look attractive on paper, her arguments for the identification of several of the draped female statues are not convincing. In particular, concerning the statue with patera in hand (therefore a priestess), the traditional identification of this statue as Regilla still seems to be most likely. The importance of Regilla as a priestess is clearly indicated in the dedicatory inscription of the nymphaeum, and it may not be mere chance that this statue of "Regilla" as a priestess was found beside the inscription which was intended to name her statue.

[78] See Rosenbaum (footnote 165 above, p. 28), pl. 76, nos. 61 and 175 (headless statue), which are shown with and compared to the stele of Lamia Viboullia. H. v. Heintze (review of Rosenbaum, *A Catalogue of Cyrenaican Portrait Sculpture*, *AJA* 66, 1962 [pp. 111–113], p. 112 and in *Das römische Weltreich* [footnote 165 above, p. 28], fig. 303) identified the well-preserved statue (Rosenbaum, no. 61) as a portrait of Faustina the Elder. Another wreathed head (no. 62) now lost could be the head of the second statue, and if so, it could then be a portrait statue of Faustina the Younger. These statues do not represent the empresses as Isis because they do not wear the necessary emblem of Isis on the head (see p. 12 above); they may represent the empresses an initiates of Isis as they wear the Attic arrangement of the costume (pp. 52–57 above).

[79] See the portrait of Lucius Verus, Athens, N.M. 3740 (Wegner, *Die Herrscherbildnisse*, pl. 45). The stele of Neike, Athens, N.M. 1303 (Conze 1934; Pl. 32) includes a portrait and hairstyle on the woman on the left which resembles the portraits of Faustina the Younger of the 160's (Wegner, *op. cit.*, p. 52, pl. 37). Even the unfinished portrait Agora S 1237 (Harrison, *Agora* I, no. 35) has similar boldly modeled features: prominent chin, high cheek bones, fleshy nose, and full lips, as well as a thick crown of hair.

[80] Sosibia: Conze 1955; her inscription offers little help. This stele has been thought to be Trajanic in date on the basis of the hairstyle (Muehsam, *Berytus* 10, 1952, p. 71; Comstock and Vermeule, *Sculpture in Stone*, p. 172, no. 276), but the hairstyle is that worn by Faustina the Younger and most frequently found on portraits of Lucilla and Crispina (Wegner, *Die Herrscherbildnisse*, pp. 75–76, pl. 64:a). The statue of Faustina the Younger with this hairstyle in Rome, Vatican Cortile del Belvedere 936 (H. v. Heintze, Helbig[4] I, no. 1304 and *Roman Art* [footnote 37 above, p. 72], pp. 156, 165, fig. 153) is an excellent comparison in pose, proportions, and snug drapery.

[81] Melitine: H. Jucker, *Das Bildnis im Blätterkelch*, Olten 1961, pp. 97–98, no. 45, pl. 38; L. Goldscheider, *Roman Portraits*, New York 1940, pl. 68; E. Michon, *Mémoires de la Société Nationale des Antiquaires de France* LXXV, 1915–1918, pp. 91–129 and front view on p. 93.

[82] See footnote 80 above.

Sosibia, which seems to lend direction and purpose to her stride. This use of space, as well as the bold three-dimensionality, naturally weighted fall of the drapery, and thick, cottony fringe in twisted strands, is characteristic of the two larger "Isis" reliefs from the Agora, **15** and **16** (Pls. 29, 30), from the same workshop as Sosibia.

These three "Isis" reliefs are from a workshop that may well have specialized in statues of Isis; one of the sculptors was responsible for the impressive statue in the Capitoline in Rome (Mus.Cap. 744; Pl. 31), possibly an idealized portrait of the empress Faustina the Younger as Isis.[83] The Capitoline statue not only is one of the few statues displaying the Athenian version of the dress of Isis with the two fringed edges caught in the knot at the chest (Fig. 1)[84] but is so strikingly similar to Sosibia in pose, proportions, and the arrangement and careful treatment of the costume that I would attribute this statue to the same sculptor. A second statue from this workshop can be recognized in a fragment from a slightly smaller statue apparently in the dress of Isis, which was found in the Agora of Athens (S 2864; Pl. 31).[85]

From the Piraeus is another exceptional "Isis" relief (Pl. 32) whose figures were five-sixths life size; this should be the work of a fine portrait sculptor.[86] In contrast to the subtle modeling of the youth's head, the drapery consists of rather ornamental, tubular folds on his mantle resembling the decorative drapery on select works of early Antonine sculpture.[87] It is likely that this sculptor served in a different workshop that was producing in that preceding period as well.

Late Antonine

The deeply drilled contours and details on the late Antonine reliefs create a harsh, linear design in place of the more natural arrangement and carefully varied rendering of the dress of Isis on the reliefs of the middle Antonine period. There is a curious change in proportions to taller, slender figures that resemble more closely those found on the early Hadrianic "Isis" reliefs.[88] This conscious borrowing or copying of certain elements of earlier

[83] See p. 57 above and footnote 80 above, p. 79. Statues from the workshop of **16**, **17**, and Sosibia include a fragment of a life-sized statue, Agora S 2864 (Pl. 31). The over life-sized Capitoline statue is regarded as an idealized portrait by Tran Tam Tinh (*Campanie*, p. 30, note 3); K. Parlasca (Helbig⁴ II, no. 1433) clarifies that it does not come from the Villa of Hadrian at Tivoli. Parlasca would date this statue to the second quarter of the 1st century after Christ, but it should be dated to the 60's of the 2nd century. As a representation of Faustina the Younger as Isis, compare with the portrait of Faustina in Dresden (Wegner, *Die Herrscherbild-nisse*, p. 52, pl. 37).

[84] See pp. 6–7 above.

[85] Agora S 2864: p.H. 0.235, W. 0.095, Th. 0.075 m.; it corresponds in pose, proportions, and placement of the strut (trace of strut preserved) to the sleeved left wrist of the second statue (Rome, Mus.Cap. 744). One could suggest that other figures such as barbarians wear long sleeved garments, but the wrist and fleshy part of the palm of both statues are positioned to hold lightly a suspended object such as the situla for the cult of Isis.

[86] Piraeus fragment: Conze 1970. Another work by this portrait sculptor could be the stele of Eukarpos and Philoxenos, Athens, N.M. 1243 (Conze 2068; Pl. 32) with figures half life size; on the inscription, see p. 47 above. The proportions, bold modeling of the facial features, and thick soft hair resemble those of the portrait of Lucius Verus, Athens, N.M. 3740; see footnote 79, p. 79 above); proportions and bold modeling of the figure and natural fall of the thick drapery also characterize other reliefs of the 160's (compare the stele of Neike, Pl. 32: see footnote 79 above, p. 79).

[87] A fine example is the early Antonine portrait of Hadrian, Athens, N.M. 249: Harrison, *Agora* I, p. 39, pl. 45.

[88] Compare the late Antonine relief of Sempronius and Agathemeris (Pl. 32; see below) with the early

monuments occurs in the 2nd century after Christ and does not appear to happen in any earlier period.

The late Antonine "Isis" reliefs are rather dry academic works possibly from two workshops. The impressive stele of Agathemeris and Sempronius (London, B.M. 630; Pl. 32) has all the textures and fine details found on official Roman portraits, but the feathering of the fringe, texture of Agathemeris' hair, and linen texture of the dress are hardly noticeable as they are so evenly executed.[89] Somewhat more innovative if less logical is the crisp treatment of the folds and textures on the second large "Isis" relief figure from the same workshop, **17** (Pl. 33). On this figure, the sharply drawn folds over the legs abruptly isolate the knee like an egg. The third "Isis" relief from this workshop, Athens, N.M. 'Aπο. 235, is a coarse, cursory version of a mantled man like Sempronius but holding a situla.[90] These three reliefs should be assigned to the late Antonine period on the basis of style and execution, tight vertical composition, and tall, slender figures with long S-curved stance, found on dated monuments in Rome and in Athens.[91]

Another very characteristic late Antonine work is the deeply drilled "Isis" relief figure **19** (Pl. 35). It may be from another workshop, one that may have made sarcophagi. The almost decorative use of the fine drill that marks the fringe and outer contour of the figure in a series of tiny holes (Pl. 35:a) is a feature of the carefully carved Attic Achilles sarcophagus in Naples (Pl. 34).[92] The "Isis" relief from the Agora has much in common with statues of Isis, popular in Asia Minor and North Africa at this time.[93] They share in the unusual

---

Hadrianic relief of Attikos (p. 75, Pl. 22).

[89] Agathemeris and Sempronius (*IG* II², 6498): figure height 1.0 m., two-thirds life size. **18** (Pl. 33) is a crisper copy of Agathemeris, possibly another work by the same sculptor. An example of official Roman portraiture, made in Athens and displaying the full range of textures, is the portrait of Marcus Aurelius from Marathon, Louvre 1161 (Wegner, *Die Herrscherbildnisse*, pp. 43, 84, 107, pl. 24; A. Datsuli-Stauridis, «Συμβολὴ στὴν εἰκονογραφία τοῦ ʿΗρώδη τοῦ ʾΑττικοῦ», *AAA* 11, 1978 [1980; pp. 214–232], p. 223, fig. 9). A very subtle and masterly rendering of all the various textures is found on the portrait of early Antonine date, Agora S 335 (Harrison, *Agora* I, no. 28).

[90] Man with situla: Conze 1972, no. 17, not published with photograph. The figure is half life size and is unusual since a mantled man holds the situla (see p. 56 above).

[91] Compare with the panel reliefs of Marcus Aurelius, A.D. 176–182, in Rome (Andreae, *Art of Rome*, p. 251, figs. 524–531); Telesphoros, Athens, N.M. 1775 (Pl. 32), which is dated by its inscription, A.D. 170 (see pp. 45–46 above); the Ostia statue of Crispina (H. v. Heintze, Helbig⁴ IV, no. 3057; Bieber, *Ancient Copies*, pl. 119, figs. 702, 703); and a statue of a young woman with the same hairstyle, Athens, N.M. 1647.

[92] **19**, although two-thirds life size like Agathemeris, is coarsely carved and riddled by deep drillwork. It is set off from the background of the relief by a drilled contour (see row of fine drill holes along edge of left shoulder). Such drilled contours are common features on Attic sarcophagi, while the unusually fine drillwork used to undercut the details, such as the shoulder contour and the fringe, is found on an Attic Achilles sarcophagus in Naples of the late 2nd century after Christ: H. Sichtermann and G. Koch, *Griechische Mythen auf römischen Sarkophagen*, Tübingen 1975, no. 1.

An earlier example of an Attic grave relief from a workshop that made sarcophagi is the middle Antonine stele of Artemidoros (Conze 2052): Muehsam, *Berytus* 10, 1952, p. 99; Dow and Vermeule, *Hesperia* 34, 1965, p. 296. It should belong with the Meleager sarcophagus, Athens, N.M. 1186: G. Koch, *Die antiken Sarkophagreliefs*, XII, vi, *Die mythologischen Sarkophage. Meleager*, Berlin 1975, p. 6, no. 160.

[93] Isis statues: a colossal Isis at Laodicea (Kahil [footnote 49 above, p. 12], pp. 189–190, pls. 61–63); a colossal Isis at Lambesis (L. C. Leschi, *Fasti archaeologici* IV, 1949, pp. 401–402, fig. 86); an under life-sized statue at Salamis, Cyprus (V. Karageorghis, *Sculptures from Salamis* I, Nicosia 1964, no. 17, pl. 22:3, 4).

flamelike fringe, the emphatic division of the figure by deeply drilled contours of the folds at the waist, and the equally harsh vertical accent given by the folds falling from the knot. If such statues served as the model for late Antonine "Isis" reliefs **18** and **19** (Pls. 33, 35), then there may have been an influence from the east.[94]

THIRD CENTURY AFTER CHRIST

The greater number and variety of Attic "Isis" reliefs occur in the 3rd century. Several, impressive in size and execution, rival the best "Isis" reliefs of the preceding two centuries.[95] The drapery becomes increasingly more ornamental and more important than the modeling of the figure. By the last third of the 3rd century, the bold pattern of the thick drapery conveys the mass of the figure.[96]

Severan

The "Isis" reliefs of the first 30 years of the 3rd century, the Severan period, vary in figure proportions and style but do share in the ornamental treatment of the drapery with folds covering the figure in flat pattern (Pl. 37).[97] At the end of this period, the folds have become thick and spongy (Pl. 42). The waist is covered by horizontal folds, dividing the figure while emphasizing its width and solidity as well as the thickness of the drapery.[98] Of this later type, **26** (Pl. 41) is so close to the early Severan relief **20** (Pl. 35) in drapery arrangement, thick cottony fringe, and figure proportions that they could be from the same workshop,[99] indicating that this workshop was in operation for at least 30 years.

Like official early Severan monuments, the Arch of Septimius Severus at Lepcis Magna of A.D. 203 and Arcus Argentarii in Rome of A.D. 204,[100] the early Severan "Isis" reliefs

[94] East–west exchange at this time is also evident in Attic sarcophagi: see H. Wiegartz, review of A. Giuliano, *Il commercia dei sarcophagi attici, Gnomon* 37, 1965 (pp. 612–617), p. 613.

[95] **23** (Pl. 39), early Severan; Trieste, Mus.Civ. 2214 (Pl. 43), reign of Balbinus, A.D. 238; **30** (Pl. 45), 240's.

[96] Riemann, no. 61 (Pl. 50); **33** (Pl. 50); Parthenope, Athens, N.M. 1244 (Pl. 50).

[97] **20** (Pl. 35); **21** (see footnote 101 below, p. 83; Pl. 36); **23** (Pl. 39); **26** (Pl. 41); Athens, N.M. 1214 (Pl. 37) and 1223 (Pl. 38; see p. 84 below for date); Riemann, no. 62 (Pl. 40); Broom Hall stele (Pl. 39).

[98] See the two reliefs on Plates 41 and 42: **26** and Athens, N.M. 2014. A third "Isis" relief, Athens, N.M. Άπο. 230 (Conze 1964), preserving most of two stout figures, is an excellent example of this spongy drapery but unfortunately has not been published with photograph. On the woman in the dress of Isis, most noticeable are the horizontal folds, nearly covering the chest, and broad knot. Her straight, thick right arm also serves to emphasize the unusual thickness of her drapery. All three reliefs should be late Severan in date: they share in the spongy drapery, figure proportions, and static posture, and the woman on Athens, N.M. 2014 has a broad-templed head and hairstyle like Julia Mamaea of Greek marble in the British Museum (B. M. Felleti-Maj, *Iconografia romana imperiale*, Rome 1958, p. 108, pl. VII:22). With this group belong the stele of Blastos (Pl. 42) and stele of Aphthonetos (Pl. 42). Both have been considered Hadrianic by Muehsam (*Berytus* 10, 1952, pp. 84, 76) as has the latter by Graindor (*Athènes sous Hadrian*, p. 281), but Aphthonetos in style, technique, and portrait closely resembles the cosmete of A.D. 231–232 (N.M. 388; *IG* II², 2241: Lattanzi, *Cosmeti*, no. 20, pl. 20; dated by Follet [*Athènes*, p. 240] and Clinton [*TAPS* 64, note 10]; see footnote 120 below, p. 85).

[99] Although these figures differ in the treatment of the folds at the waist (which on **26** are broad, horizontal grooves), they are surprisingly alike in figure proportions, arrangement of the Isis dress, and blunt execution, as well as two distinctive features: shallow slashes for shallow folds, and the unusual, thick, cottonlike fringe.

[100] J. B. Ward-Perkins, "Severan Art and Architecture at Lepcis Magna," *Journal of Roman Studies* 38–39, 1948–1949, pp. 59–80; V. M. Strocka, "Beobachtungen an den Attikareliefs des severischen Quadrifrons von Lepcis Magna," *Antiquités africaines* 6, 1972, pp. 147–172. On the Arcus Argentarii, see M. Pallotino, *L'Arco degli Argentarii*, Rome 1946, pp. 73–75, pls. 5, 6.

(Pls. 35–37) and a statue of Isis from Lakonia are characterized by the reduction of the draped figure to flat pattern.[101] The larger early Severan reliefs (Athens, N.M. Ἀπο. 54 + 231 [Pl. 37] and 232) are impressive in execution and clarity of design.[102] The statue from Lakonia, Athens, N.M. 1617, should be from the same workshop that produced **21** (Pl. 36). They share in the broadening of the figure through an awkward stride, emphasizing the front view. The few broad folds and the odd slashed texture of the densely rasped, flannel-like drapery help to increase the bulk of the figure.

Characteristic of Attic sculpture and relief of the early 3rd century and in contrast to the relief figures of the official monuments, the Attic "Isis" relief figures are not deeply drilled but, rather, are covered by broad areas of flat pattern evenly and shallowly carved. Athens, N.M. Ἀπο. 54 + 231 should be the work of a sculptor who made classicizing figures on sarcophagi such as the Attic Achilles sarcophagus in Adana.[103] Ornamental flat pattern with small folds, faceting the surface of the drapery, gives a rich, silklike appearance to several "Isis" relief figures of the second and third decades of the 3rd century (Pls. 37–39).[104] These reliefs should be assigned to a workshop that made fine draped statues. The bold modeling and very deep contours on the large figure from the Agora, **23** (Pl. 39), suggest sculpture in the round.[105] This boldly carved, large figure would have been very noticeable, even from a distance, an advantage when set up in one of the cemeteries leading from Athens.[106]

[101] Athens, N.M. Ἀπο. 54 + 231, **20**, and **21** belong with the statue of Isis of Pentelic marble found in Lakonia: Athens, N.M. 1617, under life size (Kahil [footnote 49 above, p. 12], p. 191 with photograph; Stauridis [footnote 1 above, p. 33], pp. 161–190, esp. p. 164, pl. 13). Kahil compares the Lakonia statue with the statue of Isis from Laodicea, which she recognized as late Antonine; Stauridis, however, is possibly misled by the provenience of the statue and proposes a date much too early (Hadrianic). The Lakonia statue can only be dated to the early 3rd century after Christ owing to the lack of deeply drilled folds or details and the broadening of the figure, as well as the taut planar folds of the drapery. Athens, N.M. Ἀπο. 232, published without illustration (Conze 1972, no. 8), and the Salamis relief (Pl. 37) are from a third workshop. On the island of Paros the "Isis" relief of Kleitomenes (Pl. 37) is so strikingly similar to the Attic "Isis" relief Ἀπο. 232 that it should be the work of the same sculptor, who was in Paros at the time; the relief is carved into the wall of a Hellenistic tomb (A. Orlandos, Ἀρχ Ἐφ, 1960 [1965], Χρονικά, p. 4, pl. Θ; on the re-use of these tombs for graves of Roman date, see O. Rubensohn, "Parische Künstler," *JdI* 50, 1935 (pp. 49–69), p. 67, figs. 10, 11.

[102] Athens, N.M. Ἀπο. 54 + 231 (Conze 1972, nos. 15 and 7), half life size; Athens, N.M. Ἀπο. 232 (Conze 1972, no. 8), two-thirds life size.

[103] Athens, N.M. Ἀπο. 54 + 231 is recently mended; Walters, *AAA* 12, 1979, pp. 215–221. The striking simplicity and bold design of the figures on the Adana sarcophagus, as well as the figure proportions and open composition, compare well with this "Isis" relief; L. Budde, "Ein Achilleus-Sarkophage aus Tarsus in Adana," *Festschrift Eugen v. Mercklin*, Waldsassen 1964, pp. 9–26, pl. 6.

[104] Athens, N.M. 1214, 1223, and **23**. From this workshop should also be **22** (Pl. 38); Athens, N.M. Ἀπο. 234 (Conze 1972, no. 9); **24** (Pl. 39); **25** (Pl. 40). **23–25** are emphatically three-dimensional, possibly slightly later works.

[105] **23**, from a figure of five-sixths life size. The modeling of the figure and surface of the drapery, resembling the rich sheen of silk, is more impressive than that of the contemporary statue, Athens, N.M. 707 (A. Stauridis, «Μικρὴ Ἡρακλειώτισσα ἀπὸ τὴ Ρωμαϊκὴ συλλογὴ τοῦ Ἐθνικοῦ Ἀρχαιολογικοῦ Μουσείου», *AAA* 9, 1976 [pp. 96–107], pp. 96–97, figs. 1, 2). Although more than one drapery style existed at the same time, the rich, silklike quality of the drapery seems to occur on the most prized works, such as the statue of Julia Domna from Athens, Louvre 1070 (H. J. Kruse, *Römische weibliche Gewandstatuen*, Göttingen 1975, p. 407, D 143). The latter has been considered a priestess of Isis, but there is nothing specific to the cult of Isis in dress; the hands and held objects are restorations.

[106] Concerning the cemeteries, see pp. 33–36 above.

Two small reliefs, the stele of Sophia and Eukarpos (Athens, N.M. 1214; Pl. 37) and that of the son of Soterion (Athens, N.M. 1223; Pl. 38),[107] are from the same workshop as **23** (Pl. 39). The women in the dress of Isis on the small reliefs were modeled on that of the large one, **23**. The curving contours of the figure were also emphasized by undercutting it away from the background of the relief, a feature not common among Severan "Isis" reliefs. These two small reliefs are so closely related that they should be the work of sculptors who were brothers, or father and son.[108] The date of these reliefs is based on the pose, proportions, and patterned drapery like that of the mantled man on the finely carved ephebic-decree relief of A.D. 212/3.[109]

On the middle Severan "Isis" reliefs, slender figures have a more pronounced sway and few ornamental folds. They are similar to figures on Attic sarcophagi and equally varied in execution and style. The doll-like figures on the Broom Hall "Isis" relief (Pl. 39) have much in common with bluntly carved figures on the less important, narrow ends of Attic sarcophagi,[110] but whether or not this relief is from a workshop that made sarcophagi is at the present unknown. It is more likely that the sculptor of the relief figure from the Kerameikos (Pl. 40)[111] carved relief figures on sarcophagi. This figure bears a striking resemblance to the figure in the cross-legged pose of a Muse on the left end of the Attic Hippolytos sarcophagus in Tarragona (Pl. 40).[112] The small statue of Julia Maesa as Isis (Vatican, Mus. Greg.Eg. 83; Pl. 41) in Rome should be the prized work of an Athenian sculptor contemporary with and superior to those responsible for these "Isis" reliefs.[113] The scalloped folds

[107] See footnote 108 below; for the inscriptions (IG II², 6311 and 12752, respectively) see p. 55 and footnote 138 above, p. 49.

[108] Athens, N.M. 1214 (Pl. 37) and the soldier relief, Athens, N.M. 1247 (Pl. 38) form a pair; Athens, N.M. 1223 and the soldier, Athens, N.M. 1266 (Pl. 38), also with figures of one-third life size, are a second pair. Each pair is the work of a different sculptor in view of facial types and different rendering of the facial features and details, but they are so closely related that the sculptors should be brothers or father and son: see the busts in Rome by Zenas and the father of Zenas from Aphrodisias (H. v. Heintze, Helbig⁴ II, nos. 1405 and 1408; H. Jucker, "Bildnisbüste einer Vestalin," RM 68, 1961 [pp. 93–113], p. 103, pl. 32).

[109] Ephebic-decree relief of A.D. 212–213, Athens, N.M. 1465 (IG II², 2208): Lattanzi, Cosmeti, pp. 81–82, pl. 32 and Follet, Athènes, p. 104. The close comparison with this ephebic relief makes untenable the most recent suggestion for the date of Athens, N.M. 1214: early imperial (late 1st century B.C.), offered by Stauridis (footnote 1 above, p. 33), pp. 167–168.

[110] Broom Hall relief (Conze 1966); for the inscription, see footnote 15 above, p. 7. For the differences in execution of the reliefs on the four sides of Attic sarcophagi, see Ward Perkins (footnote 75 above, p. 66), pp. 10–16. Unfortunately, Attic sarcophagi have not been fully published.

[111] Riemann, no. 62.

[112] Attic Hippolytos sarcophagus in Tarragona, Spain: H. Sichtermann, "Archäologische Funde und Forschungen in Spanien von 1940 bis 1953," AA (JdI 69), 1954, cols. 422–428, fig. 101; on its Severan date, F. Matz, review of B. G. Kallipolitis, Χρονολογικὴ κατάταξις τῶν μετὰ μυθολογικῶν παραστάσεων ἀττικῶν σαρκοφάγων τῆς ῥωμαϊκῆς ἐποχῆς, Gnomon 31, 1959 (pp. 693–698), p. 697. A grave relief from Athens, Agora S 2698 (Pl. 42), has a very similar Muse-like figure and should be contemporary.

[113] The sway of these figures in the dress of Isis is an exaggeration of the preceding "Isis" figures. Julia Maesa as Isis (height 0.92 m.): Dunand, Le Culte d'Isis I, pl. 12:1; Kruse (footnote 105 above, p. 83), pp. 405–406, D141, early Severan. The identification as Julia Maesa is clear from the coins of this empress (H. Mattingly, BMC Empire V, pl. 95:1, 2, 5) and the Agora portrait S 2435 (T. L. Shear, Jr., "The Athenian Agora: Excavations of 1971," Hesperia 42, 1973 [pp. 121–179], p. 171, pl. 37); the latter is more idealized and shallowly carved. The conical folds and sway are found on a less impressive work, a contemporary mantled statue in the Agora (S 1354: Harrison, Agora I, no. 62; see Pl. 41).

symmetrically arranged on this statue are found on the large Attic "Isis" relief in Trieste (Mus.Civ. 2214; Pl. 43), which may be a later work from the same workshop.

Mid-3rd Century

The "Isis" reliefs of the 240's and 250's are impressive in the boldness and massiveness of the figure and often have dramatic, ornamental drapery.[114] The best example and most popular figure of this group is the large one found on the relief in Trieste (Pl. 43);[115] its importance is evident from three other "Isis" reliefs. Two from the Athenian Agora, **28** and **29** (Pl. 45), are coarse, small versions of the Trieste figure and contemporary with it. The third, Athens, N.M. 3256, slightly later, retains in miniature the elegant garland and the sway of the Trieste figure, while covering the figure in lightly carved, looping folds (Pl. 46).[116]

The Trieste figure has preserved much of its original, dramatic appearance, even with the rigors of time and transport of this Attic grave relief to its final destination in Italy. The decorative drapery is rich in a variety of thick, soft folds accumulating to accentuate the pose, while thinning abruptly over the muscular, deeply bent right leg and all too slender hips. The masterly sculptor has boldly replaced the customary situla with a heavy fold that is not part of the dress of Isis but only an embellishment. The continued popularity of this figure's decorative appearance is evident in the later re-use as the Muse Erato, whose name is inscribed beside the right leg of the Trieste figure.[117]

The smaller but very dramatic figure of **27** (Pl. 43) could be the work of the same master. These two "Isis" reliefs and the life-sized statue of Isis in Dalmatia (Zagreb, Arch.Mus. 34; Pl. 44) are from a workshop that specialized in draped figures surprisingly close to those on the sarcophagus of the emperor Balbinus (Pl. 44) in Rome, A.D. 238.[118] According to Matz, Roman sarcophagi were influenced by Attic sarcophagi in the 30's of the 3rd century.[119] From the Attic "Isis" reliefs, it is evident that this ornate style in drapery was shared by Athens and Rome in the early 240's.[120]

[114] Trieste, Mus.Civ. 2214 (Pl. 43); **27** (Pl. 43); **28** (Pl. 45); **29** (Pl. 45); **30** (Pl. 45); Akropolis Mus. 3194 (Pl. 44); Riemann, no. 59 (Pl. 46); Athens, N.M. 3256 (Pl. 46); Verona relief (Pl. 46; one figure, not two as cited by Conze [1965] is preserved [see Budischovsky, *Diffusion*, p. 98, pl. 56]).

[115] Trieste, Mus.Civ. 2214; Muehsam (*Berytus* 10, 1952, p. 88) also considers this stele a fine work of the 3rd century after Christ. G. Pesce (*Il Libro dei Sfingi*, Caligliari 1977, no. 87) offers no date for this relief; for date, see below.

[116] Athens, N.M. 3256 is modeled on and should be nearly contemporary with the Trieste relief; the dramatic pose of the Trieste figure, placement of the garland, and overall decorative impact of the drapery are found in this small, Athens relief. The folds are repetitive, and the support hip has been widened on the latter.

[117] See Conze 1972.

[118] Trieste, Mus.Civ. 2214, five-sixths life size; **27**, two-thirds life size. The Trieste relief and Dalmatia Isis are included in Budischovsky (*Diffusion*, p. 163, pl. 81 and p. 176, pl. 89, respectively), but no dates are given. For the Balbinus sarcophagus, see H. Jucker, "Die Behauptung des Balbinus," *AA* (*JdI* 81), 1966 (pp. 501–514), pp. 501–504; on the possible Roman workshop of that sarcophagus, see H. Jung, "Zur Frage der Sarkophagwerkstätten in gallienischer Zeit," *AA* (*JdI* 92), 1977 (pp. 436–444), p. 438.

[119] Matz (footnote 112 above, p. 84), p. 697.

[120] G. Koch ("Zu einem Relief in der Alsdorf Foundation," *AA* [*JdI* 93], 1978 [pp. 116–135], p. 129) notes the contrast between the Piraeus statue of Balbinus and the sarcophagus of that emperor in Rome (for the Piraeus statue, see Niemeyer, *Studien*, no. 125 and pl. 46). More than one style existed in Athens at that time.

The largest "Isis" relief of this period, 240's to 250's, is unfortunately fragmentary: the torso Akropolis Mus. 3194 (Pl. 44).[121] It shares with the Trieste figure the slender torso, elegant arrangement of the costume of Isis, and delicate garland of laurel leaves, but it should be the work of a different sculptor who chose to envelop the figure in a dense mass of soft, looping folds. If the Trieste relief inspired the sculptor of the Akropolis "Isis" relief, the density of the drapery on the latter suggests that it should be somewhat later, leading towards the heavily draped figure **30** (Pl. 45) of the 50's of the 3rd century.

The "Isis" reliefs that follow the Trieste stele usually have thick, barrel-shaped torsos emphasized by the drapery.[122] **30** and **31** (Pls. 45 and 47) and a large relief in the Kerameikos are probably from workshops that made sarcophagi.[123] The relief in the Kerameikos (Pl. 46), very coarse and cursorily carved, is unusual in that a youth on the left accompanied the larger figure in the fringed costume of Isis; the uneven contours cut by the drill may suggest that the sculptor was less disciplined or had more freedom in the commission of this grave relief than his peers who made similarly blunt figures on the Pelops sarcophagus in Athens (Pl. 46).[124]

The most distinctive "Isis" relief of the mid-3rd century is preserved in the massive figure **30** (Pl. 45). The drapery is very similar to that of the women on the Pelops sarcophagus in Athens (Pl. 46),[125] but in this larger relief the same sculptor may have exercised more care. Emphasis in the Agora relief has been given to the rectangular folds. These fan out in a flat section rather than falling from the knot at the chest, almost denying the bold barrellike form of the torso. The carefully carved garland, the richest portrayed on the "Isis"

On the large grave relief of Philodamos, Berlin R 104 (Blümel [footnote 71 above, p. 41]), thick drapery, dense in folds, envelops and nearly replaces the volume of this life-sized figure; odd T-shaped furrows that punctuate his folds also occur on the Piraeus Balbinus but are less noticeable. Philodamus should be contemporary with that emperor; his portrait closely resembles the cosmete, Athens, N.M. 356 (Lattanzi, *Cosmeti*, pp. 54–55, no. 21) which Harrison (*Agora* I, p. 96) would also date late in the 30's of the 3rd century. The cosmete, Athens, N.M. 388 (Lattanzi, no. 20), also has the odd T-shaped furrows in his mantle, as well as a pronounced linear, ornamental quality to the facial features, and may be a decade earlier, *ca.* A.D. 230, as determined by the date of the archon Kasianos hierokeryx who has been reassigned (Clinton, *TAPS* 64, p. 80, no. 10; Follet, *Athènes*, pp. 240, 510).

[121] Akropolis Mus. 3194, life size: O. Walter, *Beschreibung der Reliefs im Kleinen Akropolismuseum in Athen*, Vienna 1923, pp. 167–168, no. 356; the photograph is upside down in that publication.

[122] See Pl. 46: Athens, N.M. 3256 and Verona relief. The latter is published by Budischovsky (*Diffusion*, p. 98, pl. 56), but no date or discussion is given. The larger reliefs, **30** and Riemann, no. 59, have deeply drilled folds, but the overall flat surface pattern in the arrangement of the folds and the few contrasts diminish the impact of the bold relief of each figure. These four reliefs should be from different workshops.

[123] **30**: see footnote 125 below. **31**, a figure of half life size, is strikingly similar to an Attic Dionysiac sarcophagus in Thessaloniki (Pl. 47) in the emphatic, swinging contours of the figure, loss of anatomic structure, and varied drillwork from a broad to a fine wormy incision; see Matz, *ASR* IV, i, no. 11 and H. Wiegartz, "Zu Problemen einer Chronologie der attischen Sarkophage," *AA* (*JdI* 92), 1977 (pp. 383–388), p. 388, note 90 (50's of the 3rd century after Christ for the date of this sarcophagus).

[124] The Kerameikos relief (Riemann, no. 59) shares with the draped women on the Attic Pelops sarcophagus (Athens, N.M. 1176) the coarse, yet dramatic drapery which can have oddly shaped contours. For the date of this sarcophagus, see Koch (footnote 120 above, p. 85), p. 126, fig. 13: mid-3rd century.

[125] The vertical folds on the standing women on the Pelops sarcophagus are strikingly similar to those on **30**; each fold, like a strip of wood, is rectangular in cross-section, the deeply drilled contours emphasizing this rigid arrangement.

reliefs, demonstrates the sculptor's skill in more natural forms. The abstract treatment of the drapery recurs in the Gallienian "Isis" reliefs of the 60's of the 3rd century, but the drapery on the latter has become a shell floating over slender figures.[126]

Gallienian

Slender figures return with the "Isis" reliefs preserved from the third quarter of the 3rd century.[127] With the Gallienian reliefs, the first of this group, there may have been a conscious revival of elegant figures. Their crisp drapery and long legs recall the impressive figures of the 2nd century, such as the Hadrianic (Pls. 22–25) or the late Antonine (Pls. 32–35).

Characteristic of Gallienian reliefs from Athens is the decorative, shell-like drapery.[128] The simplest version is seen on the shallow relief figure (Pl. 48) on an ephebic decree of A.D. 255/6.[129] The shell of banded folds on the Isis costume on **32** (Pl. 49) is also an exaggeration of the deep folds particularly noticeable on late Antonine reliefs (Pl. 32); the narrow folds, fanning out over the woman's feet, are so deeply separated that they appear like an abstract cage.

32 is very similar to the handsome sarcophagus of a consul in Naples, the so-called Brother sarcophagus (Pl. 48).[130] This closeness in style and execution between sculpture in Athens and contemporary imperial art in Rome indicates an active exchange between these important centers of art. A colossal statue of Isis (Pl. 49)[131] in the Piazza Venezia, Rome should be the work of a sculptor from an Attic workshop contemporary with that of **32** (Pl. 49), but this coarse piece with deep drillwork cutting into the figure suggests a somewhat later date, in the 70's of the 3rd century.[132]

Closer to the colossal Isis in Rome is a large "Isis" relief figure from the Kerameikos (Pl. 50).[133] On the latter, the shell-like drapery has been changed into thick bands that bind and cut into the figure and seem to replace its volume. A more exaggerated contrast is clearly evident in **33** (Pl. 50). Thick folds sever the torso and create the mass of the figure.

[126] **32** compares well with the late Gallienian sarcophagus in Naples (Pl. 48); see footnote 130 below.

[127] **32, 33**, Riemann, no. 61 (Pls. 49, 50).

[128] See the stele of Julios Ephebos, Athens, N.M. 3669 (Pl. 48): the man resembles the late portraits of Gallienus (see references in footnote 134 below, p. 110). Thicker drapery in a deeply drilled, shell-like arrangement is found on two Attic Dionysiac sarcophagi (Matz, *ASR* IV, i, nos. 11, 11A) that Wiegartz ([footnote 123 above, p. 86] p. 388, note 90) would date to the 50's of the 3rd century.

[129] Ephebic-decree relief dated to A.D. 255/6, Athens, E.M. 10038: *IG* II², 2245; Follet, *Athènes*, p. 84.

[130] Naples sarcophagus: N. Himmelmann-Wildschütz, "Sarkophag eines gallienischen Konsuls," *Festschrift für Friedrich Matz*, Mainz 1962, pp. 110–124; A. Geyer, "Ikonographische Bemerkungen zum Neapler 'Brüdersarkophag'," *JdI* 93, 1978, pp. 369–393. The early Gallienian date proposed by Himmelmann-Wildschutz should be corrected to late Gallienian as the bust in Ostia that he cited to date it is a late portrait of Gallienus (H. v. Heintze, Helbig⁴ IV, no. 3132).

[131] This statue, unpublished, is badly weathered but preserves the odd clawlike fringe found on a contemporary "Isis" relief in the Kerameikos (Riemann, no. 61; Pl. 50) and the snug drapery that sweeps angularly across the chest. The thick, rounded folds of the mantle on the statue are unlike the Kerameikos relief; hence, it belongs to a different sculptor or workshop. Originally the statue was of a seated figure, as indicated by the position of the left arm which once rested on a level surface.

[132] See footnote 134 below, p. 88.

[133] Riemann, no. 61.

These two "Isis" reliefs should be post-Herulian in date, after A.D. 267. They mark the transition from the shell-like drapery of Gallienian monuments to the sculpture of the late 3rd century, such as the Arch of Galerius in Thessaloniki of A.D. 303.[134] In the latter not only can folds of the drapery cut into the figure but also their mass has replaced the mass of the figure. Parts of the figure or dress can be treated separately, if not set off as segmented units.

A geometric style in Attic sculpture also appears in the second half of the 3rd century after Christ. A humble example of this style is **34** (Pl. 51), late in the 3rd or early in the 4th century, possibly as late as a grave relief in the Kerameikos (Pl. 51) which is of better quality.[135] The statuette of Athena from Epidauros (Athens, N.M. 274; Pl. 51), bearing an inscription dated A.D. 304, is one of the most masterly works of this new style.[136] Its roots lie in various abstract renderings of figures, drapery, and portraits that appeared in the course of the 3rd century, but its closest parallels are Gallienian in date.[137]

The artistic traditions of Athens did not die out with the invasion and destruction of the city by the Heruli, A.D. 267.[138] There is surprising continuity between Gallienian sculpture in Athens and official imperial monuments such as the figured ornament for the Palace of Galerius in Thessaloniki of the early 4th century.[139] The development towards the ponderous, segmented figure style of the Tetrarchic monuments such as the Arch of Galerius in Thessaloniki can be seen in the post-Herulian "Isis" reliefs (Pl. 50).[140] A prime example of

[134] **33** has thick folds that cut into the figure; the twist of the folds has replaced the anatomical structure. It is a direct development from the Gallienian relief **32** and the portrait bust, Agora S 2062 (E. Harrison, "New Sculpture from the Agora, 1959," *Hesperia* 29, 1960 [pp. 369–392], pp. 390–392, pl. 86); the drapery on the latter cuts into and replaces the body of the figure. Parthenope (Pl. 50) is separated into head and arms; the thick drapery conveys the mass of the body like figures on the Arch of Galerius in Thessaloniki of A.D. 303 (see H. P. Laubscher, *Der Reliefschmuck des Galeriusbogens in Thessaloniki*, Berlin 1975).

[135] Riemann, no. 46. It is representative of a geometric style, found in Athens in the late 3rd century; see also S 1604 (Harrison, *Agora* I, no. 52) and compare with the portrait of Galerius from Thessaloniki in Athens Kanellopoulos Museum (J. D. Breckenridge in Weitzmann [footnote 168 above, p. 52], pp. 13–14).

[136] Athens, N.M. 274: B. Staïs, «Ἀγάλματα ἐξ Ἐπιδαύρου», Ἐφ Ἀρχ, 1886, cols. 243–258, pl. 12; Karouzou (footnote 40 above, p. 38), p. 65; B. Brenk, "Die Datierung der Reliefs am Hadrianstempel in Ephesos und das Problem der tetrarchischen Skulptur des Ostens," *IstMitt* 18, 1968 (pp. 238–258), p. 252, note 36.

[137] See the figures on the ephebic-decree relief of A.D. 255/6 (Pl. 48); see footnote 129 above, p. 87.

[138] On the Herulian invasion, see Thompson (footnote 15 above, p. 59), pp. 61–72. M. Bergmann (*Studien zum römischen Porträt des 3. Jahrhunderts n. Chr.*, Bonn 1977, p. 159) suggests that the decline in Attic sculpture may not have been so severe as has been thought. The stylistic variety of portraits of the 3rd century may indicate that more were made after A.D. 267; those found built into the Late Fortification Wall in the Agora have a *terminus ante quem* of A.D. 280, the completion of the wall (see Harrison [footnote 183 above, p. 54], p. 89), but the history of the wall elsewhere in Athens is not known, and later repairs with sculpture as building material are possible (see Travlos, *Pictorial Dictionary*, pp. 62–63). Attic sarcophagi, which might contribute more information, have not been fully published.

[139] Brenk ([footnote 136 above], pp. 233–258) defines the geometric style as found in the palace's architectural ornament and very similar figures on the reliefs of the Temple of Hadrian at Ephesos. His conclusion that craftsmen from the East were responsible for this new style need not preclude a similar development in Athens; the Hygieia on a pilaster capital from the palace in Thessaloniki is encased in a shell-like drapery that is an exaggeration of the shell-like drapery popular in Athens and Rome in the mid-3rd cenury (*ibid.*, pl. 81).

[140] On the stylistic continuity between Attic sarcophagi and the Arch of Galerius in Thessaloniki, see Wiegartz (footnote 94 above, p. 82), p. 614. Increasingly we have found the Attic "Isis" reliefs of the 3rd century to be related to Attic sarcophagi; the massive Tetrarchic style is emerging in **33** and Riemann, no. 61.

ponderous Tetrarchic style is the "Isis" relief figure of Parthenope (Athens, N.M. 1244; Pl. 50).[141]

Parthenope, one of the last Attic grave reliefs, provides us evidence of the intense pride of the artist as well as that of the woman who participated in the cult. The figure is the boldest and most forceful of these late grave stelai and one of the few from the whole history of Attic grave reliefs to bear the name of the sculptor.[142] He is the proud husband of this massive, serious woman. He so boldly drilled the Athenian cross-draping of the costume that the characteristic knot and fringe were omitted. In her thick hands, Parthenope originally held a sistrum and a situla; this is the only known instance where sistrum and situla of bronze were displayed on an Attic grave relief.[143]

Fourth Century after Christ

Although the "Isis" reliefs leave us early in the 4th century after Christ, we have been introduced to changes in style that will develop in that century. We should not be surprised to find contemporary statuettes from Epidauros repeating figure types and drilled drapery found on Attic sculpture of the 40's and 50's of the 3rd century.[144] More innovative is the Athena statuette Athens, N.M. 274 (Pl. 51) from this Epidauros group, dated by its inscription to A.D. 304.[145] It is in the newer geometric style, also found among the "Isis" reliefs.

A tantalizing variety in style and execution occurs in Attic sculpture, in the round and in relief, at any given time in the Roman period. The love of marble usually prevents the sculptors from riddling the draped figures with deep drillwork or giving the undraped parts the high polish popular in Rome and other parts of the Empire.[146] The "Isis" reliefs have afforded us a survey of Attic sculpture in the Roman period.

[141] Parthenope and **33** (Pl. 50) are dated by close comparison with relief figures on the Arch of Galerius at Thessaloniki: see the heavily draped women flanking the emperor on the south side of pillar B (Laubscher [footnote 134 above, p. 89], pl. 40). The head and parted hairstyle of Parthenope compare well with the Lateran portrait of Magnia Urbica, A.D. 283–285 (H. v. Heintze, Helbig⁴ I, no. 1108 and *Römische Porträt-Plastik*, Stuttgart 1961, p. 15, pl. 36) and the portrait of Aurelia Euposia, Athens, N.M. Kabbadias Coll. 424, which also has herringbone eyebrows.

[142] Parthenope, Athens, N.M. 1244 (*IG* II², 12418). Muehsam (*Berytus* 10, 1952, p. 58) cites it as one of the few stelai with the name of the sculptor; see also Löwy (footnote 214 above, p. 57), p. 302, no. 458. For the inscription, see above (footnote 214, p. 57). See **34** (Pl. 51) for another late "Isis" relief.

[143] Conze 1954 and see p. 57 above.

[144] See Staïs (footnote 136 above, p. 88), cols. 243–258, pls. 11, 12; H. v. Schönebeck, "Die christliche Sarkophagplastik unter Konstantin," *RM* 51, 1936 (pp. 238–336), p. 333; Brenk (footnote 136 above, p. 88), p. 252, note 36; Bieber, *Ancient Copies*, p. 3. Asklepios, Athens, N.M. 264, dated by its inscription to A.D. 309, resembles the Piraeus statue of Balbinus (Niemeyer, *Studien*, no. 125, pl. 46; Pl. 45) in emphatic modeling of chest and arms, weighted sway stance, and taut folds deeply drilled. The other statuettes are drier versions of the draped figures on the Pelops sarcophagus, Athens, N.M. 1176 (Pl. 46), of the middle of the 3rd century.

[145] Athens, N.M. 274: see footnote 136 above, p. 88.

[146] See the highly polished satyr and centaur in Rome made by Aphrodisian sculptors: M. Squarciapino, *La Scuola di Afrodisia*, Rome 1943, pls. 5, 7. The statue of a satyr, Agora S 221 (T. L. Shear, "The Sculpture," *Hesperia* 2, 1933 [pp. 514–541], pp. 536–541, figs. 20–29), may be an Attic imitation of the popular, highly polished Aphrodisian sculpture. Koch ([footnote 120 above, p. 85], p. 121) and Matz (*ASR* IV, i, p. 197, note 91) would assign it to a workshop that made Attic sarcophagi in the first half of the 3rd century, in particular the Dionysiac one in Boston (Gardner Museum; Matz, no. 9).

CONCLUSION

The individuals, women and a few men, portrayed in the costume of this goddess on grave reliefs from Athens were initiates in the cult of Isis. It is clear that this knotted fringed mantle was considered exotic and feminine and appealed most to women. Its costliness and beauty when worn snug to a slender woman would also serve the interest of the family or husband. The family's social position would benefit from the display of their daughter or wife in this costume: in life, in any sculpture, and especially on the tombstone which stood in a prominent place along the major roads leading from Athens.

The Athenians not only contributed to the elaborateness of the knotted fringed dress of Isis but also made it easier to wear by securing both ends of the fringed mantle in the knot at the chest. The emphasis on this dress and hand-held attributes of sistrum and situla on Attic grave reliefs reveals the pride of the initiates in their costly costume and their coveted position in the cult. The pomp of the Isis processions may well have been best served by a throng of women in this rich attire.

A heightened production of Attic grave reliefs appears to have occurred with the reign of Augustus in the last third of the 1st century B.C. Why were the "Isis" reliefs a part of this production? Was it merely the result of greater prosperity in Athens under Roman rule, or was there greater interest and participation in the cult of Isis at that time? It is tempting to explain the cause of this popularity as the interest of a prosperous middle class, emulating the aristocratic families who had enjoyed the prestige of participation in the cult of Isis on Delos, prior to the abandonment of that island in the 1st century B.C.

The complete history of the cult of Isis in Athens may always elude us; the total number and range of participants have not come down to us. It is clear from the Attic "Isis" reliefs that there was an intense participation in the cult of Isis in Athens by members of a prosperous middle class. To judge from the inscriptions, variety of the dedications, quality of many "Isis" grave reliefs, and repeated emphasis on the costly costume, this cult continued to provide prestige to aristocrats as well. Membership in the Isis cult did capture the interest of many prosperous inhabitants of Athens. The importance of this cult, which can only be surmised, was undoubtedly greater than formerly thought.

APPENDIX 1

Catalogue of "Isis" Reliefs Found in the Athenian Agora

Findspots (in parentheses) refer to the excavation grid (Fig. 2, p. 92). All measurements are in meters.

1. Left hand with situla, period of   Pl. 4
    Augustus

S 1142. Found April 28, 1939 built into a modern house wall along the Panathenaic Way towards the north slope of the Akropolis (S 21).
Pentelic marble. P.H. 0.325, p.W. 0.145, p.Th. 0.072.
Sliver of relief preserving left hand with situla, cuff, and part of sleeve. Broken all around. Break cuts right edge of situla. Surface fresh and unweathered.

Life-sized left hand, unusually low in relief,[1] holding a very small situla. The hand, boldly modeled with a rasp, is well-proportioned with tapered fingers and nails lightly marked with a flat chisel. The contour along the thumb, carefully undercut with a narrow flat chisel, draws attention to and suggests volume, particularly convincing as the contour of the back of the hand and of the far finger on the right is barely traced. Sleeve and situla are simply modeled with a rasp. The shape of the situla is formed by opposing curves of the rasp that overlap at the bottom to suggest the customary knob.[2] Its ribbonlike handle, carved with a flat chisel, curves to the right. A broad strip, 0.015 m. wide, carefully smoothed with a chisel, separates the situla from the rough surface of the background, which is dressed with a claw chisel directed horizontally.

This summary execution is surprisingly subtle and imparts an illusion of depth and movement in space. The right contour of the hand, a fine line barely tracing the farthest finger, suggests that the hand is turning in space. This movement is convincing because of the subtle gradation of planes from the rounded forefinger and thumb highest in relief to this mere trace of the second finger holding the situla. The unusual cuplike situla and ribbonlike handle may well represent a situla of glass suspended from a ribbon.[3] The situla, tipped and swinging to the left, is shown in motion, while the curve of the ribbon gives it a twist in space.

The relief, probably a single-figure relief,[4] was impressive in size as well as execution. The figure is one of the few of life size, the largest size on Attic grave reliefs of Roman date.[5] The situla is the only one known that is shown swinging from its handle.

The relief is the work of a master sculptor. It should be Augustan in date, contemporary with if not from the same workshop as the "Isis" relief inscribed to Onesiphoron (Athens, N.M. 3036; Pl. 5) in the National Museum in Athens.[6] The latter is also unique owing to the representation of the rattle, the sistrum shown in movement. The rattling prongs of the sistrum, tilted toward Onesiphoron's head, appear to slide loosely, important to the playing of this musical instrument.[7] The execution, however, is rather coarse as the sistrum is simply incised into a

---

[1] Relief height is less than a centimeter, unusual for such a large figure.

[2] On the usual mammiform shape of the situla, see pp. 23–25 above.

[3] See pp. 23–24 above.

[4] The few stelai with figures of life size are single-figure reliefs (e.g., the Damaskenos, Conze 2038; Tryphon, Pl. 11).

[5] See footnote 11 above, p. 59.

[6] Onesiphoron (*IG* II², 7467): 1st century after Christ (Kirchner); it has not been published with photograph. Pediment with cist incised and frontal head of a woman, right forearm, and hand with sistrum; see footnote 170 above, p. 29 and pp. 67–68 above.

[7] See p. 20 above and footnote 5 above, p. 67 concerning the sistrum.

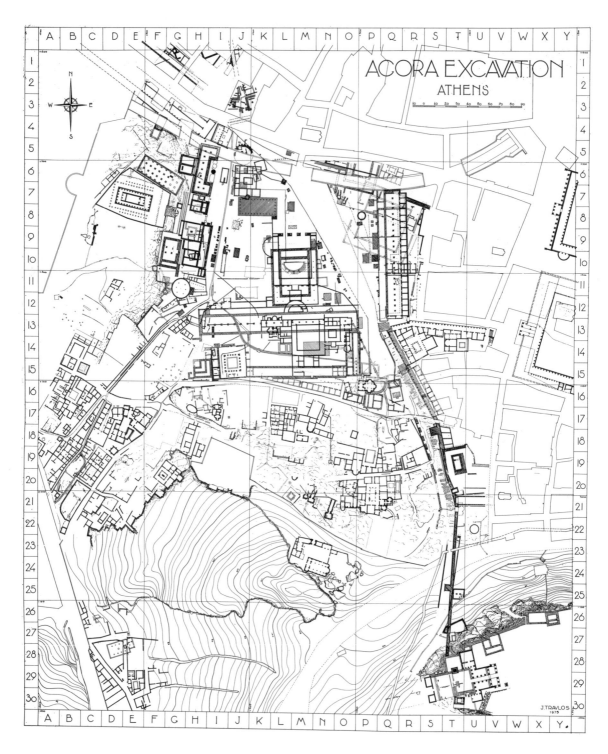

Fɪɢ. 2. Plan of the Athenian Agora

lump of marble, although the little drapery preserved and the idealized head of this young woman are carefully carved. The soft folds of the sleeve on the upraised forearm fall toward the figure as if in response to the rattling of the sistrum.

The Augustan date is based on the close comparison of Onesiphoron with a late Augustan head (Naples, M.N. 6289; Pl. 2).[8] This idealized type with late Augustan hairstyle is found again only on a second Attic grave relief, the small but well-carved stele of Demetria (Pl. 2).[9] The date of the latter, based on style, may also be confirmed by the possibility that Demetria's father was prytanis in *ca.* 50–40 B.C.[10]

2. Lower legs, period of Nero   Pl. 10

S 2264. Found July 7, 1969 in the demolition of a modern house at 36 Hadrian Street (O–P 6).
Pentelic marble. P.H. 0.129, p.W. 0.196, p.Th. 0.099.
Shin to mid-calf preserved. Broken on all sides. Center folds battered. Surface fresh and unweathered.

Draped legs, shin to mid-calf, from a figure of half life size in high relief. The thick center folds are characteristic of the costume of Isis on Attic grave reliefs;[11] the drill undercutting the center folds marks the lower edge of the mantle worn over the chiton. Each fold is varied and falls according to its thickness and weight. The surface is lightly rasped.

The figure stands in a bold three-quarter turn to the left with the left leg deeply bent; it may be from a two-figure relief. The pose, proportions, and drapery arrangement are found on a relief (of a woman) of the same size, Athens, N.M. 1270 (Pl. 10).[12] These reliefs are the work of the same sculptor, whose mastery of very sheer, clinging drapery, similar to chiffon, is evident in each fold. As the drapery

falls, it puckers slightly, and over the legs it is caught in rippling folds.

A date early in the reign of Nero, A.D. 54–68, for these reliefs is based on the close comparison with Tryphon (Pl. 11) on an Attic grave relief of large size and excellent workmanship.[13] The "Isis" relief figures share with Tryphon the pronounced three-quarter turn in bold relief, the proportions with long legs, knees high and close together, and short torso, and the weighted fall of the drapery. Tryphon, considered by Muehsam to be Claudian, should be dated slightly later because of the striking comparison with the statue of Nero from Gabii (Louvre 1221) and the portrait of Nero at Corinth (S 1088).[14]

3. Hand with sistrum, period of Nero   Pl. 11

S 1200. Catalogued May 30, 1946 from a marble pile in section S (L–N 18–19).
Pentelic marble. P.H. 0.20, p.W. 0.23, p.Th. 0.12.
Right hand with sistrum and part of background preserved. Broken on all sides. Thumb, forefinger, and uppermost prongs of sistrum battered. Traces of cement. Surface fresh and unweathered.

From a figure of two-thirds life size; the carefully smoothed hand and sistrum are bold in relief. The contour of the hand is beveled with a broad flat chisel, while the background is dressed with a chisel in even strokes nearly perpendicular to the hand. The tapered fingers and prongs of the sistrum are separated with a narrow drill. The unusually elaborate sistrum has a twisted handle, a lotus at the base of the loop, and a knob on top.[15]

The sistrum is held nearly vertically, close to the head of the figure. The contour of the cheek is preserved in the battered area on the right, indicating that the head once overlapped the upper two prongs of the sistrum and was turned sharply to the left.

[8] See p. 68 above.
[9] Demetria: p. 68 above.
[10] *IG* II², 5304; see footnote 135 above, p. 48.
[11] See pp. 6–7 above and Fig. 1.
[12] Athens, N.M. 1270: pp. 71–72 above.
[13] Tryphon: p. 72 above.
[14] Muehsam, *Berytus* 19, 1952, pp. 59–60. Louvre 1221: Niemeyer, *Studien*, no. 11, pl. 3:2. On the Corinth Nero, see De Grazia (footnote 29 above, p. 71), no. 13; Johnson, *Corinth* IX, no. 137.
[15] On sistra, pp. 20–21 above.

The pose is a contraction of that of the relief Athens, N.M. 1270 (Pl. 10), Neronian in date.[16] This Agora relief should be contemporary, if not from the same workshop. The simple bulbous shape of the right hand, the misalignment of the loop and prongs of the sistrum, and the sharply drawn contours reveal the Agora relief as the work of a bolder if less careful sculptor.[17]

4.   Head, period of Domitian   Pl. 16

S 315. Found March 22, 1933 in late Byzantine fill (J 8).
Pentelic marble. P.H. 0.225, p.W. 0.28, p.Th. 0.14.
Top of head to base of neck preserved with part of the background. Broken on all sides. Brow, left eye, mouth, and nose battered. Surface fresh and unweathered.

Head of a female figure of two-thirds life size in unusually high relief and boldly turned to the left. Part of the background dressed with a flat chisel is preserved on the left. The parted hairstyle with long locks falling to the shoulder is common on women in the dress of Isis on Attic grave reliefs,[18] but the lump on the top of the head betrays brusque, rapid modeling. Parted waved strands of hair are shallowly carved, while the pair of long locks is deeply undercut with a broad drill. Face and neck are carefully smoothed with a little rasp on the sides. Streaks of mica run vertically through the relief.[19]

The relief was probably one with a single figure.[20] The head is so high in relief that it appears to be sculptured in the round. The turn of the head and the rise in the neck show that the right arm was held high.

In proportions, hairstyle, and bold relief the Agora head belongs with two other "Isis" reliefs, one in Eleusis (Pl. 14) and one of Agathostratos and daughter in the Kerameikos (Pl. 15).[21] They should be from the same workshop but are the works of different sculptors because of differences in style and facial features.[22] A late Flavian date is likely owing to the proportions, heavy brow, and fleshiness which compare closely to those of a portrait of a young man, Agora S 1319 (Pl. 15), and the portrait of Domitian, Athens, N.M. 345 (Pl. 16).[23]

The Agora relief is the work of a fine sculptor. Unusual are the fleshy folds on the neck responding to the turn of the head and the slight fullness under the chin, caught by the turn and by the tucked-in position of the jaw. The slight puffiness at the nose, mouth, and lower eyelid are distinctive and subtly sensuous. A small hook fold at the outer corner marks the sag of flesh above the eye, while a very fine drill channel traces the curve of the parted lips. This subtle rendering of the flesh and alert, yet brooding expression are very similar to those of the portrait of Domitian. I am tempted to attribute **4** to the same sculptor.

5.   Head, period of Nerva   Pl. 17

S 847. Found March 15, 1937 in Byzantine fill of the 11th and 12th centuries below the floor of room I of building A, a Byzantine house in use to the 13th century (U 22).

---

[16] Athens, N.M. 1270: p. 71 above.

[17] For the sculptor, p. 68 above.

[18] On the hairstyle, see pp. 12, 14 above.

[19] Streaks of mica run through the relief of the Damaskenos (Conze 2038), one of the largest stelai of Roman date in Athens: see Dow and Vermeule, *Hesperia* 34, 1965, pp. 243–297; apparently such streaked marble was not avoided in the Roman period for grave reliefs as it had been in the Classical.

[20] Compare the pose to that of Sosibia, a single-figure relief middle Antonine in date (pp. 79–80, Pl. 30).

[21] Eleusis stele: Alexandri, Δελτ 22, Β′ 1, p. 125, pl. 102; Agathostratos: Riemann, no. 57.

[22] See footnotes 39 and 40 above, p. 72.

[23] *Ibid.* The young man, Agora S 1319, is considered to be early Flavian by Harrison (*Agora* I, no. 14), but he should be contemporary with the portrait of Domitian, Athens, N.M. 345 (Pl. 16), as they share in the compact head, broad jaw, heavy brow, fleshiness, and brooding expression; the latter, according to Daltrop *et al.* ([footnote 72 above, p. 41], pp. 37, 42, and 97), is thought to be early in Domitian's reign and contemporary with Naples, M.N. 6061, but better comparisons are with Rome, Mus. Naz. Rom. 115191 (*op. cit.*, pl. 30:a, b), coin portraits of A.D. 85–96 for the hairstyle (pl. 35:b–f), and particularly the fleshy face with prominent forehead on the sestertius of A.D. 95–96 (pl. 35:f).

Pentelic marble. P.H. 0.172, p.W. 0.07, p.Th. 0.125.

Sliver of head, top to mid-cheek preserved. Broken on all sides. Hair and forehead chipped. Surface fresh and unweathered.

The head of a female figure, two-thirds life size in high relief, the right side sheared away to the tear-duct of the left eye. That this head is from a relief is evident from the asymmetry of the eyes, the broadening of the forehead to the figure's left side, and the rasped edge of the figure's right cheek. The deep-set eyes are not undercut with a chisel or drill.

The head is from a figure turned to the right, probably from a single-figure relief.[24] Unlike **4**, this head has a low crown, and the tight, narrow waves of hair are sharply and deeply cut. This crisp execution occurs on classicizing reliefs such as the "Isis" relief of Alexandra (Pl. 24), late Hadrianic in date.[25] The identification of **5** as from an "Isis" relief is based on the tightly waved, parted hairstyle.[26]

The Agora head should be contemporary with and from the same workshop as the stele of Titus Flavius Onesiphoros (Athens, N.M. 3725; Pl. 17).[27] They are very close in execution and have the same proportions and deep-set, long, and thick-lidded eyes. The tall figures of Titus Flavius and his wife, with small heads and long limbs, seem to be suspended in their ornamental drapery, bold in relief and yet barely recording their pose. A late Flavian date, possibly as late as Nerva, A.D. 96–98, is very likely. In proportions, drapery, and crisp execution, they compare well and should be contemporary with draped figures on late Flavian monuments in Rome, such as the Cancelleria relief[28] and the frieze of the Forum Transitorum dedicated in A.D. 98.[29] The long narrow head of Titus Flavius with eyes deep set and locked under the straight brow is similar to but

less harsh than a portrait of a man, Agora S 1182, of the early 2nd century after Christ.[30]

6. Fringed mantle, period of Trajan   Pl. 18

S 455. Found March 29, 1934 in disturbed fill with Turkish sherds in all levels to bedrock (H 15).

Pentelic marble. P.H. 0.222, p.W. 0.193, p.Th. 0.084.

Left side of chest, base of neck to waist, preserved. Broken on all sides. Center folds and knot battered.

From a large female figure in high relief, probably of life size;[31] the break on the right is along the inner contour of the left arm snug to the side but cuts into the folds at the waist. To judge from the broad curve of its right upper edge, the knot was large. The drapery has a rich, mat surface, lightly and carefully rasped, while the neck is very smooth.

A broad section of folds and long fringe covers the left breast, expanding laterally with the emphasis on the clarity of the arrangement and flat pattern of drapery. These narrow folds, tightly drawn and caught under the ridge of folds at the waist, are evenly and shallowly drilled and lightly creased. The drapery has the appearance of being soft and thick. The long fringe and few folds above the waist are lightly carved with a flat chisel. The strands of the fringe are broadly curved and overlap at the ends, varied in their fall.

The figure would have been impressive in size and execution, the work of a master sculptor. Related in drapery arrangement, execution, and style is the relief of Mousaios and Amaryllis (Athens, N.M. 1233; Pl. 19).[32] This carefully carved relief should be assigned to the same workshop but is the work of a different sculptor as the emphasis is on the

---

[24] See the single-figure relief, Sosibia, Pl. 30.

[25] Alexandra: pp. 75–76 above.

[26] On hairstyle, see p. 18 above; instead of the tight, crisp waves on this head, the woman on the contemporary stele of Titus Flavius Onesiphoros (p. 72 above, Pl. 17) has a loosely waved coiffure and does not wear the dress of Isis.

[27] Titus Flavius Onesiphoros (*IG* II², 12377): p. 72 above; Theophanides (footnote 1 above, p. 58), p. 12, fig. 16; on inscription, see p. 47 above.

[28] See footnote 41 above, p. 73.

[29] *Ibid.*

[30] Agora S 1182: Harrison, *Agora* I, no. 18.

[31] The length of this fragment is greater than the comparable area on Alexandra of five-sixths life size, the largest well-preserved "Isis"-relief figure (Pl. 24).

[32] Mousaios and Amaryllis: p. 74 above; figure height 0.69 m., half life size.

thickness of the drapery and the massiveness of the figures.

The two reliefs should be dated to the Trajanic period. The relief of Mousaios and Amaryllis has securely dated parallels in composition, figure proportions, and portrait types.[33] The compact composition is found in the panel reliefs of the monument of Philopappos (Pl. 22), A.D. 114–116,[34] and with the massive figures on the ephebic-decree relief Athens, N.M. 1469, A.D. 115/6.[35] Mousaios is very close to the portrait of the cosmete Heliodoros (Athens, N.M. 384), dated to the first decade of the 2nd century.[36]

7.   Fragment from right shoulder, period   Pl. 18
            of Trajan

S 2551. Catalogued August 16, 1977 from a marble pile in section A (G–H 5–6).
Pentelic marble. P.H. 0.105, p.W. 0.105, p.Th. 0.025.
Five folds from right shoulder preserved with end of long lock and edge of neck. Broken on all sides. Surface fresh and unweathered.

From a life-sized female figure; the upper break follows the shallowly drilled contour of the shoulder. To judge from the upper break there seems to have been only one lock of hair on the shoulder. The lock twists to the left, lightly carved with a flat chisel. The drapery is tautly drawn with narrow folds shallowly and evenly drilled. Single folds alternate with paired folds. The drapery, lightly rasped, has the same rich, mat surface as **6** (Pl. 18), while the neck has a slightly greater polish.

This small fragment is so similar to **6** in scale and execution that they could be from the same figure.

The opposing slope of the neckline, however, prevents this reconstruction. The striking resemblance between the two fragments does indicate that they are the work of the same master sculptor. He then would have been responsible for two relief figures of the unusual life size.

8.   Small figure with situla, period Trajan   Pl. 20

S 202. Catalogued March 14, 1932 from a marble pile in section Δ (D–F 13–15).
Hymettian marble with light streaks. P.H. 0.33, p.W. 0.24, p.Th. 0.07.
Mid-chest to mid-calf preserved with part of the background. Broken on all sides. Right breast, left hand, and handle of situla battered. Folds chipped. Surface fresh and unweathered.

A frontal female figure of one-third life size in low relief, cut into a curved surface, a cylindrical monument 0.39 m. in diameter.[37] The relief may have been carved into an earlier monument, one of the numerous columnar gravestones of the Hellenistic and Roman periods.[38] A trace of the right edge of the relief panel remains along the nearly vertical break 0.06 m. from the figure. Originally the figure was displayed in a rectangular panel, possibly framed by antae and pediment.[39]

The relief is the work of a competent sculptor. Although the figure is bluntly cut with a flat chisel and spreads at the hips with the curve of the monument, the folds, fringe, and knot are lightly and evenly carved. Fine parallel striations of the rasp run the length of the folds. The background is dressed with a chisel.

The Agora relief is contemporary with the impressive Trajanic relief of Mousaios and Amaryllis

[33] See p. 74 above and footnotes 34 and 35 below. The drilled-curl, "sponge" wig on the woman on the left is a Flavian-Trajanic hairstyle: see Harrison, *Agora* I, p. 27.

[34] Santangelo (footnote 56 above, p. 75), pp. 197–198 (*IG* II², 3451, A, line 4); Kleiner (footnote 56 above, p. 75).

[35] Athens, N.M. 1469 (*IG* II², 2017); Lattanzi, *Cosmeti*, p. 80, pl. 35:b.

[36] Heliodoros (*IG* II², 2021); Lattanzi, *Cosmeti*, p. 34, pl. 2.

[37] The cylindrical form is evident from the curved surface of the figure that is parallel to that of the background. See Conze 1796–1821 for other columnar grave markers; also Melisia, Pl. 21. For others with "Isis" reliefs, see **14** and **30**.

[38] See p. 58 above and Conze, pp. 1–6, 10 and nos. 1796, 1798, 1806, and 1815. Fragmentary ones from the Agora show the use of this size from the 3rd century B.C. to at least the 2nd century after Christ: Bradeen, *Agora* XVII, no. 311 (III/II a.), no. 803 (II/I a.), and no. 251 (II p.).

[39] Compare with Agora I 3205: B. Meritt, "Greek Inscriptions," *Hesperia* 30, 1961 (pp. 205–292), p. 205, pls. 33, 34.

(Athens, N.M. 1233; Pl. 19), if not a lesser work from the same workshop.[40] The symmetrical arrangement of the fringed mantle, with nearly parallel folds tautly drawn over the legs and fanning out from the vertical strip of the center double fold, repeats that worn by Amaryllis. The large knot is marked by a reversed "C" for the triple-puffed sections of the knot on Amaryllis. The softer, broader shape of the end of the mantle that falls from the knot, the short strands of the fringe that do not cover the breast, and the even thicker left arm that nearly merges with the broad, globular situla[41] are simplifications by a different sculptor.

9. Torso, period of Hadrian   Pl. 22

> S 437. Found March 6, 1934 in demolition of the Church of the Prophet Elias (H–I 14).
> Pentelic marble. P.H. 0.31, p.W. 0.17, p.Th. 0.12.
> Shoulders to mid-thigh preserved. Broken on all sides. Left breast, knot, and center folds battered. Folds chipped. Surface fresh and unweathered.

A torso from a female figure of half life size in low relief which was used as building material in the Church of the Prophet Elias. The arms are sheared away, but the upper break runs below the top of the right shoulder and follows the contour of the left. Although it is common to find long locks falling to the shoulders of women in the dress of Isis on Attic grave reliefs, the shallowly carved long locks that spread over the top of the left shoulder and cover the fringe are unusual in that they almost merge with the fringed mantle. The drapery is rasped, while the base of the neck is very smooth.

The slender figure stands with support hip jutting angularly to the side and left leg slightly bent. The drapery is snugly drawn, smooth over breasts and hips and in thin loops at the waist. Taut triangular folds with flared upper edge are on the thighs. Each

fold is creased by a fine incision, diagonally placed. This incised surface represents the linen texture of the garment.[42]

In style and execution this figure has much in common with Alexandra (Athens, N.M. 1193; Pl. 24). The latter is one of the most impressive "Isis" reliefs, a striking example of late Hadrianic classicism.[43] The Agora relief lacks the precision in execution of Alexandra and should be the work of a lesser sculptor. It is a crisp copy of the female figure on a third "Isis" relief from this workshop, the stele of Attikos (Mantua, Duc.Pal. 6677; Pl. 22).[44] **9** and the stele of Attikos would have preceded the massive, monumental figure of Alexandra. Their slender, long-legged figures and angularly jutting support hip correspond well to that of the small, well-carved figure on the ephebic-decree relief, Athens, E.M. 10040, A.D. 120 (Pl. 23).[45] Their proportions and angular pose recall those of the mantled men on the panel reliefs on the Philopappos monument, A.D. 114–116 (Pl. 22).[46] This angular pose, meant to convey a stride, is most lifelike in the woman on the stele of Attikos in Mantua; as such it is a helpful criterion. In the later Hadrianic figure of Alexandra, the stride has lost its effect. She has become monumental, more compact, and an established type.

10. Sistrum, period of Hadrian   Pl. 25

> S 486. Found May 5, 1934 built into a rubble wall possibly of early Byzantine date (M 14).
> Pentelic marble. P.H. 0.21, p.W. 0.26, p.Th. 0.107.
> Part of sistrum, loop and three prongs, preserved with left edge of relief. Broken on all other sides. Iron pin in background. Surface fresh and unweathered.

A large sistrum bold in relief, bluntly shaped and heavily rasped. Although the hooked ends of the

---

[40] Mousaios and Amaryllis: p. 74 above; see under **6**.

[41] This globular situla is a simplification; cf. p. 23.

[42] Sharp incisions mark the linen texture of the fringed mantle; footnote 11 above, p. 7.

[43] Alexandra: pp. 75–76 above.

[44] Stele of Attikos: p. 75 above; it is an outstanding work of a third sculptor in this workshop. Unlike **9** and Alexandra, figures and drapery on the Mantua stele appear to have a soft surface, folds are rounded, and fringe is cottony.

[45] Athens, E.M. 10040 (*IG* II², 2018): Graindor (footnote 55 above, p. 75), fig. 31; on the revised date, see Follet, *Athènes*, p. 204.

[46] Philopappos monument on Mouseion hill in Athens: see footnote 56 above, p. 75.

prongs of the sistrum are barely indicated, two are turned up, and the lowest is turned down. The background and left edge of the relief are carefully dressed, the former with a flat chisel and the latter with a claw chisel.

Although little is preserved, the original relief was unusual not only in size but also in the lack of a frame.[47] There is a slot in the side where an iron pin was placed and later robbed out. Above the sistrum an iron pin remains in the background. Iron pins, usually a pair, were placed in the sides of finished stelai to hold wreaths or garlands in honor of the deceased, like the pins in the background that often frame the relief figure.[48]

The sistrum is one of the largest preserved and was probably once held by a figure at least two-thirds life size.[49] An expansive pose is suggested by the position of the sistrum which is tipped away from the figure. The stele would probably have been a single-figure relief.[50]

In execution and style this relief is very close to the well-preserved stele of Epigonos and Elate (Athens, N.M. 1308; Pl. 24).[51] They should be contemporary with but probably not from the same workshop as the impressive late Hadrianic "Isis" relief of Alexandra (Athens, N.M. 1193; Pl. 24).[52] The figure of Elate, although based on Alexandra, is the antithesis of the precisely carved and crisply contoured Alexandra. The folds of Elate's drapery have been reduced to coarse arcs marked with a broad drill, while heavy raspwork models and nearly obscures figure and drapery when viewed from a distance. Upon close inspection, surprising detail is found in Elate's ornate sistrum and strong, bony hands and feet. The sistrum 10, less carefully defined, is from a second heavily rasped "Isis" stele, originally larger and possibly bolder than the relief of Elate whose figure is half life size. The tipped sistrum also indicates that its figure had an unusually expansive pose.

11. Torso with garland, early Antonine   Pl. 26
        period

S 428. Found February 12, 1934 built into a wall of a modern house (L 12).
Pentelic marble. P.H. 0.223, p.W. 0.176, p.Th. 0.12.
Shoulders to hips preserved. Broken on all sides. Left arm battered. Right breast and knot worn. Right hip and lower folds pitted. Cement on lower folds. Surface fresh and unweathered.

Part of the torso from a female figure, one-third life size in low relief. The upper break follows the contour of the right shoulder and cuts across the neck and below the top of the left shoulder. A ropelike garland[53] is worn over the left shoulder. Equally minimal is the definition of figure and drapery. Light rasp-work covers all areas. The tightly draped mantle is reduced to narrow folds forming a "U" around the breast, and fringe is omitted. Long fringe is incised along the edge of the folds falling from the characteristic knot of the Isis costume. Over the hips the folds are sharp ridges caught by thick folds at the waist.

The figure stands with right leg bent, left arm snug to the side, and right arm upraised. This small figure shares with Lamia Viboullia (Piraeus Mus. 1160; Pl. 27)[54] in pose (high left support hip and vertical left arm as if suspended from the shoulder), shallow even treatment of the folds of the mantle, over-all flatness and simplicity of the torso, and the unusual absence of the characteristic long locks of hair on the shoulders. The omission of the deep drill to mark folds worn over the figure in both reliefs is also rare. All these features suggest that these reliefs

---

[47] An excellent example of a stele without a frame is one of a youth in Corinth (S 187 + 196): Johnson, *Corinth* IX, no. 247, pp. 121–122; and see footnote 72 above, p. 41.

[48] See pp. 42–45 above.

[49] Its width (0.135 m.) is comparable to that held by Agathemeris of two-thirds life size, London, B.M. 630 (Pl. 32).

[50] No other "Isis" relief shows the sistrum tilted away from the figure; the stele of Sosibia (Boston, M.F.A. 1971.209; Pl. 30) shows the broad spacing of the figure and the usual pose on a single-figure "Isis" relief.

[51] Epigonos and Elate: pp. 76–77 above.

[52] Alexandra: pp. 75–76 above.

[53] For garlands worn with the dress of Isis, see pp. 26–28 above.

[54] Piraeus Mus. 1160; figure height 1.03 m. See p. 78 above.

may have been made in the same shop,[55] but the use of incisions rather than carved folds over the breast on **11** points to a different sculptor.

They should be dated to the early Antonine period, the 40's of the 2nd century, as Lamia Viboullia has the S-curve sway, slender torso with long arms, and linear drapery found on the statue of Regilla in Olympia, A.D. 150–153,[56] and on the small figures on the ephebic-decree relief (Athens, N.M. 1483, A.D. 143/4).[57] **11** may be a slightly earlier work. It has the thick torso and tautly drawn U-shaped folds around the breast recalling those of the late Hadrianic relief of Alexandra (Athens, N.M. 1193; Pl. 24).[58]

12.   Torso, early Antonine period   Pl. 26

S 1728. Catalogued May 1953 from a marble pile in section T (K–Q 15–17).
Pentelic marble. P.H. 0.29, p.W. 0.27, p.Th. 0.12.
Shoulders to mid-thigh, left arm, and part of right anta preserved. Broken on all sides. Left half of chest, wrist and hand, and right anta battered. Knot, center folds, and end of hair worn. Lower folds pitted. Surface fresh and unweathered.

Part of a female torso, half life size, in high relief and framed by a thick anta on the right. Although this frame is sheared away to the level of the background, the anta appears to be all too massive for the slender figure. There is a slot in the side of the anta where an iron pin was set and later robbed out.[59] The inner edge of the anta near the shoulder preserves part of an impost block from which an arch would spring.[60] The original relief was probably of a single figure with antae and low arch.[61] The background and side of the anta are very smooth, while the figure is lightly rasped.

The figure stands with left leg bent and stiffly holds a situla from the long, nearly vertical arm. On the right shoulder is the tip of a thick, long lock of hair. Although the fringe is hatched into the edge of the U-shaped folds around the breast, long, soft fringe is draped unusually low over the left arm. The snugly draped mantle has soft, thick, looping folds bunching at the waist and the hips. Short folds are shallowly cut into the breast, while diagonal slashes mark the snug, long sleeve.

This relief may be a lesser work from the early Antonine workshop of Lamia Viboullia (Piraeus Mus. 1160; Pl. 27).[62] The smaller, more loosely constructed figure **12** has the same sway, proportions, and drapery arrangement with stance reversed, garland omitted, and folds thicker. The unusual feature of the double sleeve and the low draping of the fringe are exaggerations of those worn by Lamia Viboullia.[63] The sculptor of this small, poorly modeled figure must have known the larger relief quite well, as the feature of the double sleeve is not only rare but also is barely visible on the shallowly carved, large figure of Lamia Viboullia. The scooped-out folds of the double sleeve are very similar to those on the small figure of the maid on the stele of Lamia Viboullia.[64]

13.   Torso with garland, early Antonine   Pl. 28
          period

S 2393. Two fragments found July 16, 1970: one built into a green lime wall (N 10) and one from the demolition of a modern house (N 6).

[55] In contrast to the closeness of **11** and Lamia Viboullia's stele is the contemporary relief, Athens, N.M. Ἀπο. 237 + **13**; see Pl. 28 and p. 78 above with footnote 75.

[56] The statue of Regilla is from the exedra of Herodes Atticus (Treu [footnote 29 above, p. 71], pl. 67:5), dated to A.D. 150–153: Bol (footnote 63 above, p. 76), pp. 26–28, no. 41, pl. 45 (traditionally known as Regilla), and date, 98–100; see footnote 77 above, pp. 78–79.

[57] Athens, N.M. 1483 (IG II², 2050): Lattanzi, Cosmeti, p. 82, pl. 36.

[58] Alexandra: pp. 75–76 above and under **9**.

[59] Possibly in gouging out the pin, the raised surface of the anta was broken off. The slot (0.03 × 0.03 m.) has two blunt cuts. On iron pins, see pp. 42–45 above.

[60] A trace of the inner edge of the block remains. The background extends to the right allowing the anta a maximum width of 0.06 m., 0.02 m. narrower than the impost block.

[61] Compare with Lamia Viboullia (Pl. 27).

[62] Lamia Viboullia: see p. 78 above and under **11**.

[63] Pl. 27; on the double sleeve, see p. 7 above and under **13**.

[64] The small figure on the left is a maid with open jewel box, a popular motif for grave stelai of the 5th and 4th centuries B.C.; see p. 55 above.

Pentelic marble. P.H. 0.50, p.W. 0.28, p.Th. 0.175.

Mended from two fragments. Hips to above knees preserved with garland. Broken on all sides. Section of folds and garland missing at joint. Chips in folds and fringe. Surface fresh and unweathered.

Torso of large female figure in high relief preserved in two fragments. The upper part, shoulders to waist, is in the Athens National Museum (N.M. Ἀπο. 237; Pl. 28) and was formerly stored in the Library of Hadrian,[65] while the adjoining lower part (13), hips to above knees, is in the Agora Museum. Together they would measure 0.80 m. in length and be from a figure of five-sixths life size. The lightly rasped surface is on drapery, garland, and background.

The slender figure stands with right leg bent and right arm upraised. A garland of laurel leaves bound by clusters of flowers, lightly and carefully carved and with centers of flowers occasionally marked with a fine drill, is worn diagonally from the left shoulder to just above the right knee. Falling from the upraised right arm is a thick, soft fold, the loose material of the chiton which would appear to be a second sleeve.[66]

The drapery is rich in texture and unusually varied in execution, each part of the figure treated as a separate unit and isolated by drilled contours. Although soft, thick folds nearly envelop the chest, the folds are thinner over the legs; over the left, support hip they are scratched into the marble. The right breast is pierced by deeply drilled folds, while the left is sunk into thick folds. Across the figure the fringe is short and coarsely hatched, but the fringe is long and broadly carved as it falls freely on the side of the figure below the right arm.

This large figure is the work of a talented if erratic sculptor. His unfamiliarity with the dress of Isis is evident from the disparity in the length of the fringe and illogical placement of the end of the mantle below the folds at the waist, rather than falling from the knot.[67] The finely carved garland and soft looping folds over the right leg have been given greater care.

This relief should be early Antonine in date. The figure has the pose, proportions, basic arrangement of the dress of Isis, and long garland of Lamia Viboullia (Piraeus Mus. 1160; Pl. 27).[68] The latter is covered by shallow, evenly carved folds and has a plain, ropelike garland, the work of a different sculptor probably from another workshop. The early Antonine date is evident from the swaying pose and loose-limbed lanky figures that compare well with the center figure on the ephebic-decree relief Athens, N.M. 1483, A.D. 143/4[69] and the statue of Regilla from the nymphaeum of Herodes Atticus at Olympia, A.D. 150–153.[70]

14. Legs and hand with situla, early   Pl. 29
       Antonine period

S 2543. Catalogued August 27, 1975 from a marble pile in section Ψ (O–Q 17–19).
Pentelic marble. P.H. 0.19, p.W. 0.29, p.Th. 0.11.

Hips to mid-calf, left hand with situla, and part of background preserved. Broken on all sides. Center folds and left leg battered. Forefinger and lip of situla worn. Surface fresh and unweathered.

Figure of one-fourth life size in high relief on a columnar monument. On the right is part of the curved surface of the monument, carefully dressed with a fine-toothed claw chisel and originally 0.47 m. in diameter. The relief, probably a second use of the columnar grave marker,[71] has been simply carved without a frame: instead, a recessed area has been beveled into the curved surface with a broad flat chisel. A narrow strip beside the figure is dressed smooth and serves to set off the carefully carved, soft, well-rounded folds of the Isis costume falling over

[65] Athens, N.M. Ἀπο. 237: Walters, *AAA* 12, 1979, pp. 215–221.

[66] This second sleeve is shown snug to the arm on Lamia Viboullia (Pl. 27) and **12** (Pl. 26).

[67] The end of the mantle should be caught by the knot and fall from it; see Figure 1 and explanation of the drapery on p. 7 above.

[68] See p. 78 above and under **11** and **12**.

[69] Athens, N.M. 1483 (*IG* II², 2050): see Lattanzi, *Cosmeti*, p. 82, pl. 36; for the date, see Follet, *Athènes*, p. 174.

[70] See footnote 77 above, p. 78.

[71] The coarse treatment of the relief ground is in contrast to the evenly dressed surface of the columnar monument, indicating re-use. Other columnar markers are **8** and **30**; see also Athens, N.M. 3724, Pl. 21.

the legs of the figure. The situla held in the left hand clearly identifies this as an "Isis" relief.

The figure stands with right leg bent and holds a round situla on the side just above the left knee. The spread of the legs, giving the impression that both are bent, is awkward and also distorted by the curve of the monument. The drapery is so soft and thick that the looping folds barely separate at the right knee, while those on the left leg are broad and flat. The hand and the situla are carefully modeled. The little finger is extended, and the nails are carved. The drapery is lightly rasped.

This relief could be assigned to the same early Antonine workshop as the large "Isis"-relief figure **13**. The drapery arrangement, dependent upon the large figure, has thicker soft folds over the right leg, while those on the left are flattened and sharply drawn. A second small relief by the sculptor of **14** may be the upper figure on the stele of Eisias (Athens, N.M. 1249; Pl. 28).[72] It may be slightly later because of the modeling of the figure and the exaggerated loose fall of the gown.[73]

15. Right arm with sistrum, middle   Pl. 29
       Antonine period

S 754. Found May 15, 1936 in modern fill (P 7). Pentelic marble. P.H. 0.414, p.W. 0.259, p.Th. 0.198.

Right arm with sistrum preserved with background and part of left anta. Broken on all other sides. Forearm, thumb, fingertips, loop of sistrum, and front of anta battered. Surface fresh and unweathered.

Right arm with sistrum from a figure of half life size in bold relief. The upper break across the anta may have been made when the iron pin, of which the tip remains, was robbed out.[74] The relief is carefully worked with figure and drapery well modeled and lightly rasped. The background is dressed smooth with a broad flat chisel and the left side of the anta with a claw chisel.

The right arm is unusually bold in relief with wrist sharply arched and handle of the sistrum undercut with a drill, giving the figure the appearance of being sculptured in the round. One of the few elaborate sistra[75] is held by this figure. This large rattle, outlined with a fine drill, has a lotus top, floral base for the loop, and double-beaded end on the handle. It is tipped back towards the figure, and the end of the handle rests on the anta.

Originally the figure stood in a bold three-quarter turn to the left, probably a single-figure relief.[76] It is the work of a fine sculptor. Even the fringe has a lively, three-dimensional twist with each strand thick and curling, bluntly carved with a flat chisel. It should be assigned to the same workshop as the evenly carved relief of Sosibia (Boston, M.F.A. 1971.209; Pl. 30),[77] if not to the same sculptor. A date in the 160's is definite. Sosibia wears the deep-waved hairstyle of Crispina and Lucilla[78] and also has the proportions and narrow stance of the statue of Faustina the Younger as Venus,[79] again with the same deep-waved coiffure. Sosibia resembles the portrait of Melitine from Piraeus (Louvre MA 3068), A.D. 164, in proportions and placement of the facial features.[80]

16. Fringe, middle Antonine period   Pl. 30

S 1920. Catalogued May 1955 from a marble pile in the southeast corner of section T (P–Q 16–17). Pentelic marble. P.H. 0.25, p.W. 0.18, p.Th. 0.09.

---

[72] Eisias: figure height 0.40 m.; p. 78 above.

[73] Eisias' loose arrangement of the drapery recalls Hellenistic prototypes; see p. 8 above and also the Hellenistic grave relief of Isias from Smyrna (London, B.M. 639; Pl. 1).

[74] On iron pins, see pp. 42–45 above.

[75] For sistra see pp. 20–21 above.

[76] Compare with Sosibia (Pl. 30).

[77] Sosibia is smaller, one-third life size, and less detailed but is evenly and masterfully carved. **15** and Sosibia are so strikingly similar in proportions, bold three-dimensional pose, and treatment of the drapery that they should be the work of the same sculptor; see pp. 79–80 above.

[78] See Wegner, *Die Herrscherbildnisse*, p. 75, pl. 64:a, e (Lucilla) and p. 76, pl. 64:l, p (Crispina). Muehsam (*Berytus* 10, 1952, p. 71) and Comstock and Vermeule (*Sculpture in Stone*, p. 172, no. 276) mistook this hairstyle on Sosibia for Trajanic and dated Sosibia to that period.

[79] Vatican, Cortile del Belvedere 936: H. v. Heintze, Helbig I⁴, no. 241 and *Roman Art*, New York 1971, pp. 156, 164, fig. 153.

[80] Melitine: see Jucker (footnote 81 above, p. 79).

Fringe and folds preserved with part of background. Broken on all sides. Some cement on folds and background. Upper strand of fringe worn. Surface fresh and unweathered.

Lower left edge of the fringed mantle with part of the background. Five long strands of fringe, selvage, and two pairs of nearly vertical folds are from the lower left corner of the mantle that falls along the right side of the figure.[81] A carefully rasped, mat surface covers fringe, folds, and background.

The fringe, 0.10 m. in length, is the longest preserved and would be from a large figure, possibly of life size.[82] The original must have been a single-figure relief because of the space to the left of the fringe.[83] On this vivid work, masterfully carved, each cottony strand of fringe has a different twist. The upper strand falls over a coiled strand and flips up to the left, while the lowest is loosely braided. The folds, low in relief, have carefully rounded edges, while the double fold nearest the fringe is a decorative abbreviation of a tubular fold with its edge an inverted Ω and inner folds shown.

This large relief is contemporary with and may belong to the same workshop as the middle Antonine relief of Sosibia (Boston, M.F.A. 1971.209; Pl. 30).[84] **16** may have been the model for Sosibia and for **15**, a larger relief by the sculptor of Sosibia. The crimped "pie-crust" fringe of the latter is a bold abbreviation of the twisted strands on **16**.

17.   Left arm and right leg, late Antonine   Pl. 33
period

S 261. Left arm found in 1933 in the demolition of a modern house (K 7).
S 1584 a, b. Right leg from hip to knee, mended from two pieces: a) lower part catalogued February 14, 1952 from a marble pile from the demolition of a modern house north of Holy Apostles Street (P 14); b) upper part catalogued August 27, 1975 from a marble pile in section EΛ (U 19–21). Pentelic marble. S 261: P.H. 0.27, p.W. 0.09,

p.Th. 0.16. S 1584: p.H. 0.59, p.W. 0.26, p.Th. 0.18.
Two fragments, broken on all sides. Long locks on shoulder worn. Chips in folds. Rust stain on lower folds of leg. Right hip battered. Trace of right arm and left anta. Surface fresh and unweathered.

Two parts of a figure, five-sixths life size, including the left upper arm and right leg, hip to knee; they are very bold in relief. The lower contour of the bent, upraised right arm and a trace of the edge of the left anta are preserved. The fringed mantle falling cape-like on the left of the figure is in very low relief, shallowly and carefully carved with crisp, finely textured fringe.

The figure stood with right arm sharply bent and high above the hip of the support leg, overlapping the anta at the wrist. Originally it may have been a two-figure relief, as the arm with sistrum overlaps the frame like that of Agathemeris on the "Isis" relief London, B.M. 630 (Pl. 32).[85] The tall, slender figure stood slightly turned to the left, to judge from the placement of the right knee.

The drapery snug to the figure is unusually varied in texture and detail. On the shoulder, a broad deep drill formed the tightly arranged, narrow folds and cut the contours of the long spaghetti-like locks of hair, while the rasp modeled taut folds wrapped over the arm, giving them a gauzelike texture. Although the fringe on the shoulder is carefully and shallowly carved, the fringe falling from the capelike part of the mantle on the left is crisply carved and metallic in texture. Even the knee is peculiar, isolated and resembling an egg capped by a sharp triangular fold. The taut folds over the legs are illogically pierced by a fine incision, rather than varied in thickness to show the crease of the linen dress.

This figure belongs with the stele of Agathemeris and Sempronius (London, B.M. 630) in pose, drapery arrangement, and proportions.[86] If they are from the same workshop, the larger relief figure **17**, more noticeable with its idiosyncrasies, should be the work

---

[81] See the drapery arrangement, Figure 1, p. 4 above.

[82] The fringe is longer than that of Agathemeris (London, B.M. 630), which is two-thirds life size (Pl. 32).

[83] Compare with Sosibia (Pl. 30).

[84] Sosibia: Comstock and Vermeule, *Sculpture in Stone*, pp. 174–175, no. 276; and see pp. 79–80 above.

[85] On the stele of Agathemeris and Sempronius the capelike section of the drapery meets the anta; on **17** the narrow band of space between the anta and capelike section of the drapery need not imply a single-figure relief.

[86] Agathemeris and Sempronius: a date at the beginning of the 2nd century after Christ is given by Muehsam (*Berytus* 10, 1952, p. 90, note 1) without valid reasons; see p. 81 above for the date of this relief.

of a different sculptor. They are contemporary with the late Antonine stele of Telesphoros (Athens, N.M. 1775; Pl. 32), dated by its inscription to A.D. 170.[87] With that figure and the figures on the panel reliefs of Marcus Aurelius in Rome, A.D. 176–180,[88] they share in the tight vertical composition, tall figures with long S-curve stance, and dry, academic drapery.

18.   Torso, late Antonine period   Pl. 33

S 2544. Catalogued August 27, 1975 from a marble pile in section M (K–L 11–12).
Pentelic marble. P.H. 0.19, p.W. 0.22, p.Th. 0.11.
Base of neck to waist preserved with right upper arm. Broken on all sides. Left side, knot, and center folds battered. Folds and fringe on right shoulder worn. Surface pitted and weathered.

Torso of a female figure of two-thirds life size in bold relief. It is weathered gray and granular with only the hollows of the folds preserving the original, carefully rasped surface. The figure is slightly turned to the right. The right arm is snug to the torso, probably sharply bent at the elbow. The crisply cut contour on the left side indicates that the left arm hung free.

In pose, proportions, drapery arrangement, and fringe this figure is very close to Agathemeris on the late Antonine stele London, B.M. 630 (Pl. 32).[89] They should be from the same workshop, if not by the same sculptor. As the Agora torso is rounded in cross-section and does not recede like that of Agathemeris, **18** may have been a single-figure relief.

19.   Left shoulder and legs, late Antonine   Pl. 35
period

S 2771. Catalogued August 23, 1977 from a marble pile in section OO (D–E 16–17).
Pentelic marble. Left shoulder: p.H. 0.245, p.W. 0.22, p.Th. 0.08. Legs: p.H. 0.40, p.W. 0.24, p.Th. 0.114.
Two fragments: left shoulder and upper arm; legs from hips to knees. Broken on all sides. Some cement on folds. Pitted and weathered.

Female figure, two-thirds life size in high relief, in two fragments: left shoulder with arm and legs from hips to knees. Both fragments are very weathered. Curiously fine drillwork is evident in the shoulder's contour, the fringe, and lock of hair.

This deeply drilled figure is a harsher version of Agathemeris of the same size on the late Antonine stele London, B.M. 630 (Pl. 32).[90] They should be contemporary but not from the same workshop, in view of the extensive use of a deep drillwork that riddles the drapery and cuts into the figure on **19**, as well as the singular flamelike fringe.[91] Like **18**, this relief could also have been a single-figure stele.

The unusual use of the drill suggests that **19** may have been made in a workshop that produced sarcophagi. A series of very fine drill holes inserted in a row, rather than a running-drill channel, cuts the contours of the figure (Pl. 35:a). By dividing and undercutting the fringe and piercing the long lock of hair on the shoulder, this staccato use of the fine drill has a particularly ornamental effect, which is found on the contemporary Attic Achilles sarcophagus Naples, M.N. 124325 (Pl. 34),[92] from the frilly edges of

---

[87] Telesphoros: pp. 45–46, 47 above.

[88] Andreae, *Art of Rome*, p. 251, figs. 524–531. In style and execution, **17** and London, B.M. 630 resemble these official reliefs in Rome.

[89] Agathemeris and Sempronius: p. 81 above; see also **17** (Pl. 33) for another work from this workshop but by a different, less disciplined sculptor.

[90] Agathemeris and Sempronius: p. 81 above; figure height 1.0 m.

[91] The flamelike fringe is characteristic of contemporary statues of Isis in Asia Minor and North Africa; see pp. 81–82 above.

[92] Attic sarcophagus in Naples, M.N. 124325; see footnote 92 above, p. 81. Sichtermann and Koch (footnote 92 above, p. 81) would date this sarcophagus to the late 2nd century, but a date early in the 3rd century is more likely owing to the spreading width of the figures and drapery which emphasizes the plane and the flat ornamental appearance of both; compare with the panel-relief figures of Septimius Severus and Julia Domna on the Arcus Argentarii, Rome, A.D. 204 (Andreae, *Art of Rome*, fig. 555). As **19** lacks the spreading width of the figure, characteristic of the early 3rd-century reliefs, it should still be late Antonine, late 2nd century in date.

the drapery to the hair of the figures and the rosettes in the border above them.

20. Torso, early Severan period   Pl. 35

S 262. Found in 1933 in the demolition of a modern house (K 7).

Pentelic marble. P.H. 0.32, p.W. 0.23, p.Th. 0.14.

Mid-neck to hips preserved with left upper arm and part of right. Broken on all sides. Right shoulder, knot, and left arm battered. Traces of cement. Surface fresh and unweathered.

Torso of a female figure of half life size in low relief. The double fringe is unusual. Each fold is thick and given a crease parallel to the edge with a flat chisel. The folds across the chest are vertically arranged. On the left shoulder is a thick lock of hair. A rasped, flannel-like surface is on both figure and drapery.

The broad figure, bluntly carved, stands with right arm bent and upraised, while the left is snug to the side. The end of the mantle which should fall from the knot is illogically shown below the folds at the waist.[93] The knot is large and round, while the neckline is simply a straight edge.

Originally **20** would have been a single-figure relief, similar to the "Isis" relief Athens, N.M. Ἀπο. 54 + 231 (Pl. 37).[94] The latter, masterfully and evenly carved, should be from a different workshop.[95] They should be dated to the early 3rd century on the basis of the figure proportions, the reduction of the drapery to flat pattern, and the repetitive shape of the folds. These characteristics are

found on the Attic stelai of Hermione, Timokrates, and Praxiteles (Pl. 36), as well as on the relief panel of Septimius Severus and Julia Domna on the Arcus Argentarii in Rome, A.D. 204.[96] Hermione also has the hairstyle of Julia Domna on imperial coins of A.D. 193–209.[97]

21. Legs, early Severan period   Pl. 36

S 297. Found March 7, 1933 built into a modern wall (J 8).

Pentelic marble. P.H. 0.25, p.W. 0.35, p.Th. 0.18.

Just below knees to just above ankles preserved with part of background. Broken on all sides. Center folds chipped. Traces of cement. Surface fresh and unweathered.

Lower legs of a female figure of half life size in low relief. The thick center folds indicate that this fragment is from an "Isis" relief; the chiton folds under the mantle are only found on women in the dress of Isis on Attic grave reliefs.[98] The drapery has an unusual linear pattern of parallel incisions cut with a flat chisel that flare up and out from the center folds. On the left shin these lines meet vertical ones. The incisions represent the linen texture of the mantle,[99] but the diagonal arrangement emphasizes the spreading stance of the figure.

The relief should be dated to the early 3rd century. Like the figures of Hermione, Timokrates, and Praxiteles (Pl. 36) of that period, this "Isis" figure has an awkward and broad stance, odd paddle-shaped calves, and the reduction of the drapery to flat pattern.[100] **21** also resembles the under life-sized

---

[93] On the arrangement of the drapery, see p. 6 above and Figure 1.

[94] Athens, N.M. Ἀπο. 54 + 231 has been mended: Walters, *AAA* 12, 1979, pp. 215–221.

[95] See p. 83 above.

[96] The stelai of Hermione, Athens, N.M. 3396 (Conze 1914), Timokrates, Athens, N.M. 3316, and Praxiteles were found in 1904 built into a 3rd-century grave (see p. 35 above). They compare well with Septimius Severus and Julia Domna on the Arcus Argentarii in Rome of A.D. 204 (McCann [footnote 56 above, p. 13], p. 73, pl. 15:2). The patterned drapery is also found on the mantled man on the ephebic-decree relief of A.D. 212/3, Athens, N.M. 1465; Lattanzi, *Cosmeti*, pp. 81–82, pl. 37.

[97] Coins of A.D. 193–209: K. Buchholz, *Die Bildnisse der Kaiserinnen der severischen Zeit nach ihren Frisuren*, Frankfurt am Main, 1963, p. 10, pl. 4:3.

[98] On the dress of Isis shown on the Attic grave reliefs, see p. 5 above and Figure 1; when a man wears the knotted, fringed mantle, the chiton as undergarment is not worn: see the Paros relief (Pl. 37) and p. 56 above.

[99] See footnote 11 above, p. 7.

[100] See the early 3rd-century stelai of Hermione (Conze 1914), Timokrates, and Praxiteles; on the date, see footnote 96 above.

statue of Isis, Athens, N.M. 1617 (Pl. 34), in stance and particularly in the treatment of the drapery with few broadly spaced folds, thick curved mantle, and the densely rasped, flannel-like texture.[101] Both could be from the same workshop as **20**, because of these features, as well as the blunt rendering of the figure and the peculiar texture with parallel incisions in the folds.

22.   Pediment, early Severan period   Pl. 38

I 4776. Found April 21, 1937 in a modern context west of the Stoa of Attalos (P 11–12).
Pentelic marble. P.H. 0.432, p.W. 0.333, p.Th. 0.155. Letter height 0.016.
Right half of pediment with inscription and part of relief preserved. Broken on all sides. Center and upper right edge battered. Surface fresh and unweathered.

[- - - - - - - - -]   Πῶλλα Ζωΐλο[υ]
[- - - - - - - - -]   ᾽Ιφιστιάδου Θυγ[άτηρ]

Published by B. Meritt, "Greek Inscriptions," *Hesperia* 26, 1957 (pp. 198–221), p. 221, no. 82, pl. 57; Bradeen, *Agora* XVII, no. 162.

The center and right half of the pediment are preserved with part of the relief. Head of a female figure of half life size in high relief, sheared away from the waved hair over her forehead to that just above the ears. The sistrum lies on her right with prongs touching her hair. The pediment with center disk and the relief, background and figure, are carefully smoothed with a flat chisel.

Originally the pediment would have measured 0.66 m. in width and accommodated a two-figure relief.[102] The inscription on the architrave names the woman Polla, the daughter of Zoïlos of Iphistiadai, otherwise unknown. No date has been given on the basis of the inscription, only the designation of belonging to the Roman period.[103]

The little that remains of the relief is not only carefully carved but also strikingly similar to two "Isis" reliefs with figures of the same size, the reliefs of Sophia and Eukarpos and of the son of Soterion (Athens, N.M. 1214 and N.M. 1223; Pls. 37, 38).[104] In execution, the sistrum with long prongs outlined by a drill, and the careful inclusion of the waves at the side of the head, the Agora figure is closer to the figure of Sophia. The woman on the other relief has less detail and a softer surface, probably the work of another sculptor in the same workshop.[105] These three "Isis" reliefs should be dated to the second decade of the 3rd century by the close parallel with the mantled man on the carefully carved ephebic-decree relief Athens, N.M. 1465, A.D. 212/3.[106] They have the same proportions, swaying stance, and treatment of the drapery. These slender figures are in definite contrast to the broad figures of the early 3rd-century reliefs but share in the flat pattern of the drapery and the thick cottony fringe.[107]

23.   Torso with garland, early Severan   Pl. 39
           period

S 1917. Found April 11, 1955 in a modern house wall along the south side of Asteroskopeiou Street (Q 17).
Pentelic marble. P.H. 0.21, p.W. 0.37, p.Th. 0.255.
Waist to hips of torso preserved with garland, left arm, and part of right anta. Broken on all other sides. Front of anta battered. Chips in folds. Surface fresh and unweathered.

Torso of female figure of five-sixths life size in bold relief. The garland draped from the left shoulder has simple, round flowers lightly carved and separated by drilled holes. The contours of the figure, deeply drilled on the right, emphasize the bold relief. The drapery is carefully varied with thick folds at the waist and down the center, marked by a broad

---

[101] Athens, N.M. 1617 of Pentelic marble, found in Lakonia (see footnote 101 above, p. 83).
[102] The head is placed to the right of center, permitting a second figure on the left; it measures 0.075 m. in width, comparable to that of the women on the two-figure "Isis" reliefs Athens, N.M. 1214 and 1223; their figure height is 0.58 m. and 0.56 m., respectively, slightly under half life size.
[103] See publication references above.
[104] See footnote 104 above, p. 83.
[105] See footnote 108 above, p. 84.
[106] Athens, N.M. 1465 (*IG* II², 2208): Lattanzi, *Cosmeti*, pp. 81–82, pl. 37.
[107] See **20** (Pl. 35) and p. 83 above with footnote 101.

drill, while those over the support hip and arm are shallowly carved. Each fold differs in thickness and tautness and has a richly rasped surface. The lightly carved fringe is barely visible.

The slender figure stands with left leg bent and leans against the very narrow anta. Owing to the snugness of figure to frame, the stele may have originally been a two-figure relief.[108] It should be from the same workshop as two early Severan "Isis" reliefs, Athens, N.M. 1214 and N.M. 1223 (Pls. 37, 38), as they are very close in pose, proportions, drapery arrangement, and rich surface of the drapery.[109] 23 should be slightly later in view of the pronounced sway of the figure.[110] The size of 23 as well as the masterly rendering of figure and drapery suggests that the sculptor made fine draped statues.

24. Sistrum, middle Severan period   Pl. 39

S 2029. Catalogued April 7, 1959 from a marble pile in section ΕΛ (U 19–21).
Pentelic marble. P.H. 0.15, p.W. 0.26, p.Th. 0.10.
Part of sistrum preserved with background. Broken on all sides. Ends of prongs battered. Surface of loop worn. Surface fresh and unweathered.

Loop and prongs of a large sistrum in bold relief with part of the background. The prongs, separated by a drill, are rounded rods with hooked ends pierced by a large drill. The background is dressed with short strokes of a broad flat chisel. On the right, the raised area touching the uppermost prong and higher in relief, is a remnant of the figure's head. The few strokes of the flat chisel dipping down to the left of the sistrum are traces of the curved contour of a second figure. Originally it was a two-figure relief.

The sistrum would have been held by a figure of at least two-thirds life size,[111] closely flanked by a second and shorter figure, to judge from the trace of the latter to the left and below the loop of the sistrum. It would have resembled the Broom Hall "Isis" relief (Pl. 39) in composition.[112] The shape of

the sistrum and boldness in relief are also like the Broom Hall relief. It is possible that these two are contemporary, middle Severan in date.[113] The Agora sistrum 24 in size and bold relief might be thought to be from the same relief as 23, but the width of the shoulder on the latter is too broad to allow the overlapping by the head of the figure which occurs with the sistrum fragment.

25. Pediment with cist, middle Severan   Pl. 40
     period

I 3348 + 3532. I 3348 found February 4, 1936 in a late wall west of the Stoa of Attalos, over Shop XV (Q 8); I 3532 catalogued February 1936 from the area of the Stoa of Attalos (P–Q 7–13).
Pentelic marble. P.H. 0.312, p.W. 0.53, p.Th. 0.187. Letter height 0.026.
Pediment with inscription mended from two fragments: I 3348, center with cist, and I 3532, right half with top of anta. Center, top of right acroterion, and relief ground battered. Inscription worn away on I 3532. Surface fresh and unweathered.

Στεφηφό[ρος----]

I 3348 published by Meritt (footnote 139 above, p. 49), p. 281, no. 171, pl. 59; Bradeen, *Agora* XVII, p. 172, no. 981.

The pediment originally would have been 0.70 m. in width. Of the relief, only a trace of a broadly rasped contour remains, possibly that of the head of a figure slightly right of center. The monument may have been a single-figure relief with a figure of two-thirds life size. A cist in high relief is in the center of the pediment. A broad rectangular panel was cut into the pediment and center acroterion to receive this cist. The sides are slotted with a pick, while the cist is well rounded and carefully detailed and the background is dressed smooth. The left handle of the cist is preserved.

---

[108] See Athens, N.M. 1223 (Pl. 38). A little space is left between left arm and anta on the "Isis" relief Trieste, Mus.Civ. 2214 (Pl. 43), the only example of a single figure nearly filling the stele while overlapping the frame.

[109] Athens, N.M. 1214 and N.M. 1223: see under 22, for date, and p. 83 above.

[110] Slender figures with a pronounced sway are found on the "Isis" reliefs of the middle Severan period such as the Broom Hall relief (Pl. 39) and a relief in the Kerameikos (Riemann, no. 62; Pl. 40); see p. 84 above.

[111] The sistrum is the same size as that held by Agathemeris (London, B.M. 630; Pl. 32), whose figure height is two-thirds life size. The loop is 0.11 m. long, and the prongs, hooked end to hooked end, measure 0.12 m.

[112] Broom Hall relief: p. 84 above.

[113] *Ibid.*

The inscription on the architrave is preserved in the center (I 3348). There are traces of letters ΣΙΔΣ of an earlier inscription which was erased to receive the name of Stephepho[ros]. Meritt proposed a Stephephoros of Aixone who was prytanis in A.D. 174/5,[114] but the inscription on this stele naming Stephephoros should be later.

The bold inscription of Stephepho[ros] and the intrusive cist are indicative of re-use of this grave monument. If these two are contemporary, they would then mark this stele as belonging to a man named Stephepho[ros]; the cist would have been added to emphasize his membership in the cult of Isis.[115] The re-use may have occurred as early as the first quarter of the 3rd century since this tall cist with thick coils is similar to the cist on the pediment Athens, E.M. 9730 (Pl. 36), early 3rd century.[116] A later date is more likely because the cist on **25** is the most three-dimensional of those on Attic grave reliefs and should be contemporary with the boldly modeled reliefs **23** and **24** of the middle Severan period.

26. Torso, late Severan period   Pl. 41

S 2451. Catalogued November 11, 1971 from the Panathenaic Way (R 18).
Pentelic marble. P.H. 0.30, p.W. 0.31, p.Th. 0.16.
Mid-neck to waist, right arm, and part of left

preserved with part of background. Broken on all sides. Right breast, knot, center folds, and long locks battered. Fingers and right fringe worn. Surface fresh and unweathered.

Torso of a female figure of two-thirds life size in high relief. The upper break cuts across the top of the handle of the sistrum held by the right hand. The background is smooth, while the draped figure has a rasped, flannel-like surface. Unusual is the Venus fold on the neck, marked by a straight line.[117]

The drapery is thick and coarsely rendered with rectangular folds framing the chest and horizontal ones at the waist marked with a broad drill. The fringe is long and cottony, lightly carved with a flat chisel as is the pair of long locks on the shoulders, but the latter have curled ends marked with a drill. The sleeves are marked with parallel incisions to represent the linen texture of the dress.

The figure is turned slightly to the left and probably was the only one on this relief. The arrangement of the drapery with bold rectangular folds at the chest, long cottony fringe, and parallel incisions closely resembles that of two early 3rd-century "Isis" reliefs, **20** and **21**, indicating that **26** may be a later work from the same workshop. A later date for this relief is likely as it displays the thick horizontal folds at the waist that flatten and broaden the woman in the dress of Isis on a two-figure "Isis" relief in the Athens National Museum.[118] The thick, "spongy"

[114] See publication references above and Oliver (footnote 147 above, p. 50), p. 55, no. 21, line 37, for the prytanis.

[115] See p. 30 above.

[116] Athens, E.M. 9730 (*IG* II², 7431, II/III *p.*): by style it should be early 3rd century in date. The cist is presented as flat pattern with coils as bands, shallowly and evenly carved. It may be from the same workshop as Athens, N.M. Ἀπο. 54 + 231 (Pl. 37); on the date see p. 83 above.

In contrast to the bold cist on **25**, the other cists of the 3rd century include one other basketlike example, Athens, N.M. 2067 (Conze 2139), which has coils marked by narrow, wormy drillwork and should be contemporary with **31** (Pl. 47) of the 250's. The odd, rounded cist in low relief, Athens, E.M. 9706 (Conze 2140), and its rambling inscription (*IG* II², 5909) may be contemporary with the stele of Aurelios Eutyches, Athens, N.M. 1207 (Conze 2042), dated by Muehsam (*Berytus* 10, 1952, pp. 77–78) to the 260's. The third cist with inscriptions, Athens, E.M. 1036 (Conze 2141), is coarsely rendered with planar body jutting out beyond lid and base and may be as late as the abbreviated cist on **34** (Pl. 51) of the end of the 3rd century after Christ.

The coiled cist of the 2nd century is in low relief and heavily rasped: e.g. Athens, N.M. 1308, footnote 171 above, p. 29, Pl. 24.

[117] The other "Isis" relief with such folds is **4** (Pl. 16) where two are well modeled and fleshy, not a mere line as on **26**.

[118] Athens, N.M. Ἀπο. 230 (Conze 1964; see footnote 98 above, p. 82) is briefly described by Conze but has not been published with a photograph. This stele, although broken and missing the heads and top of the monument, is otherwise well preserved and has much in common with late Severan reliefs (Pl. 42; see footnote 119 below, p. 108): the very large knot and broad straight folds at the waist on the woman in the dress of Isis nearly obscure her torso, and the stoutness of the two figures is also emphasized by the awkward straight-arm embrace, simple ponderous stance, "spongy" drapery, and well-spaced position of the figures.

drapery and stout figure proportions on these two "Isis" reliefs correspond well to the drapery and figures on Attic grave reliefs of the late Severan period.[119]

27.   Knees, period of Balbinus   Pl. 43

S 2280. Found August 26, 1969 in the east wall of a modern house (O 5–6); joined to S 2284 found September 23, 1969 in the wall of another modern house (M 5–6).
Pentelic marble. P.H. 0.214, p.W. 0.253, p.Th. 0.167.
Knees to mid-calf preserved (S 2284, fragment of right leg). Broken on all sides. Center folds battered. Some cement on knees. Surface fresh and unweathered.

From a female figure of two-thirds life size in bold relief. The drapery is decoratively arranged and deeply drilled. The dense cluster of thick spaghetti-like folds in the center sweeps up over the calves and frames the broad, jutting knees. A tubular, pincer-like fold floats above the left knee rather than being placed beside it as material caught at the end of the leg. The surface of the drapery is smooth, but in the hollows there is heavy rasping.

The figure stands with left leg deeply bent, but the left knee is only slightly lower than the right, impossible anatomically. The pose and decorative drapery are almost a mirror image of that on the large and impressive figure (Pl. 43) in Trieste, Mus.Civ. 2214.[120] They should be from the same workshop and date to the late 30's of the 3rd century. Like that of the statue of Balbinus, Piraeus Mus. 278, A.D. 238 (Pl. 45),[121] the drapery on these "Isis" reliefs creates the majesty of the figure, while revealing and playing against the odd pose and figure proportions. In dramatic drapery, these "Isis" reliefs are far more sophisticated than the Piraeus Balbinus and are strikingly similar to the draped figures on the sarcophagus of that emperor in Rome (Pl. 44).[122]

28.   Torso, period of Balbinus   Pl. 45

S 2900. Catalogued August 23, 1977 from a marble pile in section Ψ (O–Q 17–19).
Pentelic marble. P.H. 0.36, p.W. 0.20, p.Th. 0.15.
Mid-neck to hips preserved with part of right arm and background. Broken on all sides. Center folds on arm and knot worn. Some white paint on chest. Surface fresh and unweathered.

Torso of a female figure of half life size in high relief. Traces of the right prongs of the sistrum held high on the left are found at the level of the head of the figure, which overlapped the edge of the frame; its trace is on the left. The drapery is soft and thick with puckering folds falling from the very large knot and in the capelike section of the mantle on the left. On each side of the neck is a long lock of hair. The folds have been shallowly drilled, and the original lightly rasped surface is found in the hollows and on the right hip.

The figure stands frontally in a narrow frame. It may have been a single-figure relief. In pose, drapery arrangement, and snug composition, this figure belongs with the impressive "Isis" relief Trieste, Mus.Civ. 2214 (Pl. 43), dated to the reign of Balbinus, A.D. 238.[123] **28** may be a minor work from another, contemporary workshop in view of the simplicity and soft thickness of the drapery.

29.   Torso, period of Balbinus   Pl. 45

S 434. Found March 3, 1934 in surface fill (M 14).
Pentelic marble. P.H. 0.35, p.W. 0.33, p.Th. 0.16.
Base of neck to hips, right arm, left upper arm, and left anta preserved. Broken on all sides. Knot, folds on chest, and anta battered. Thumb and loop of sistrum worn. Surface fresh and unweathered.

Female figure of one-third life size in high relief, framed by a narrow anta. The very smooth, curved

---

[119] Good examples of late Severan reliefs are the stele of a man and a woman, Athens, N.M. 2014 (Pl. 42); Aphthonetos, Brussels, Musées Royaux d'Art et d'Histoire (Pl. 42); and Blastos, Piraeus Museum (Pl. 42). These stelai display the "spongy" drapery characteristic of late Severan reliefs (see p. 82 above) as well as the limited use of a broad drill, so emphatic on **26**.

[120] Trieste, Mus.Civ. 2214, five-sixths life size, pp. 85, 86 above. The Trieste figure is the only "Isis" relief where the woman in the dress of Isis does not hold a situla; the ornamental drapery is so important to the sculptor that the left hand holds a thick, festoonlike fold instead.

[121] Statue of Balbinus: Niemeyer, *Studien*, no. 125.

[122] Balbinus sarcophagus in Rome: see Jucker (footnote 118 above, p. 85).

[123] Trieste, Mus.Civ. 2214: see pp. 85, 86 above and **27** (Pl. 43), another relief from the same workshop.

surface of the columnar monument into which the relief was carved is beyond the anta on the left. Re-use is indicated by the contrast between the smooth surface of this columnar grave marker[124] and the un-even curve of the background beside the figure, roughly dressed with a claw chisel. The figure is coarsely carved with a flat chisel, the abruptly slashed folds on stumpy limbs. Two parallel, vertical drill channels mark the fringed edge of the capelike section of the mantle falling on the left.

This re-use of a columnar monument took place in the late 230's. The figure is a coarse version of the handsome "Isis" relief in Trieste, Mus.Civ. 2214 (Pl. 43).[125] It shares with **28** the thicker torso and more upright posture. It is possible that both are from the same workshop, but this coarse figure on the columnar marker is far less well executed, as if unfinished, and yet that it was finished is evident from the very fine drillwork to mark the prongs of the sistrum and the careful rendering of the equally miniature fingers of the right hand.

30. Torso with garland, 40's of the 3rd   Pl. 45
     century after Christ

S 984. Found November 17, 1937 in a modern house in section Ψ (O 17).
Pentelic marble. P.H. 0.331, p.W. 0.275, p.Th. 0.238.
Base of neck to hips preserved with left upper arm and garland. Broken on all sides. Locks and upper part of garland battered. Chips in folds. Surface fresh and unweathered.

Stout female figure, five-sixths life size, very bold in relief. In contrast to the massive figure, an unusual-ly elaborate and delicate garland over the left shoul-der displays carefully carved grape leaves, pierced with a fine drill, and sets of buds bound by a fillet. On each shoulder is a thick, straggly lock of hair. Equally blunt is the treatment of the thick, toothlike fringe separated by drillwork. The drapery is dense with narrow folds rectangular in cross-section; each fold is marked by a fine line. The vertical fall of the mantle

from the knot fans out to the sides. The surface of the drapery and garland is lightly rasped, while the neck is smooth.

This large, barrel-shaped torso is probably from a single-figure relief owing to its mass and frontality. It is an exaggeration of the Trieste "Isis"-relief fig-ure (Mus.Civ. 2214; Pl. 43)[126] and should be later, in the 40's of the 3rd century, on the basis of the loss of movement, stout proportions, and planar treat-ment of the drapery. The stacked, narrow folds and stumpy figure resemble those on the Attic Pelops sarcophagus, Athens, N.M. 1176 (Pl. 46).[127] This "Isis" relief may have been made in the workshop of that sarcophagus.

31. Torso with garland, 50's of the 3rd   Pl. 47
     century after Christ

S 2396. Catalogued March 22, 1971 from a mar-ble pile in section Ω (Q 21).
Pentelic marble. P.H. 0.385, p.W. 0.21, p.Th. 0.20.
Base of neck to hip, left arm, and part of background preserved. Broken on all sides. Left shoulder and part of upper surface of garland worn. Cement on shoulder. Surface pitted and weathered.

Torso of a female figure of half life size in high relief. The lower break cuts the left hand across the knuckles of the fingers bending to hold a situla. Over the left shoulder is draped a floral garland covered with shallow scalloped decoration. Wispy strands of hair are barely visible on the garland at the level of the neckline of the dress. The contour of the figure is deeply drilled, while very fine drillwork pierces the folds at the waist and traces a wormy path in the folds at the chest and in the unusual oval folds falling from the knot. The original lightly rasped surface is preserved in the hollows and on the hand.

The figure stands with left leg as support leg and left arm bent at the elbow. It is the only Attic "Isis" relief to have the knot off-center and the mantle drawn over only one shoulder. There is also

---

[124] The diameter of the columnar monument would have been 0.60 m.; on columnar grave markers, see p. 58 above. Other re-used columnar markers include **8**, **13**, and **14**.

[125] Trieste, Mus.Civ. 2214, dated to the late 30's of the 3rd century after Christ: pp. 85, 86 above.

[126] See footnote 125 above.

[127] The Pelops sarcophagus has been dated to the mid-3rd century by Koch ([footnote 120 above, p. 85], pp.126–129; see also footnotes 124, 125 above, p. 86).

no fringe on the edge of the mantle. That these omissions are not owing to lack of ability is evident from the well-modeled arm and arched wrist. This relief could be the work of a sculptor who made relief figures on sarcophagi such as the Attic Dionysiac sarcophagus Thessaloniki, Arch.Mus. 1247 (Pl. 47).[128] 31 is not only similarly inconsistent in the scale of parts of the body but also shares in the emphasis on elegant bold curves of the figure. At first glance, these distinctive figures seem well knit owing to the sinuous curves that unite the disproportionate parts and stress the movement of the pose, but the shoulders are too narrow for the broad necks, the hips are placed too far to the left, and the limbs are too long for the short torsos. 31 also employs in the drapery the fine, wormy drillwork found on the Dionysiac sarcophagus in Thessaloniki, and the peculiar cottony texture of the garland on the Agora figure is common on the leafy borders on other Attic sarcophagi of the 3rd century.[129] I would assign this "Isis" relief to the workshop of the Dionysiac sarcophagus and accept the date, offered by Wiegartz, in the mid-3rd century for that sarcophagus as the date of 31.[130]

A more carefully carved garland, also wrapped by a fillet, is on the small "Isis" relief Athens, N.M. 3256 (Pl. 46), but its barrel-shaped torso and decorative drapery belong to the 40's of the 3rd century.[131] A better possibility for a second "Isis" stele possibly from the same workshop as 31 is a fragment, Athens, E.M. 2067.[132] It preserves a pediment with basketlike cist again marked by wormy drillwork and also lacking volume.

32. Lower part of two-figure relief,   Pl. 49
        period of Gallienus

S 341. Mended from three fragments: right (woman), found April 13, 1933 built into a Byzantine cistern (J 8); left two found February 10, 1933 used as threshold for pottery kiln east of 19th-century church of Panagia Blassaraou (K 11).
Pentelic marble. P.H. 0.51, p.W. 0.72, p.Th. 0.17.
Lower part of relief preserved with base and antae. Broken just above the knees of the figures. Right anta and lower front edge of base battered. Some cement on folds. Surface fresh and unweathered.

Two figures of half life size in high relief, framed by columnar antae. On the left is a man with mantle caught high over his bent left leg,[133] and on the right a woman in the dress of Isis has the same dancelike pose. The latter is closer to the frame, her left foot touching the base of the anta and a round-bodied situla snug between left leg and anta. Figures and frame are carefully carved and lightly rasped, while the background is dressed with a broad-toothed claw chisel.

The drapery of the two figures is decorative, consisting of banded folds sweeping up and forming a shell. A bow-shaped fold frames the woman's bent left leg, and numerous narrow bands flare out over her feet, deeply separated by a broad drill channel. Each of the folds of her drapery is rectangular in cross-section and creased, recalling the severe treatment on the stout torso 30. The drapery of her companion seems less complicated and consists simply of a few flat bands.

A date in the 60's of the 3rd century is evident from the shell-like drapery that floats over the figures.[134] This relief is strikingly similar to that on a sarcophagus of a consul in Naples, late Gallienian in date (Pl. 48).[135] The figures share in the ornamental drapery, the slender figure proportions, and the graceful, dancelike pose.

[128] Dionysiac sarcophagus: see footnotes 123 and 128 above, pp. 86, 87.

[129] Compare with the acanthus molding on the short sides of the Amazonomachy sarcophagus, Thessaloniki, Arch.Mus. 1245 (Giuliano and Palme [footnote 151 above, p. 26], pl. XLIII, fig. 103).

[130] See footnote 123 above, p. 86.

[131] Athens, N.M. 3256: for the date, see p. 85 above.

[132] Athens, E.M. 2067: the fragmentary inscription is not included by Kirchner. On "Isis" reliefs with cists in the pediment, see pp. 29–30 above and 25.

[133] See the relief of a man in the Kerameikos, Riemann, no. 74.

[134] The shell-like drapery is found on the ephebic-decree relief of Athens, E.M. 10038, A.D. 255/6 (Pl. 48; IG II², 2245; Follet, Athènes, p. 84) and on the stele of Julios Ephebos, Athens, N.M. 3669 (Pl. 48; Theophanides [footnote 1 above, p. 58], p. 10, fig. 17). Julios resembles late portraits of Gallienus, A.D. 260–268 (Bergmann [footnote 138 above, p. 88], pl. 13) and particularly Rome, Mus.Naz.Rom. 644 (H. v. Heintze in Helbig⁴ III, no. 2315).

[135] The so-called Brother sarcophagus; for the date, see p. 87 above.

33. Torso, last third of the 3rd century   Pl. 50
after Christ

S 1987. Found April 15, 1957 in modern fill under Areopagus Street (O 22).

Pentelic marble. P.H. 0.34, p.W. 0.26, p.Th. 0.13.

From base of neck to hips preserved with right arm and part of left. Broken on all sides. Knot and center folds worn. Chips in folds. Back of relief worn smoth. Surface fresh and unweathered.

A slender torso from a female figure of two-thirds life size in high relief. The most unusual drapery, snug to the chest and right hip, is cluttered with sharp hatched incisions, while heavy looping folds, each rounded and separated by a row of fine drill holes, fall at the waist and cut into the left hip of the figure. The knot at the chest is high and large, but the mantle's fringe is short and hatched by sharp diagonal lines, cut with a flat chisel. A small, rubbery, curved end represents the tip of a long lock of hair on the right shoulder. The drapery is heavily rasped.

This curiously distorted figure has an abrupt twist to the left, which in part is the result of the heavy folds at the waist that cut into and replace the left hip. The slender figure vaguely recalls the pose of the late Gallienian "Isis" relief figure Riemann, no. 61 (Pl. 50).[136] **33** has a less compact pose. The right arm is held out boldly to the left, a pose often found on single-figure reliefs.[137] The distortion found in **33**, where hips are too narrow and conical and folds cut into the hips, indicates the transition from the discrete, patterned, shell-like drapery of the Gallienian relief figure to the replacement of the body by thick, boldly patterned folds which occurs in Tetrarchic monuments of the late 3rd century.[138] A date

in the last third of the 3rd century after Christ is likely for the Agora relief.

34. Pediment with cist, late 3rd century   Pl. 51
after Christ

S 1281. Found July 3, 1947 in the wall of a Byzantine house of the 11th to 12th centuries (B–C 16–17).

Pentelic marble. P.H. 0.30, p.W. 0.285, p.Th. 0.11.

Center and right edge of pediment preserved with head of relief figure. Broken on all other sides. Right acroterion broken off. Left side of figure's head battered. Back of monument worn smooth. Surface fresh and unweathered.

Small pediment with a cist in low relief, close to the head of a relief figure of one-third life size. The pediment originally measured 0.40 m. in width. The stele may be unfinished in view of the rough preliminary shaping by point on the cist, and moldings have been barely removed with the flat chisel in carving the background around the cist. The relief ground is also rough with point marks, while the head of the relief figure is given the final smooth finish.

The rectangular cist with triangular lid is the simplest type occurring on pediments of Attic "Isis" reliefs.[139] This abbreviated cist is the only one that lacks handles on the sides. Together with the high pitch of the pediment, it may indicate a date in the second half of the 3rd century,[140] while the frontal head on this single-figure relief is very similar to that of Parthenope (Athens, N.M. 1244; Pl. 50) which should be dated to the late 3rd or beginning of the 4th century.[141] They are the last of the preserved "Isis" reliefs and belong with the few Attic grave reliefs made after the Herulian invasion in A.D. 267.[142]

[136] Riemann, no. 61, a coarse version of **32** (Pl. 49), probably from the same workshop; see also p. 87 above.

[137] See Sosibia, Boston, M.F.A. 1971.209 (Pl. 30).

[138] This development can be seen in the following examples: **32** and the stele of Julios Ephebos, Athens, N.M. 3669 (Pls. 49, 48), for Gallienian shell-like drapery; a late Gallienian bust, Agora S 2062 (Harrison [footnote 134 above, p. 88]), where the bands of folds cut into the torso instead of forming a shell; greater distortion is seen in **33**, which therefore would be later. In the Tetrarchic monuments such as the reliefs on the Arch of Galerius in Thessaloniki, the heavy and frequently patterned drapery replaces the figure and often breaks up the figure into segments (see pp. 88–89 above).

[139] On cists, see pp. 29–30 above and **25** with footnote 116, above, p. 107.

[140] For the pitch of the pediment, see Conze 1976 where the little boy has wormlike, drilled contours like babies on the Attic Dionysiac sarcophagus in Thessaloniki (footnote 123 above, p. 86; Pl. 47). Closer in the geometric style of the figures is the stele of a man and woman in the Kerameikos (Riemann, no. 46; Pl. 51) that Riemann would date after the Herulians and that compares well with Agora S 1604, which Harrison (*Agora* I, no. 52) places late in the 3rd century.

[141] Parthenope: half life size; on the date, see p. 89 above.

[142] Pp. 59 and 88–89 above.

APPENDIX 2

Types of Dress for Isis on Representations in the Roman Period

I. Knotted fringed mantle
    A. With chiton as undergarment:
        Dalmatia, Zagreb, Arch.Mus. 34   Pl. 44

    B. With chiton as undergarment and *veil* on head:
        Rome, Mus.Cap. 744   Pl. 31

    C. With chiton as undergarment and plain mantle over left arm and shoulder,
        often Isis-Fortuna: Luxor Sarapieion   Pl. 52

    D. With chiton as undergarment and plain mantle drawn over head:
        Naples, M.N. (A. de Franciscis, *Il Museo Nazionale di Napoli*,
        Naples 1963, pl. C)   Pl. 52

    E. With chiton as undergarment, plain mantle and *veil* on head:
        Rome, Vatican, Mus.Greg.Eg. 83   Pl. 41

    F. Without undergarment:
        Isis Pelagia relief, Rome, Mus.Cap. 2448 (K. Parlasca, "Ein Isiskultrelief in Rom," *RM* 71, 1964,
        pp. 195–205, pls. 55, 56)

    G. Without undergarment and mantle over lap, often Isis Lactans:
        see Tran Tam Tinh, *Isis Lactans*, pls. 26–27

II. Chiton with plain mantle over left shoulder, often Isis-Fortuna:
        Rome, Pal.Cons. (H. S. Jones, *A Catalogue of the Ancient Sculptures preserved in the Municipal
        Collections of Rome*, II, *The Sculptures of the Palazzo dei Conservatori*, Oxford 1926, p. 94, no. 31,
        pl. 33)

III. Peplos with mantle over right shoulder and *veil* on head:
        Herakleion Mus. 260 from Gortyna Isieion   Pl. 19

IV. Archaizing dress
    A. Chiton with mantle folded and clasped on right shoulder:
        statue from Sabratha Isieion and grave relief of Balullia Varilla, Naples,
        M.N. 2929   Pls. 24, 51

    B. Chiton snug to figure recalling Archaic korai:
        Naples, M.N. 976 from Pompeii Iseum (J. B. Ward-Perkins and A. Claridge, *Pompeii A.D. 79*,
        pp. 192–193, fig. 191)

V. Narrow *stole* over left shoulder
    A. Worn over knotted fringed mantle and chiton:
        Isis Barberini, Naples, M.N. (A. Levi, "L'Iside Barberini," *Monumenti antichi* 28, 1922,
        cols. 157–170, figs. 1–3)   Pl. 52

B. Worn over chiton and plain mantle:
    terracotta from Abella, Campania, London, B.M. D285 (Tran Tam Tinh, *Campanie*, pp. 81–82, pl. 21)

C. Worn over chiton:
    wall painting from Pompeii, Casa degli Amorini dorati (VI 16, 7; Tram Tan Tinh, *Essai*, p. 129, no. 17, pl. XV: 1)

APPENDIX 3

Chronological List of Attic "Isis" Reliefs

FIRST CENTURIES BEFORE AND AFTER CHRIST
Augustan (27 B.C.–A.D. 14)
1
    Athens, N.M. 3036
Tiberian (A.D. 14–37)
    Athens, N.M. Θησ. 140
Caligulan (A.D. 37–41)
    Athens, N.M. Ἀπο. 233
Claudian (A.D. 41–54)
    Athens, N.M. 1296
Neronian (A.D. 54–68)
    Athens, N.M. 1270
2, 3
    Kerameikos, Riemann, no. 58
Flavian (A.D. 68–98)
    Athens, Third Ephoria, Kallo and Synpheron
4, 5
    Kerameikos, Riemann, no. 57
    Eleusis relief
    Aigina stele pediment

SECOND CENTURY AFTER CHRIST
Trajanic (A.D. 98–117)
    Athens, N.M. 1233
6, 7, 8
    Hadrianic (A.D. 117–138)
    Mantua, Duc.Pal. 6677
9, 10
    Athens, N.M. 1193
    Athens, N.M. 1308
    Athens, Third Ephoria 1160
Early Antonine (A.D. 138–161)
    Piraeus Mus. 1160
    Athens, N.M. 1249
11, 12, 13, 14
    Laurion relief (Conze 1967)
Middle Antonine (A.D. 161–180)
    Boston, M.F.A. 1971.209
15, 16
    Piraeus fragment (Conze 1970)
Late Antonine (A.D. 180–193)
    London, B.M. 630
17, 18, 19
    Athens, N.M. Ἀπο. 235

THIRD CENTURY AFTER CHRIST
Early Severan (A.D. 193–217)
    Athens, N.M. Ἀπο. 54 + 231
    Athens, N.M. Ἀπο. 232
20, 21
    Salamis relief (Conze 1959)
    Paros relief
    (teens)
22, 23
    Athens, N.M. 1214
    Athens, N.M. 1223
    Athens, N.M. Ἀπο. 234
Middle Severan (A.D. 217–220)
24, 25
    Kerameikos, Riemann, no. 62
    Broom Hall relief (Conze 1966)
Late Severan (A.D. 222–235)
26
    Athens, N.M. Ἀπο. 230
Balbinus (A.D. 238)
    Trieste, Mus.Civ. 2214
27, 28, 29
    Akropolis Mus. 3194
Forties of the 3rd century
30
    Kerameikos, Riemann, no. 59
    Athens, N.M. 3256
    Verona relief (Conze 1965)
Fifties of the 3rd century
31
    Athens, E.M. 2067
Sixties (late Gallienian)
32
    Athens, E.M. 9706
Last third of the 3rd century
    Kerameikos, Riemann, no. 61
33
    (end of the 3rd century)
    Athens, N.M. 1244
34
    (possibly Athens, E.M. 1036)

INDEX I: GENERAL

Proper names by which sculptures may be identified are included here for convenience; the reader is referred to the location under which they are listed in Index II, given in parentheses; for the Kerameikos Museum, Riemann numbers (*Kerameikos* II) are given in brackets, in lieu of inventory numbers. For the reliefs from the Athenian Agora, the page reference to the catalogue entry in Appendix 1 is italicized.

ACHILLES SARCOPHAGUS (II: Naples, M.N. 124325)
Achilleus of Eupyridon. *See* Kallo
Achilleus son of Euphrosynos, ephebe 49
Agathemeris and Sempronius (II: London, B.M. 630)
Agathostratos and Ma (II: Athens, Kerameikos [57])
Agrippa (II: Boston, M.F.A. 99.347; Butrinto; Nikopolis)
Agrippina the Younger (II: Olympia)
Ailia Epilampsis 48
Alexandra (II: Athens, N.M. 1193)
Alexandria, imperial coins with Isis 12$^{47, 49}$ 13^{57}, 16
Alexandria, Serapieion 13
Alexandros, Paramonos and (II: Piraeus Mus. 222)
Alexandros of Sphettos. *See* Demetrios
Amarna relief (II: Cairo)
Amaryllis, Mousaios and (II: Athens, N.M. 1233)
Amazon sarcophagus (II: Thessaloniki, Arch.Mus. 1245)
Amenemhet I, situla (II: Berlin, Staat.Mus. 18492)
Ammia (II: Athens, N.M. 1163)
Andros, Hymn to Isis 1, 16–17
Antipatros son of Mousaios, ephebe, prytanis, and agoranomos 50
Aphelia and Zosimos (II: Salamis)
Aphrodeisia (II: Broom Hall); alias Epilampsis 48. *See also* Index II (Cambridge, Fitzwilliam Museum GR 5.1919); daughter of Demetrios (II: Athens, N.M. Θησ. 140)
Aphthonetos (II: Brussels)
Apuleius: account of Isis processions 56; description of Isis 16–17
Ara Pacis, Rome 69
Arcus Argentarii, Rome 82, 103^{92}
Aristo, Neikias and (II: Piraeus Museum storeroom)
Aristogora (II: Athens, N.M. Θησ. 146)

Arsinoe II 10–11, 19^{97}. *See also* Index II (Chicago; New York, M.M.A 20.2.1)
Arsinoe III 9^{24}, 19^{97}
Artemidoros (II: Athens, N.M. 1192)
Asklepias (II: Athens, N.M. 1259)
Asklepios (II: Athens, N.M. 264)
Athena (II: Athens, N.M. 274)
Athens, cemeteries 33–35, 39
Athens, cult of the Egyptian gods 30–31, 57, 60–64
Athens, Isieion 60^{25}, on Akropolis south slope 16^{72}, 63
Athens, Sarapieion 62
Attikos son of Zotikos of Phlya (II: Mantua)
Attis. *See* Cybele
Augustus (II: Corinth, S 1116 a–e)
Aurelia Euposia (II: Athens, N.M., Kabbadias Coll. 424)
Aurelios Eutyches (II: Athens, N.M. 1207)
Aurelius 47

BAKCHIS-SABAZIOS 30
Balbinus (II: Piraeus Museum 278)
Balbinus sarcophagus (II: Rome, Pretextatus Catacomb)
Balullia Varilla (II: Naples, M.N. 2929)
Bathyllos, actor 47–48; Gaius Silios 47–48. *See also* Index II (Verona)
Beneventum, Arch of Trajan 73^{46}, 75^{53}
Berenice II 19^{97}
Blastos (II: Piraeus Mus.)
Brother sarcophagus (II: Naples, M.N.)
Bryaxis 13
Butrinto head 69^{15}

CALIGULA 16, 70. *See also* Index II (Herakleion Museum 64)
Chloe (II: Athens, N.M. Θησ. 144)

Cists (*cistae mysticae*) 29–30, 107[116]
Claudia. *See* Claudii
Claudii 57[209], 63[51]
Claudius as Zeus (II: Olympia)
Claudius Phokas of Marathon, neokore 63
Cleopatra (II: New York, M.M.A. 89.2.660)
Cleopatra II 8[21], 11[44]
Cleopatra III 8[21], 11
Cleopatra VII 11, 31–32
Corinth, Isis titles 14–15
Cornelia (II: Athens, Kerameikos)
Costoboci 46
Costume 4–8
Crispina 79[80, 82]. *See also* Index II (Athens, N.M. 1647; Ostia)
Cybele and Attis 29
Cyrene, Isieion 79. *See also* Faustina

Damaskenos, the (II: Athens, American School of Classical Studies)
Dancer stele (II: Athens, N.M. 1896)
Delos: cult of the Egyptian gods 14–15, 31, 61–62; Isieion 15, 63; Sarapieion C 31
Demetria daughter of Diotimos 48. *See also* Index II (Athens [Conze])
Demetria and Sarapias [Smyrna] (II: Oxford)
Demetrios of Phaleron 39, 58
Demetrios son of Alexandros of Sphettos, thesmothete 48, 50, 69[16]
Diodotos (II: Athens, Kerameikos [52])
Diogenes of Eitea, presbis 48
Dion, Mika and (II: Athens, N.M. 765)
Dionysia and Synpherousa (II: Athens [Conze])
Dionysiac sarcophagus (II: Boston, Gardner Museum; Thessaloniki, Arch.Mus. 1247)
Dionysios of Marathon, cosmete and iakchagogos 63, ephebe 49[137]
Dionysios of Phyle. *See* Eukarpos
Dionysos, mystery cult 25[145, 146], 29
Diotimos of Azenia, prytanis 48
Domitian 16, 72, 94[23]. *See also* Index II (Athens, N.M. 345; Corinth, S 2272; Rome, Mus.Naz. Rom. 115191)
Dress. *See* Costume

Eisias (II: Athens, N.M. 1249)
Eision 51
Elate daughter of Menodoros 49; Epigonos and (II: Athens, N.M. 1308)
Eleusinian Mysteries 25[145], 30, 34, 56, 63
Epaphroditos (II: Athens, N.M. 1867)

Epigonos and Elate (II: Athens, N.M. 1308)
Epilampsis 47–48. *See also* Ailia; Aphrodeisia
Erato 52
Eukarpos son of Dionysios of Phyle, zakore and hagiaphore 56[199], 60[25]
Eukarpos son of Euporos of Miletos 56[199], 60[25]. *See also* Index II (Athens, N.M. 1958)
Eukarpos son of Philokratos 49. *See also* Index II (Athens, N.M. 1195)
Eukarpos, Sophia and (II: Athens, N.M. 1958)
Eukarpos and Philoxenos 47. *See also* Index II (Athens, N.M. 1243) and Telesphoros
Euphrosynos. *See* Achilleus
Euphrosyne (II: Athens, N.M. 1232; Eretria)
Euporos of Miletos. *See* Eukarpos
Eupyridon. *See* Achilleus

Fabia Aconia Paulina, sarcophagus in Ravenna 57
Fabia Stratonice, altar of (II: Karlsruhe)
Faustina the Elder, in Cyrene 57, 79; Faustina the Younger, in Cyrene 57, 79[78], 80, as Venus (II: Rome, Vatican, Cortile del Belvedere 936)
Flaccus, L. Valerius, of Magnesia 45[100]
Forum Transitorium, Rome, frieze 73[41]

Gaios and Hilaros (II: Athens, N.M. 1250)
Galatea (II: Rome, Vatican, Loggia Scoperta)
Galerius (II: Athens, Kanellopoulos Museum); Arch of (II: Thessaloniki); Palace of (II: Thessaloniki, Arch.Mus.)
Gallienus (II: Ostia; Rome, Mus.Naz.Rom.)
Garlands 26–29
Glykon of Berenikidai father of Menodoros. *See* Elate
Gnome (II: Athens, N.M. Θησ. 142)
Gortyna: Isieion 73; Isis statues 73–74
Grave wreaths 44–45

Hadrian 2, 60, 77[69], Temple at Ephesos 88[139]. *See also* Index II (Athens, N.M. 249)
Heliodoros, cosmete (II: Athens, N.M. 384; Kerameikos [51])
Hellenistic Isis types 11–15
Herculaneum Isiac scenes 22[114]
Hermione (II: Athens, N.M. 3396)
Herulian invasion of Greece 46, 59, 88, 111
Hieronis (II: Istanbul)
Hilara (II: Athens [Conze])
Hilaros, Gaios and (II: Athens, N.M. 1250)
Hippolytos sarcophagus (II: Tarragona)
Hymns of Isidorus (Medinet Madi, Egypt) 1, 17[85]

IOBAKCHOI 46

Iseum Campense, Rome. *See* Rome

Isias daughter of Metrodoros of Laodikea (II: London, B.M. 639)

Isidotos (II: Athens, N.M. 1024)

Isieion: at Cyrene 79; at Gortyna 73; at Ras-el-Soda 7[14]; at Sabratha 76; at Thessaloniki 74. *See also* Athens, Isieion; Delos, Isieion

Isis: black stole (*palla nigerrima*) 16–17, 20[99], 24[133]; emblem 12; epithets 14–15, 17, 31–32; hairstyle 12, 14, 16–17; initiates 52–53, 56–57, 63; priests 24[133], 53, 55, 62; priestesses 52–56, 62; tunic (*tunica multicolor*) 16–17

Isis (II: Athens, N.M. 224, N.M. 1617; Delos Museum; Delos Isieion; Gortyna; Hamburg; Herakleion Museum 260; Istanbul; Laodicea at Lycos; Lepcis Magna; Munich, Glyptothek 250 [Rome]; Naples [n.n.], 6372; Rome, Mus. Cap. 744, (?); Rome, Pal.Cons.; Rome, Piazza Venezia; Sabratha; Salamis [Cyprus]; Thessaloniki, Arch.Mus. 843; Tunis, Bardo Museum C 982; Vienna; Zagreb, Arch.Mus. 34)

Isis Barberini (II: Naples, M.N.)

Isis-Demeter 13[51]

Isis-Fortuna 13[51]. *See also* Index II (Alexandria; Gortyna, Prytaneion; Luxor)

Isis Taposiris, priestess of 62

JULIA DOMNA (II: Paris, Louvre 1070)

Julia Maesa as Isis (II: Rome, Vatican, Mus.Greg. Eg. 83)

Julia Mamaea, statue in British Museum 82[98]

Julia Titi 72[38]

Julios Ephebos (II: Athens, N.M. 3669)

KALLO (II: Athens, N.M. 1164)

Kallo daughter of Achilleus of Eupyridon 49; and Synpheron (II: Athens, Third Ephoria)

Kasianos, archon and hierokeryx 86[120]

Kenchreai 64

Kleitomenes (II: Paros)

Kokkeia. *See* Onasas

Kom el Hisn stele (II: Cairo, Egyptian Museum CG 22186)

Ktesilaos, relief 64[59]

LAMIA VIBOULLIA 47, 49. *See also* Index II (Piraeus Mus. 1160)

Lepcis Magna, Arch of Septimius Severus 13[56], 82

Livia (II: Lepcis Magna); as Ceres (II: Lepcis Magna)

Lucilla 79[80, 82]

Lucius Verus (II: Athens, N.M. 3740)

MA, AGATHOSTRATOS AND (II: Athens, Kerameikos [57])

Ma-Bellona 29

Magnia Urbica, portrait 89[141]

Marcus Aurelius (II: Paris, Louvre 1161); panel reliefs in Rome 81[91], 103

Megiste (II: Athens, N.M. 710)

Meleager sarcophagus (II: Athens, N.M. 1186)

Melisia (II: Athens, N.M. 3724)

Melitine (II: Paris, Louvre MA 3068)

Menodoros son of Glykon of Berenikidai. *See* Elate

Methe daughter or wife of Herakleides of Kephale 50. *See also* Index II (Athens, Third Ephoria)

Metrodoros of Laodikea. *See* Isias

Mika and Dion (II: Athens, N.M. 765)

Mousaios and Amaryllis (II: Athens, N.M. 1233)

Mousaios son of Antipatros of Alopeke 50

Mousonis (II: Brussels, M.R.A.H.)

NAOS (II: Paris, Louvre C 123)

Neike (II: Athens, N.M. 1303, N.M. 2558)

Neikias and Aristo (II: Piraeus Museum storeroom)

Neikon (II: Athens, Kerameikos [56])

Nero (II: Corinth, S 1088; Paris, Louvre 1221)

Nikopoulos head 69[15]

Nostimos, Zosas and (II: Marathon)

Noummia Kleo. *See* Nummii

Nummii 57[209]

OLYMPIA, nymphaeum of Herodes Atticus, sculpture 76[63], 78, 100

Onasas, Kokkeia, and Kokkeia (II: Athens, N.M. 3342)

Onesiphoron (II: Athens, N.M. 3036). *See also* Zosas

Orphic Sabazios 29

PARAMONOS AND ALEXANDROS (II: Piraeus Mus. 222)

Parthenope (II: Athens, N.M. 1244)

Patron son of Zotikos 49

Pelops sarcophagus (II: Athens, N.M. 1176)

Phileros, son or brother of Euphrosyne, ephebe 76[63]

Philodamos (II: Berlin, Staat.Mus. R 104)

Philokratos. *See* Eukarpos

Philopappos Monument (II: Athens, Mouseion Hill)

Philostrate, stele 71[28]

Philoxenos, Eukarpos and (II: Athens, N.M. 1243)

Pithom stele (II: Cairo, Egyptian Museum CG 22183)

Plutarch, *de Is. et Os.* 16, 19

Polla daughter of Zoïlos of Iphistiadai *105*

Pompeia Isias 48. *See also* Index II (Athens, N.M. 1224)

Pompeii: Iseum 17, 17[84], 20[99], 22[114], 112; Isis in wall paintings 17, 113

Pontike, Thallos and (II: Athens, N.M., Karapanos Coll.)

Poseidon of Melos 64[59]

Praxiteles son of Sotos of Iphistiadai 35[18]. *See also* Index II (Athens [Conze])

Ptolemaic-Egyptian statues 8–11, 18

Ptolemaic oinochoai 9

Ptolemaic queens assimilated to Isis 10–11

Ptolemy III 11

Ptolemy V 12

Ptolemy VII (II: Kom Ombo)

Ptolemy X, west pylon (II: Qus)

REGILLA (II: Olympia)

Rhodes, Isis representations 14–15. *See also* Index II (London, B.M. 2150; Rhodes; Vienna)

Rome: Cancelleria relief 71, 73[41], 95; Iseum Campense 15, 62, 70[20, 21]

SABINA (II: Athens, N.M. 449)

Sarapias, Demetria and (II: Oxford)

Sarapiastai, cult association 55[193]

Sarapieion: at Alexandria 13, 13[55], at Athens 62, on Delos 24, 31, at Luxor 7[14]

Sarapis (II: Herakleion Mus. 259)

Seconda Serulia (II: Piraeus Mus.)

Sempronius, Agathemeris and (II: London, B.M. 630)

Septimius Severus. *See* Lepcis Magna

Serapias (II: Athens, N.M. 1319)

Sistrum 20–21, 57

Situla 20–22, 57

Smirna (II: Athens, N.M. 2700)

Sophia and Eukarpos (II: Athens, N.M. 1214)

Sosibia (II: Boston, M.F.A. 1971.209)

Sosipatros and Epiteugma (II: Laurion)

Soterion, son of (II: Athens, N.M. 1223)

Stephephoros of Aixone 49, *106–107*

Stratonike (II: Athens, N.M. 1300)

Syncheron, Kallo and (II: Athens, Third Ephoria)

Synpherousa, Dionysia and (II: Athens [Conze])

TARSUS RELIEF (II: Athens, N.M. 1158)

Telesphoros son of Eukarpos 47. *See also* Index II (Athens, N.M. 1775)

Teti I, sistrum (II: New York, M.M.A. 26.7.1450)

Thallos and Pontike (II: N.M. Karapanos Coll.)

Theophilos (II: Athens, N.M. 1309; Riemann, no. 50)

Timokrates (II: Athens, N.M. 3316)

Titiana of Sinope 54[181]

Titus (II: Athens, N.M. 4915; Olympia); and wife (II: Rome, Vatican, Braccio Nuovo 2282 and 417)

Titus Flavius Onesiphoros 47. *See also* Index II (Athens, N.M. 3725)

Tivoli, caryatids at Villa of Hadrian 76

Tiye (II: Cairo, Egyptian Museum JE 38257)

Trajan (II: Piraeus Mus. 276). *See also* Beneventum

Tryphon (II: Cambridge)

VESPASIAN 15. *See also* Index II (Copenhagen)

Vibullii 47, 63[51]

YOUTH, long locks of, as dedication 25

ZENAS AND FATHER, sculptors from Aphrodisias, in Rome 84[108]

Zoïlos of Iphistiadai *105*. *See also* Zosas son of Zoilos

Zosas and Nostimos 47. *See also* Index II (Marathon)

Zosas son of Zoilos, Zoilos son of Teichippos, and Onesiphoron (II: Athens, N.M. 1230)

Zosimos, Aphelia and (II: Salamis)

INDEX II: SITES AND MUSEUMS

For Riemann numbers, see Athens, Kerameikos Museum. Page numbers of the catalogue entries in Appendix 1 are italicized.

Location		Page No.	Illustration
Adana			
Achilles sarcophagus		83	
Alexandria, Graeco-Roman Museum			
1332	statue	8[21]	
4780	Isis-Fortuna from Upper Egypt	7[14], 28[164]	Pl. 52:d
14941	statue	9[24]	
25724	head	12[50]	
25783	Isis from Ras-el-Soda	7[14], 12[49], 22[114], 23[125]	Pl. 52:a
Aigina Museum			
pediment		21[112], 25, 25[170], 37, 49[138], 58[1], 73[41]	Pl. 14:d
Askelon, Israel			
Isis		53[177]	
Athens, Agora Museum			
S 166	Hadrian	77[67]	
S 202	relief **8**	7[11], 38[46], 35[50, 53], 67[5], 74, *96–97*, 100[71], 109[124]	Pl. 20:c
S 221	satyr	89[146]	
S 258	relief	77[70]	
S 261, S 1584	relief **17**	7[11], 59[11], 81, *102–103*	Pl. 33:a–c
S 262	relief **20**	37[30], 66[69], 82, 82[97], *104*, 107	Pl. 35:d
S 297	relief **21**	83, *104–105*	Pl. 36:a
S 315	relief **4**	38[43], 65[62], 71[31], 72, *94*, 107[117]	Pl. 16:a–c
S 333	head	62[36], 63[44]	
S 335	head	81[89]	
S 341	relief **32**	38[43], 40[63], 87, *110*, 111[138]	Pl. 49:a, b
S 362	portrait	65[68]	
S 428	relief **11**	26[147, 150], 56[200], 78, *98–99*	Pl. 26:a
S 434	relief **29**	38[43, 46], 39[52], 85, *108–109*	Pl. 45:b
S 437	relief **9**	7[11], 38[43], 75, 97	Pl. 22:c
S 455	relief **6**	38[43], 59[11], 65[65], 73–74, *95–96*	Pl. 18:a, b
S 486	relief **10**	38[43], 41[72], 43[83], 44[87], 73, *97–98*	Pl. 25:a, b
S 553, S 554	herms from Odeion	69[17]	
S 584	relief	74[49]	
S 754	relief **15**	20[104], 21[105], 38[43], 41[72], 44[87], 80, *101*	Pl. 29:c
S 847	relief **5**	38[43], 71[5], 72	Pl. 17:b–d
S 880	relief	74[49]	
S 984	relief **30**	26[147], 65[63], 85[114], 86, 96[37], 100[71], *109*	Pl. 45:d

S 1118	relief	64[61]	Pl. 21:f
S 1142	relief **1**	23–24, 59, 65[62, 67], 67–69, *91*, *93*	Pl. 4:a
S 1182	portrait	95[30]	
S 1200	relief **3**	20[104], 71[30], *93–94*	Pl. 11:a
S 1281	relief **34**	29[170, 173], 38[43], 52[164], 59[13], 88, 89[142], 107[116], *111*	Pl. 51:a
S 1319	head	72[39], 94[23]	Pl. 15:d, e
S 1354	statue	84[113]	Pl. 41:a
S 1584	relief **17**	*See* S 261	
S 1604	head	88[135], 111[140]	
S 1728	relief **12**	44[87], 56[200], 78[72], *99*	Pl. 26:b
S 1917	relief **23**	26[147], 83, 84, *105–106*	Pl. 39:a
S 1920	relief **16**	80, *101–102*	Pl. 30:d
S 1987	relief **33**	59[13], 87, 88[134, 140], *111*	Pl. 50:a
S 2029	relief **24**	82, 83[104], *106*	Pl. 39:b
S 2062	bust	88[134], 111[138]	
S 2264	relief **2**	71[30, 34], *93*	Pl. 10:b, c
S 2280	relief **27**	85, *108*, 108[123]	Pl. 43:a, b
S 2393	relief **13**	7[11, 12], 26[147–149], 28[165], 38[46], 39[51], 56[200], 64[59], 78–79, *99–100*, 109[124]	Pl. 28:b
S 2396	relief **31**	7[11], 26[147], 65[63], 86, 107[116], *109–110*	Pl. 47:a
S 2435	portrait	84[113]	
S 2443	relief	41[68], 44[89], 69[17]	Pl. 3:c, d
S 2451	relief **26**	66[69], 82, 82[98], *107–108*	Pl. 41:e
S 2543	relief **14**	7[11], 23[121], 38[46], 39[51, 53], 56[200], 78, 96[37], *100–101*, 109[124]	Pl. 29:a
S 2544	relief **18**	65[66], 81[89], *103*	Pl. 33:d
S 2551	relief **7**	59[11], 65[65], 73–74, *96*	Pl. 18:c
S 2698	relief	18[91], 36[22], 84[112]	Pl. 42:b
S 2771	relief **19**	65[63, 64], 81–82, *103–104*	Pl. 35:a–c
S 2864	statue	80[83, 85]	Pl. 31:c–e
S 2900	relief **28**	7[11], 38[46], 39[52, 53], 85, *108*	Pl. 45:a
I 3348 + 3532	pediment **25**	29[170, 171], 30, 49, 51, 83[104], *106–107*	Pl. 40:c
I 4776	pediment **22**	20[103], 49[138], 83[104], *105*	Pl. 38:d

Athens, Akropolis Museum
674	kore	19[96]	
680	kore	19[96]	
3194	relief	26[147, 148], 38[41], 59[11], 65[63], 85[114], 86	Pl. 44:a, b
reliefs		2[15], 26[147], 38[41], 58[1]	Conze 1957 b–d

Athens, Akropolis South Slope
| Isis | | 7[14], 12[49], 16[72, 73], 63, 70 | |

Athens, American School of Classical Studies
| the Damaskenos | | 33[1], 41[71], 42[74, 79], 43[84], 44[87], 59[11], 66[71], 75[56], 94[19] | Conze 2038 |

Athens, Epigraphical Museum (E.M.)

186	inscription	47[116]	
396	inscription	57[209]	
1036	pediment	2[15], 29[173], 38[41], 49[138], 58[1], 107[116]	Conze 2141
2067	pediment	2[15], 29[170, 171], 38[38], 49[138], 58[1], 65[63], 107[116], 110[132]	Conze 2139
8159	inscription	55[191]	
8160	inscription	55[191]	
8187	inscription	46[112]	
8299	inscription	57[209, 210]	
8426	Isis Dikaiosyne	31, 32, 70[27]	Pl. 1:a
8488	inscription	46[111]	
8653	inscription	46[111]	
9706	pediment	2[15], 29[170, 173], 38[41], 49[138], 58[1], 107[116]	Conze 2140
9730	pediment	2[15], 29[170, 171], 49[138], 58[1], 107[116]	Pl. 36:d
10038	inscription	87[129], 87[137], 110[134]	Pl. 48:c
10040	inscription	75, 97[45]	Pl. 23:a

Athens, Kanellopoulos Museum

Galerius	88[135]	

Athens, Kerameikos

Cornelia	40	

Athens, Kerameikos Museum

Riemann, no. 46 relief	28[164], 44[87], 52[164], 88, 111[140]	Pl. 51:b Conze 2085
Riemann, no. 50 Theophilos	25[144]	
Riemann, no. 51 Heliodoros	40[61]	
Riemann, no. 52 Diodotos	25[144], 69	Pl. 7:a
Riemann, no. 56 Neikon	40[61], 44[87]	
Riemann, no. 57 Agathostratos and Ma	29[170, 173], 38[42], 44[87], 49[138], 51[153], 65[62], 71[31], 72[36, 39], 90[21]	Pl. 15:a
Riemann, no. 58 relief	38[42], 71[30], 72[36],	Pl. 11:b
Riemann, no. 59 relief	38[42], 65[63], 82[124]	Pl. 46:c
Riemann, no. 61 relief	38[42], 87[127, 131, 133], 88[140], 111[136]	Pl. 50:c
Riemann, no. 62 relief	38[42], 84[111], 106[110]	Pl. 40:a
Riemann, no. 70 relief	66[73]	Pl. 9:b
Riemann, no. 74 relief	110[133]	

Athens, Metropolitan Church

relief	41[69]	Conze 1936

Athens, Mouseion Hill

Philopappos Monument	75[56], 96	Pl. 22:a

Athens, National Museum (N.M.)

224	Isis	14[60], 15[64]	
249	Hadrian	80[87]	
264	Asklepios	89[144]	
274	Athena	88	Pl. 51:c

345	Domitian	72[39]	Pl. 16:d, e
356	cosmete	82[98], 86[120]	
384	cosmete Heliodoros	74[51], 96[36]	
388	cosmete	82[98], 86[120]	
420	bust	74[53]	Pl. 20:a, b
449	Sabina	76[64]	
707	statue	83[105]	
710	Megiste	44[89], 68[6]	
715	Salamis relief	41[73]	
765	Mika and Dion	36, 41[70]	Conze 157
870	relief	41[71], 42[74]	
1024	Isidotos	68[6]	Conze 1973
1158	Tarsus relief	19[94], 54[180]	
1163	Ammia	69	Pl. 6:d Conze 1836
1164	Kallo	46[115, 116]	Conze 1857
1176	Pelops sarcophagus	86, 89[144], 109[127]	Pl. 46:a
1186	Meleager sarcophagus	81[77]	
1192	Artemidoros	42[81], 44[87], 51[154], 81[92]	Conze 2052
1193	Alexandra	2[15], 19[96], 35[15], 36, 37[30], 39, 41[71], 42[79], 43[81, 82, 85], 44[87], 49[138], 58[1], 60[18], 65[64], 66[72], 74[47], 75[55], 75–76, 97, 98	Pl. 24:a, b Conze 1969
1195	Eukarpos	78[74]	Conze 2078
1207	Aurelios Eutyches	107[116]	Conze 2042
1214	Sophia and Eukarpos	2[15], 7[9], 20[103], 38[36], 43[87], 49[138], 55[199], 58[1], 60[18, 25], 64[60], 66[70], 78[97], 84, 105, 106	Pl. 37:e Conze 1958
1223	Son of Soterion	2[15], 20[103], 38[39], 49[138], 58[1], 60[18], 64[60], 66[70], 84, 105, 105[102]	Pl. 38:a Conze 1961
1224	Pompeia Isias	46[115], 48	Pl. 2:a Conze 1860
1230	Zosas, Zoilos, and Onesiphoron	47[118], 50[152]	Conze 2120
1232	Euphrosyne	44[87], 46[115], 76[63]	Conze 1902
1233	Mousaios and Amaryllis	2[15], 24, 38[37], 41[70], 42[80], 43[85], 44[87], 46[115], 47[118], 50, 51[153], 60[18], 65[62], 72[36], 74, 95–97	Pl. 19:a Conze 1971
1243	Eukarpos and Philoxenos	42[79], 44[87], 47, 80[86]	Pl. 32:a Conze 2068
1244	Parthenope	2[15], 18[92], 24[135], 28[164], 38[37], 40[61], 43[87], 46[111], 49[138], 57, 58[1], 59[13, 14], 60[18], 89, 111	Pl. 50:d, e Conze 1954
1247	soldier relief	66[70], 84[108]	Pl. 38:b Conze 2124
1249	Eisias	2[15], 19[94], 38[38], 49[138], 51–52, 55, 56[200], 58[1], 60[18], 78, 101	Pl. 28:c Conze 1955
1250	Gaios and Hilaros	37[29], 40[61], 42[75, 79], 44[87, 88], 47[119], 71[29]	Pl. 9:a Conze 2066
1259	Asklepias	46[116]	Conze 1837

1266	soldier relief	66[70], 84[108]	Pl. 38:c
			Conze 2127
1270	relief	2[15], 7[9], 43[86], 44[87], 58[1], 71, 72[36], 93, 94	Pl. 10:a
			Conze 1968
1296	relief	2[15], 5[1], 19[94], 58[1], 68[9], 70–71	Pl. 8:a, b
			Conze 1868
1300	Stratonike	37[30], 46[115]	Conze 1906
1303	Neike	40[62], 43[82, 85], 44[87], 46[115], 79[79], 80[86]	Pl. 32:c
			Conze 1934
1308	Epigonos and Elate	2[15], 7[9], 19[96], 20[104], 29[170, 171], 30[186], 38[37], 42, 43[87], 49, 51, 52[165], 58[1], 60[18], 76–77, 98, 107[116]	Pl. 24:d
			Conze 1962
1309	Theophilos	44[87], 49[137]	Conze 2003
1319	Serapias	68[6]	Conze 1844
1390	votive relief	42[81]	
1465	ephebic decree relief	84[109], 105	
1469	ephebic decree relief	74[51], 96	
1470	ephebic decree relief	46[110]	
1483	ephebic decree relief	78, 99, 100	
1617	Isis	83, 105	Pl. 34:c, d
1647	Crispina	81[91]	
1663	relief	64[61]	Conze 2023
1775	Telesphoros	45–46, 81[91], 103	Pl. 32:d
			Conze 2048
1867	Epaphroditos	25[144]	Conze 1987
1896	dancer stele	64[61]	
2014	relief	46[115], 82[98], 108[119]	Pl. 42:a
			Conze 2084
2558	Neike	46[115], 69	Pl. 6:c
			Conze 1929
2700	Smirna	40[63], 44[87]	Conze 1913
2725	relief	41[72]	Conze 2008
3036	Onesiphoron	2[15], 29[170, 173], 49[138], 58[1], 59[10], 67–68, 91, 93	Pl. 5:a, b
			Conze 1972, no. 23
3081	relief	41[69]	Conze 1866
3085–3087	relief	59[11]	
3256	relief	2[15], 26[147], 37, 58[1], 85, 85[114], 86[122], 110	Pl. 46:b
			Conze 1957a
3316	Timokrates	35[14, 19], 104	Pl. 36:b
			Conze 2011
3342	Onasas, Kokkeia, and Kokkeia	47[118]	Conze 2119a
3396	Hermione	35[14, 15, 19], 37[30], 46[115], 104	Conze 1914
3552	relief	64[61]	Pl. 21:d, e
3669	Julios Ephebos	18[91], 41[69], 87[128], 110[134], 111[138]	Pl. 48:b
3724	Melisia	42[80], 96[37], 100[71]	Pl. 21:a, b
3725	Titus Flavius Onesiphoros	18[91], 40[62], 44[87], 47, 72, 95, 95[26]	Pl. 17:a

3740	Lucius Verus	79[79], 80[86]	
4464	horse and groom relief	58[7]	
4915	Titus	72[39]	Pl. 15:b, c
Ἀπο. 54 + 231	relief	2[15], 20[103], 38[36], 58[1], 64[60], 65[63], 83, 104, 107[116]	Pl. 37:a, b Conze 1972, nos. 15, 7
Ἀπο. 230	relief	2[15], 23[128], 58[1], 82[98], 107[118]	Conze 1964
Ἀπο. 232	relief	2[15], 38[37], 58[1], 83[101, 102]	Conze 1972, no. 8
Ἀπο. 233	relief	2[15], 38[39], 58[1], 70	Conze 1972, no. 13
Ἀπο. 234	relief	2[15], 38[39], 58[1], 83[104]	Conze 1972, no. 9
Ἀπο. 235	relief	2[15], 38[37], 56[204], 58[1], 81[90]	Conze 1972, no. 17
Ἀπο. 237	relief	2[15], 7[12], 38[37], 58[1], 64[59], 78, 99[55], 100	Pl. 28:a Conze 1972, no. 3
Θησ. 140	Aphrodeisia	37, 39–40, 48, 50, 69	Pl. 6:a, b
Θησ. 142	Gnome	35[15], 37[30]	
Θησ. 143	relief	35[15], 37[30]	
Θησ. 144	Chloe	37[30]	
Θησ. 145	Aristogora	37[30]	
Θησ. 146	relief	37[29]	

Athens, National Museum, Kabbadias Collection
424	Aurelia Euposia	89[141]	

Athens, National Museum, Karapanos Collection
Thallos and Pontike		18[91], 58[5]	Conze 1869

Athens, Third Ephoria
Kallo and Synpheron		2[15], 37[34], 38, 44[87], 49, 56, 58[1], 65[62], 71[31], 72	Pl. 13:a–d Conze 2077
1160	Methe	21[112, 113], 29[171], 30[186], 43[81], 44[87], 49[138], 50, 76, 77[71]	Pl. 23:b–d

Athens (according to Conze)
Demetria		48, 68, 93	Pl. 2:b Conze 1838
Dionysia and Synpherousa		18[91], 35[20], 36[21, 22], 47[119]	Conze 1940
Hilara		18[91], 35[20], 36[21, 23], 47[116, 117], 74[49]	Pl. 20:d Conze 1951
Praxiteles		35[14, 18], 104	Pl. 36:c Conze 2086

Berlin, Staatliche Museen (Staat.Mus.)
1462	relief	44[91], 67[2]	
18492	situla of Amenemhet I	25	
R 104	Philodamos	41[71, 72], 86[121]	

Boston, Gardner Museum
Dionysiac sarcophagus		89[146]	

Boston, Museum of Fine Arts (M.F.A.)
 01.8191 statue 71^{34} Pl. 9:c, d
 37.100   relief 47^{119}
 88.384   bust 64^{61}
 99.347   Agrippa   68–69   Pl. 4:b, c
 1971.209 Sosibia 2^{15}, 7^{11}, 18^{92}, 19^{95}, 20^{104}, 21^{105}, 23^{121}, Pl. 30:a–c
             35–36, 42^{81}, $43^{82, 83, 87}$, 46^{115}, 48^{131}, Conze 1955
             49^{138}, 58^{1}, 60^{18}, 64^{60}, 65^{65}, 73^{43}, 79–80,
             94^{20}, 98^{50}, $101^{76, 77}$, 111^{137}
 1972.875 relief 28^{166}

Brooklyn Museum
 70.132   relief 5^{4}, 28^{166}

Broom Hall, England
 Aphrodeisia 2^{15}, 7^{15}, 20^{104}, 23^{128}, 40^{61}, 44^{87}, 49^{138}, 51, Pl. 39:c
             58^{1}, 82^{97}, 84, 106, 106^{110} Conze 1966

Brussels, Mariemont
 E 51   statue $9^{24, 25}$

Brussels, Musées Royaux d'Art et d'Histoire (M.R.A.H.)
 Mousonis 40^{61} Conze 1985
 Aphthonetos 82^{98}, 108^{119} Pl. 42:c
                           Conze 2049

Cairo, Egyptian Museum
 CG 2317 offering table 23^{125}
 CG 3547 situla 23^{129}
 CG 3560 situla 23^{131}
 CG 3562 situla 23^{131}
 CG 3582 situla 23^{129}
 CG 22183 Pithom stele 10^{38}, 11^{39}
 CG 22186 Kôm el Hisn stele 8^{21}
 CG 27472 statue 8^{21}
 CG 33281 mummy portrait 5^{4}
 CG 54517 Amarna relief 12^{48}
 CG 69316 sistrum $21^{105, 109}$
 JE 38257 statue of Tiye 12^{48}
 JE 39517 head 12^{50}, 19^{93}

Cambridge, Fitzwilliam Museum
 GR 5.1919 Aphrodeisia alias 40^{61}, 42^{80}, 44^{87}, 48 Conze 1930
       Epilampsis
 Tryphon 43^{86}, 44^{87}, $72^{34, 35}$, 93 Pl. 11:c
                           Conze 2005

Chicago, Oriental Institute
 10158   Arsinoe II 8^{20}, 9^{26}, 10^{33}

Copenhagen, Ny Carlsberg Glyptotek (Ny Carlsberg Glyp.)
 2585   Vespasian 72^{38}

Corinth Museum
 S 1116 a–e Augustus 71^{29}
 S 1088   Nero 72^{35}, 93

S 2272 Domitian 72
S 187+196 relief of youth 41[72], 59[11], 98[47]
sarcophagus 42[81]
statuette 15[64]

Cyrene
Faustina the Elder and 26[149], 28, 53[176], 57, 66, 78–79 Pl. 27:d
Faustina the Younger

Delos, Isieion
colossal Isis 15, 63[48]

Delos Museum
A 378 Isis statuette 14[60, 62], 15[64]
A 2255 Isis statuette 14[60, 62]
A 5370 Isis statuette 14[60, 62]
A 5373 Isis statuette 14[60, 62]

Edfu
seal 12[50]

Eleusis Museum
relief 36–37, 43[83], 44[87], 71[31], 72, 94 Pl. 14:a–c
relief bust 74 Pl. 19:b
Conze 2133

Eretria
Euphrosyne 22[114], 28, 30[184], 53[179], 67

Gortyna, Crete
Isis statuette 27[152], 28[164]
Prytaneion, Isis-Fortuna 27[152], 28[164], 66[76], 73–74

Grenoble
relief 46[115], 57[214], 75[56] Pl. 22:b
Conze 2096

Hamburg, Museum für Kunst und Gewerbe
1968.38 Isis 53[177]

Herakleion Museum
64 Caligula 70
259 Sarapis from Gortyna 73 Pl. 19:c
260 Isis from Gortyna 12[49], 27[152], 28[164], 66[76], 73–74, 112 Pl. 19:c, d
314 statue 7[9], 53[176], 66[76], 71[30], 72 Pl. 12:a–c

Istanbul, Archaeological Museum
Hieronis 52[163]
Isis figurine 27[152]

Karlsruhe, Badisches Landesmuseum
64/134 altar of Fabia Stratonice 53[178]

Karnak
Propylon of Temple of Khonsu 8[21]
statue reinscribed to Cleopatra II 11[44]

Köln
N 126 situla 24[132]

Kom Ombo, Temple of Khnum
    relief of Ptolemy VII   8[21]

Kos
    statuette of Isis   14[60, 64]

Lambesis
    Isis   81[93]

Laodicea at Lycos
    Isis   12[49], 65[64], 81[93]

Laurion
    Sosipatros and Epiteugma   2[15], 37[35], 47[118], 49[138], 56, 58[1], 78   Pl. 29:b
                                                                                            Conze 1967

Leiden, Rijksmuseum
    F 1960/3, 1   statue   6[8], 8[16], 10[31-33]

Lepcis Magna
    Isis   17[82]
    Livia (as Ceres) from Theater temple   70, 71[29]

London, British Museum (B.M.)
    379   Memphis stele   11[39]
    630   Agathemeris and   2[15], 7[11], 19[95], 37[30, 34], 40[63], 42[81],   Pl. 32:e
                 Sempronius   43[83, 84, 87], 49[138], 58[1], 60[18], 65[66], 73[43],   Conze 1963
                                          81, 98[49], 102-103, 106[111]
    639   Isias from Smyrna   20[99], 22[114], 31, 53-54, 70[27], 101[73]   Pl. 1:b
    1054   Tanis stele   9[24]
    2150   Rhodes votive relief 14[63]
    D 285   Abella terracotta   17[84], 113

Luxor
    Sarapieion, Isis-Fortuna   7[14], 112   Pl. 52:d

Ma'amra
    statue   9[24]

Mantua, Ducal Palace (Duc.Pal.)
    6677   Attikos   2[15], 7[9], 23[121], 43[84, 87], 49, 51, 58[1], 65[67],   Pl. 22:d
                                          66[72], 75, 97   Conze 1960

Marathon Museum
    Zosas and Nostimos   44[87], 47, 77   Pl. 25:d
                                                                                            Conze 2069

Munich, Glyptothek
    250   Isis from Rome   16[72], 17[84], 66[76], 70   Pl. 7:b
    relief   46[115], 70[23]   Pl. 7:c
                                                                                            Conze 2093

Munich, Museum antiker Kleinkunst (Mus.Ant.Kl.)
    512   situla from Pompeii   22[114], 24[134]

Naples, Museo Nazionale (M.N.)
                 Isis   112   Pl. 52:c
    976   Isis   112
    2929   Balullia Varilla   53[178], 112   Pl. 51:d

6061	portrait	94[23]	
6141	male head	19[93]	
6289	female head	68, 93	Pl. 2:c, d
6372	Isis	16[72, 73]	Pl. 7:d
124325	Achilles sarcophagus	81[92], 103	Pl. 34:a, b
	"Brother" sarcophagus	87, 110[135]	Pl. 48:a
	Isis Barberini	17[84], 112	Pl. 52:e

Nikopolis

| | Agrippa | 69[15] | |

New York, Metropolitan Museum of Art (M.M.A)

13.198.6	fluted bottle	24[134]	
17.194.193	aryballos	24[133]	
20.2.21	Arsinoe II	8[20], 9[26], 10[33]	
26.7.1450	sistrum of Teti I	21[107]	
60.11.2	amphora-situla	23[120]	
60.11.3	psykter	23[120]	
68.44	sistrum	20[101]	
86.1.6a	coffin lid of Iyanafery	6[7]	
89.2.660	Cleopatra	10[33]	
1972.118.157	bowl	22[115]	
1973.11.10	situla	22[116]	

Olympia Museum

Agrippina the Younger	71[29]	
Claudius as Zeus	42[75], 71[29]	
Regilla	78, 99, 100	
Titus	41[72]	

Ostia, Archaeological Museum

| Crispina | 57[212], 81[91] | |
| Gallienus | 87[130] | |

Oxford, Ashmolean Museum

| Demetria and Sarapias from Smyrna | 20[99], 22[114], 31, 53[179] | Pl. 1:c |

Palermo, Museo Nazionale (M.N.)

| 704 | statue | 10[33], 22[114], 57[212] | Pl. 51:f |

Paris, Louvre

1070	Julia Domna	83[105]	
1161	Marcus Aurelius	81[89]	
1221	Nero	72[35], 93[14]	
C 123	naos	11[39]	
C 124	stele	11[39]	
E 11201	sistrum	21[105]	
E 14.268	relief	13[56]	
E 25908	relief	5[4]	
MA 3068	Melitine	79, 101	
MA 3546	head	19[93]	
MND 2087	head	28[165]	
	grave relief	50[152], 77[69]	Conze 2098

Paros
    Kleitomenes   56, 66, 83[101], 104[98]   Pl. 37:c

Piraeus
    relief   2[15], 37[34], 44[87], 58[1], 80   Pl. 32:b
                                                                  Conze 1970

Piraeus Museum (Piraeus Mus.)
    222   Paramonos and   47[118], 50[153], 64[59]   Pl. 21:c
                    Alexandros   Conze 2067
    223   relief, man with siren   44[89]   Pl.3:a, b
                                                               Conze 2053
    276   Trajan   64[59]
    278   Balbinus   85[120], 89[144], 108   Pl. 45:c
    388   relief   44
    1160   Lamia Viboullia   2[15], 7[12], 19, 23, 26[147, 150], 37[34], 42[81],   Pl. 27:a–c
                                       43[82–85], 47, 49, 55, 56[200], 58[1], 66, 78, 98 Conze 1957
    Blastos   82[98], 108[119]   Pl. 42:d
                                                                  Conze 1975
    Seconda Serulia   46[116]   Conze 1863
                                                                 (Athens)

Piraeus Museum storeroom
    Neikias and Aristo from Oropos   77–78   Pl. 25:c

Qus
    West pylon of Ptolemy X   8[21], 18[89]

Rhodes, Archaeological Museum (Arch.Mus.)
    funerary altar   31, 53[179]   Pl. 1:d
    statuette   14[60]

Rome, Museo Capitolino (Mus.Cap.)
    744   Isis   7[9], 53[176], 54[184], 66[76], 80, 112   Pl. 31:a, b
    2448   Isis Pelagia relief   112
    4371   relief   7[14], 13[56]
                  Isis (?)   17[82]

Rome, Museo Nazionale Romano (Mus.Naz.Rom.)
    644   Gallienus   110[134]
    115191   Domitian   94[23]

Rome, Palazzo dei Conservatori (Pal.Cons.)
    Isis   17[82], 112

Rome, Piazza Venezia
    Isis   87   Pl. 49:c

Rome, Pretextatus Catacomb
    Balbinus sarcophagus   85, 108   Pl. 44:c

Rome, Vatican:

  Braccio Nuovo
    2282 and 417   Titus and wife   71[30], 72[37]
  Cortile del Belvedere
    936   Faustina the Younger   79[80], 101[79]
                  (as Venus)

Loggia Scoperta
    Galatea 17^{82}, 22^{114}, 53^{178}, 54, 55   Pl. 51:e

Museo Gregoriano Egizio (Mus.Greg.Eg.)
    83   Julia Maesa as Isis 7^9, 17^{82}, 53^{176}, 54^{184}, 66^{76}, 84–85, 112   Pl. 41:b–d
    107   statue $9^{24, 25}$

Sabratha
    Isis   76, 112   Pl. 24:c

Salamis
    Aphelia and Zosimos 2^{15}, 18^{92}, 37^{34}, 49^{138}, 58^1, 83^{101} Pl. 37:d
                                                                                             Conze 1959

Salamis, Cyprus
    Isis 81^{93}

Syros
    relief 22^{114} Pl. 14:e

Tanis
    statue 9^{24}

Tarragona
    Hippolytos sarcophagus   84   Pl. 40:b

Thasos
    relief 20^{99}

Thessaloniki
    Arch of Galerius   88, 89^{141}, 111^{138}

Thessaloniki, Archaeological Museum (Arch.Mus.)
    843   Isis   74
    1245   Amazonomachy 26^{151}, 110^{129}
                    sarcophagus
    1247   Dionysiac sarcophagus 86^{123}, 87^{128}, 110, 111^{140} Pl. 47:b, c
                    Decoration from Palace of Galerius   88

Trieste, Museo Civico (Mus.Civ.)
    2214   relief 2^{15}, $26^{147, 148}$, 52, 58^1, 82^{95}, 85–86, 106,   Pl. 43:c
                                                108, 109   Conze 1972

Tunis, Bardo Museum
    C 982   Isis 7^{14}, 53   Pl. 52:b

Turin
    statuette 14^{60}

Verona, Museo Lapidario
    Bathyllos stele   47–48, $64^{60, 61}$, 71^{29} Pl. 8:c
                                                                                             Conze 2113
    relief 2^{15}, 58^1, 85^{114}, 86^{122} Pl. 46:d
                                                                                             Conze 1965

Vienna, Kunsthistorisches Museum
    Isis from Catajo $14^{63, 64}$

Zagreb, Archaeological Museum (Arch.Mus.)
    34   Isis 7^9, 53^{176}, 66^{76}, 85, 112   Pl. 44:d

INDEX III: ATTIC GRAVE RELIEFS PUBLISHED BY A. CONZE

(*Die attischen Grabreliefs*, Berlin/Leipzig 1893–1922)

Conze No.	Location	Page and Plate Nos.
157	Athens, N.M. 765: Mika and Dion	36, 41[70]
1570f	Proxenos	46[116]
1749		40[64]
1796		96[38]
1798		96[38]
1806		96[38]
1815		96[38]
1836	Athens, N.M. 1163: Ammia	69; Pl. 6:d
1837	Athens, N.M. 1259: Asklepias	46[116]
1838	Athens: Demetria	48, 68, 93; Pl. 2:b
1843	Athens [Kerameikos]: Cornelia	40[65]
1844	Athens, N.M. 1319: Serapias	68[6]
1857	Athens, N.M. 1164: Kallo	46[115, 116]
1860	Athens, N.M. 1224: Pompeia Isias	46[115], 48; Pl. 2:a
1863	Athens [Piraeus Museum]: Seconda Serulia	46[116]
1866	Athens, N.M. 3081	41[69]
1868	Athens, N.M. 1296	2[15], 5[1], 19[94], 58[1], 68[9], 70–71; Pl. 8:a, b
1869	Athens, N.M. Karapanos Collection: Thallos and Pontike	18[91], 58[5]
1870		58[5]
1887		58[5]
1888		58[5]
1902	Athens, N.M. 1232: Euphrosyne	43[87], 46[115], 76[63]
1906	Athens, N.M. 1300: Stratonike	37[30], 46[115]
1913	Athens, N.M. 2700: Smirna	40[63], 44[87]
1914	Athens, N.M. 3396: Hermione	35[14, 15, 19], 37[30], 46[115], 104[96, 100]
1921		46[115]
1929	Athens, N.M. 2558: Neike	46[115], 69; Pl. 6:c
1930	Cambridge, Fitzwilliam Museum GR 5.1919: Aphrodeisia alias Epilampsis	40[61], 42[80], 44[87], 48
1934	Athens, N.M. 1303: Neike	40[62], 43[82, 85], 44[87], 46[115], 79[79], 80[86]; Pl. 32:c
1936	Athens, Metropolitan Church	41[69]
1939		18[91]
1940	Athens: Dionysia and Synpherousa	18[91], 35[20], 36[21, 22], 47[119]
1941		18[91]
1942		18[91]

1943		18^{91}
1951	Athens: Hilara	18^{91}, 35^{20}, $36^{21, 23}$, $47^{116, 117}$, 74^{49}; Pl. 20:d
1954	Athens, N.M. 1244: Parthenope	2^{15}, 18^{92}, 24^{135}, 28^{164}, 38^{37}, 40^{61}, 43^{87}, 46^{111}, 49^{138}, 57, 58^1, $59^{13, 14}$, 60^{18}, 89, 111; Pl. 50:b, d
1955	Boston, M.F.A. 1971.209: Sosibia	2^{15}, 7^{11}, 18^{92}, 19^{95}, 20^{104}, 21^{105}, 23^{121}, 35–36, 42^{81}, $43^{82, 83, 87}$, 46^{115}, 48^{131}, 49^{138}, 58^1, 60^{18}, 64^{60}, 65^{65}, 73^{43}, 79–80, 94^{20}, 98^{50}, $101^{76, 77}$, 111^{137}; Pl. 30:a–c
1956	Athens, N.M. 1249: Eisias	2^{15}, 19^{94}, 38^{38}, 49^{138}, 51–52, 55, 56^{200}, 58^1, 60^{18}, 78, 101; Pl. 28:c
1957	Piraeus Museum 1160: Lamia Viboullia	2^{15}, 7^{12}, 19, 23, $26^{147, 150}$, 37^{34}, 42^{81}, $43^{82–85}$, 47, 49, 55, 56^{200}, 58^1, 66, 78, 98; Pl. 27:a–c
1957a	Athens, N.M. 3256	2^{15}, 26^{147}, 37, 58^1, 85, 85^{114}, 86^{122}, 110; Pl. 46:b
1957b–d	Athens, Akropolis Museum	2^{15}, 26^{147}, 38^{41}, 58^1
1958	Athens, N.M. 1214: Sophia and Eukarpos	2^{15}, 7^9, 20^{103}, 38^{36}, 43^{87}, 49^{138}, 55^{199}, 58^1, $60^{18, 25}$, 64^{60}, 66^{70}, 78^{97}, 84, 105, 106; Pl. 37:e
1959	Salamis: Aphelia and Zosimos	2^{15}, 18^{92}, 37^{34}, 49^{138}, 58^1, 83^{101}; Pl. 37:d
1960	Mantua, Duc.Pal. 6677: Attikos	2^{15}, 7^9, 23^{121}, $43^{84, 87}$, 49, 51, 58^1, 65^{67}, 66^{72}, 75, 97; Pl. 22:d
1961	Athens, N.M. 1223: Son of Soterion	2^{15}, 20^{103}, 38^{39}, 49^{138}, 58^1, 60^{18}, 64^{60}, 66^{70}, 84, 105, 105^{102}; Pl. 38:a
1962	Athens, N.M. 1308: Epigonos and Elate	2^{15}, 7^9, 19^{96}, 20^{104}, $29^{170, 171}$, 30^{186}, 38^{37}, 42, 43^{87}, 49, 51, 51^{165}, 58^1, 60^{18}, 76–77, 98, 107^{116}; Pl. 24:d
1963	London, B.M. 630: Agathemeris and Sempronius	2^{15}, 7^{11}, 19^{95}, $37^{30, 34}$, 40^{63}, 42^{81}, $43^{83, 84, 87}$, 49^{138}, 58^1, 60^{18}, 65^{66}, 73^{43}, 81, 98^{49}, 102–103, 106^{111}; Pl. 32:e
1964	Athens, N.M. ᾽Απο. 230	2^{15}, 23^{128}, 58^1, 82^{98}, 107^{118}
1965	Verona, Museo Lapidario	2^{15}, 58^1, 85^{114}, 86^{122}; Pl. 46:d
1966	Broom Hall: Aphrodeisia	2^{15}, 7^{15}, 20^{104}, 23^{128}, 40^{61}, 44^{87}, 49^{138}, 51, 58^1, 82^{97}, 84, 106^{110}, 106; Pl. 39:c
1967	Laurion: Sosipatros and Epiteugma	2^{15}, 37^{35}, 47^{118}, 49^{138}, 56, 58^1, 78; Pl. 29:b
1968	Athens, N.M. 1270	2^{15}, 7^9, 43^{86}, 44^{87}, 58^1, 71, 72^{36}, 93, 94; Pl. 10:a
1969	Athens, N.M. 1193: Alexandra	2^{15}, 19^{96}, 35^{15}, 36, 37^{30}, 39, 41^{71}, 42^{79}, $43^{81, 82, 85}$, 44^{87}, 49^{138}, 58^1, 60^{18}, 65^{64}, 66^{72}, 74^{47}, 75^{55}, 75–76, 97, 98; Pl. 24:a, b
1970	Piraeus	2^{15}, 37^{34}, 44^{87}, 58^1, 80; Pl. 32:b
1971	Athens, N.M. 1233: Mousaios and Amaryllis	2^{15}, 24, 38^{37}, 41^{70}, 42^{80}, 43^{85}, 44^{87}, 46^{115}, 47^{118}, 50, 51^{153}, 58^1, 60^{18}, 65^{62}, 72^{36}, 74, 95–97; Pl. 19:a
1972	Trieste, Mus. Civ. 2214	2^{15}, $26^{147, 148}$, 52, 58^1, 82^{95}, 85–86, 106, 108, 109; Pl. 43:c
1972, no. 3	Athens, N.M. ᾽Απο. 237	2^{15}, 7^{12}, 38^{37}, 58^1, 64^{59}, 78, 99^{55}, 100; Pl. 28:a
1972, nos. 7, 15	Athens, N.M. ᾽Απο. 231 + 54	2^{15}, 20^{103}, 38^{36}, 58^1, 64^{60}, 65^{63}, 83, 104, 107^{116}; Pl. 37:a, b
1972, no. 8	Athens, N.M. ᾽Απο. 232	2^{15}, 38^{37}, 58^1, $83^{101, 102}$
1972, no. 9	Athens, N.M. ᾽Απο. 234	2^{15}, 38^{39}, 58^1, 83^{104}
1972, no. 13	Athens, N.M. ᾽Απο. 233	2^{15}, 38^{39}, 58^1, 70
1972, no. 15.	See 1972, nos. 7, 15	
1972, no. 17	Athens, N.M. ᾽Απο. 235	2^{15}, 38^{37}, 56^{204}, 58^1, 81^{90}

1972, no. 23 Athens, N.M. 3036: Onesiphoron 2[15], 29[170, 173], 49[138], 58[1], 59[10], 67–68, 91, 93; Pl. 5:a, b

1973 Athens, N.M. 1024: Isidotos 68[6]

1975 Piraeus Museum: Blastos 82[98], 108[119]; Pl. 42:d

1976 111[140]

1985 Brussels, M.R.A.H.: Mousonis 40[61]

1987 Athens, N.M. 1867: Epaphroditos 25[144]

1989 58[5]

1990 58[5]

1995 58[5]

2003 Athens, N.M. 1309: Theophilos 44[87], 49[137]

2005 Cambridge, Fitzwilliam Museum: Tryphon 43[86], 44[87], 72[34, 35], 93; Pl. 11:c

2008 Athens, N.M. 2725 41[72]

2011 Athens, N.M. 3316: Timokrates 35[14, 19], 104; Pl. 36:b

2022 57[214]

2023 Athens, N.M. 1663 64[61]

2029 43[87]

2031 43[87]

2038 American School of Classical Studies: the Damaskenos 33[1], 41[71], 42[74, 79], 43[84], 44[87], 59[11], 66[71], 75[56], 94[19]

2042 Athens, N.M. 1207: Aurelios Eutyches 107[116]

2048 Athens, N.M. 1775: Telesphoros 45–46, 81[91], 103; Pl. 32:d

2049 Brussels, M.R.A.H.: Aphthonetos 82[98], 108[119]; Pl. 42:c

2052 Athens, N.M. 1192: Artemidoros 42[81], 44[87], 51[154], 81[92]

2053 Piraeus Museum 223: man with siren 44[89]; Pl. 3:a, b

2066 Athens, N.M. 1250: Gaios and Hilaros 37[29], 40[61], 42[75, 79], 44[87, 88], 47[119], 71[29]; Pl. 9:a

2067 Piraeus Museum 222: Paramonos and Alexandros 47[118], 50[153], 64[59]; Pl. 21:c

2068 Athens, N.M. 1243: Eukarpos and Philoxenos 42[79], 44[87], 47, 80[86]; Pl. 32:a

2069 Marathon Museum: Zosas and Nostimos 44[87], 47, 77; Pl. 25:d

2070 57[214]

2077 Athens, Third Ephoria: Kallo and Syncheron 2[15], 37[34], 38, 44[87], 49, 56, 58[1], 65[62], 71[31], 72; Pl. 13:a–d

2078 Athens, N.M. 1195: Eukarpos 78[74]

2079 43[87]

2084 Athens, N.M. 2014 46[115], 82[98], 108[119]; Pl. 42:a

2085 Athens, Kerameikos Museum: Riemann, no. 46 28[164], 44[87], 52[164], 88, 111[140]; Pl. 51:b

2086 Athens: Praxiteles 35[14, 18], 104; Pl. 36:c

2092 58[5]

2093 Munich, Glyptothek 46[115], 70[23]; Pl. 7:c

2096 Grenoble 46[115], 57[214], 75[56]; Pl. 22:b

2098 Paris, Louvre 50[152], 77[69]

2106 43[87]

2113 Verona: Bathyllos stele 47–48, 64[60, 61], 71[29]; Pl. 8:c

2119a	Athens, N.M. 3342: Onasas, Kokkeia, and Kokkeia	47[118]
2120	Athens, N.M. 1230: Zosas, Zoilos, and Onesiphoron	47[118], 50[152]
2124	Athens, N.M. 1247: soldier	66[70], 84[108]; Pl. 38:b
2127	Athens, N.M. 1266: soldier	66[70], 84[108]; Pl. 38:c
2133	Eleusis Museum	74; Pl. 19:b
2139	Athens, E.M. 2067	2[15], 29[170, 171], 38[38], 49[138], 58[1], 65[63], 107[116], 110[132]
2140	Athens, E.M. 9706	2[15], 29[170, 173], 38[41], 49[138], 58[1], 107[116]
2141	Athens, E.M. 1036	2[15], 29[173], 38[41], 58[1], 107[116]
2142	Athens, E.M. 9730	2[15], 29[170, 171], 49[138], 58[1], 107[116]; Pl. 36:d

INDEX IV: INSCRIPTIONS

Inscr. No.	Page No.	Inscr. No.	Page No.	Inscr. No.	Page No.
IG II[2]		*IG* II[2]		*IG* II[2]	
337	31[187, 190]	5540	48[136]	10106	35[20]
1051	48[136]	5568	47[118], 50[147], 51[153]	10181	49[138]
1292	55[193]	5895	51[154]	10182	49[138], 51[158]
1368	46[112]	5909	49[138], 107[116]	10746	37[30]
1729	48[134], 50[146], 69[16]	6148	49[140]	10890	46[116]
1794	49[144]	6299	35[18]	11148	36[23]
1950	55[191], 61[28], 62[40]	6311	49[138], 56[199], 60[25], 84[107]	11329	35[19]
1990	46[111]	6367	46[116]	11441	35[20]
2017	74[51], 96[35]	6441	49[138]	11546	47[118], 50[152]
2018	75[57], 97[45]	6458	49[142, 143], 51[155]	12129	36[23]
2020	50[147]	6498	49[138], 81[89]	12367	47[118]
2021	96[36]	6692	47[118], 50[153]	12377	47[117, 124], 95[27]
2022	49[137]	6725	48[129]	12418	49[138]
2050	78[76], 99[57]	6789	36[23, 25]	12726	47[118], 49[138]
2052	49[143]	6797	49[137]	12752	49[138], 84[107]
2068	49[140]	6842	47[116]	12794	35[19]
2069	49[141]	6945	49[138]		
2086	76[63]	7042	18[91], 36[22]	*IG* III	
2124	46[111]	7349	76[63]	3647	49[138]
2130	46[110]	7431	49[138], 107[116]		
2208	84[109], 105[106]	7441	47[125], 49[144]	Athenian Agora	
2241	82[98]	7467	49[138], 67[4]	I 3205	96[39]
2245	87[129], 110[134]	7507	48[134], 50[145], 69[16]	I 4776	49[138], **22**
3451	96[34]	7667	49[141], 51[157]	I 3348 +	49[139], **25**
3681	63[50]	7704	47[116]	3532	
3687	48[129]	8837	25[144]		
3733	63[49]	9324	68[6]		
4068	57[209], 63[51]	9410	50[152], 77[69]		
4070	57[209, 210], 63[51]	9599	47[121, 122]		
4702	31[189]	9631	47[120]		
4714	68[6]	9681	36[23]		
4771	55[199], 60[25], 63[47, 49]	9683	47[117]		
4772	56[199], 61[25]	9687	47[119]		
5044	63[49]	9697	49[138], 51[161]		
5302	48[127]	9721	46[116]		
5304	48[135], 68[8], 93[10]	9734	40[65]		
5403	49[138], 51[153]	9803	69[17]		
5447	40[64]	9818	35[20]		
5484	40[64]	9898	45[106, 107], 47[122]		

PLATE 1

a. Athens, N.M. 8426: Isis Dikaiosyne

c. Oxford: Demetria and Sarapias
   (Smyrna)

b. London, B.M. 639: Isias (Smyrna)

d. Rhodes: funerary altar

PLATE 2

a. Athens, N.M. 1224: Pompeia Isias

b. Athens: Demetria

c, d. Naples, M.N. 6289

PLATE 3

a, b. Piraeus Museum 223: man with siren

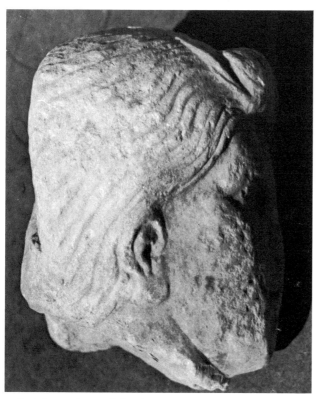

c, d. Athens, Agora S 2443

PLATE 4

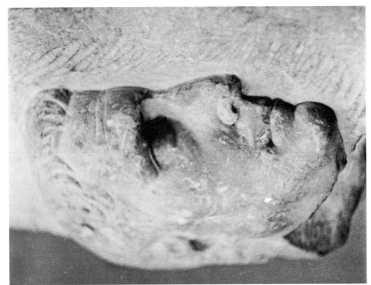

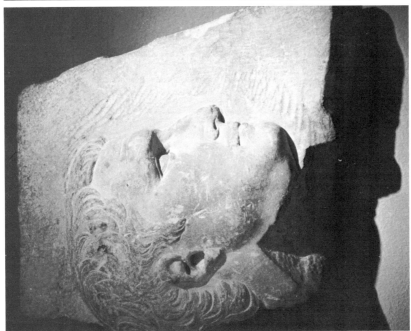

b, c. Boston, M.F.A. 99.347: Agrippa

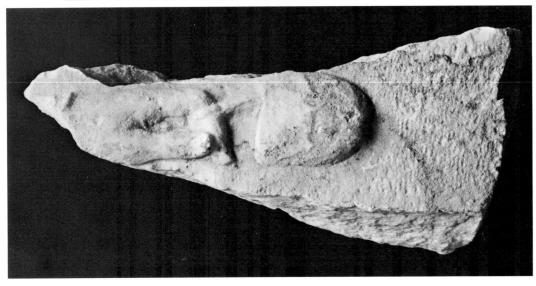

a. 1 (Agora S 1142): left hand with situla

PLATE 5

a, b. Athens, N.M. 3036: Onesiphoron

PLATE 6

a, b. Athens, N.M. Θησ. 140:
 Aphrodeisia

c. Athens, N.M. 2558: Neike

d. Athens, N.M. 1163: Ammia

PLATE 7

a. Athens, Kerameikos (Riemann, no. 52):
   Diodotos

b. Munich, Glyp. 250: Isis (Rome)

c. Munich stele

d. Naples, M.N. 6372: dark-stone
   Isis

PLATE 8

a. Athens, N.M. 1296 (detail)

b. Athens, N.M. 1296

c. Verona, Museo Lapidario: Gaius Silios Bathyllos

PLATE 9

b. Athens, Kerameikos (Riemann, no. 70)

a. Athens, N.M. 1250: Gaios and Hilaros

c, d. Boston, M.F.A. 01.8191

PLATE 10

b, c. **2** (Agora S 2264):
lower legs

a. Athens, N.M. 1270

PLATE 11

c. Cambridge, Fitzwilliam Museum: Tryphon

b. Athens, Kerameikos (Riemann, no. 58)

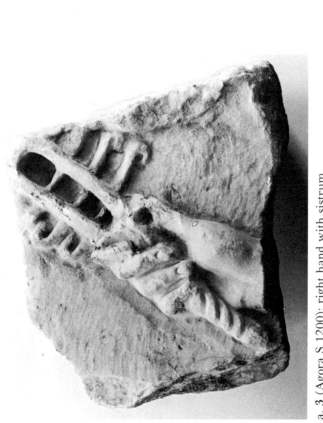

a. 3 (Agora S 1200): right hand with sistrum

PLATE 12

a–c. Herakleion Museum 314

PLATE 13

a. Photograph published as Conze 2077

b.

c.

d.

a–d. Athens, Third Ephoria: Kallo and Synpheron

PLATE 14

a.

d. Aigina stele pediment: sistrum and situla

e. Syros stele top: sistrum and situla

b.

a–c. Eleusis stele

c.

PLATE 15

a. Athens, Kerameikos (Riemann, no. 57): Agathostratos and Ma

b, c. Athens, N.M. 4915: Titus

d, e. Athens, Agora S 1319

PLATE 16

a–c. **4** (Agora S 315): head

b.

d, e. Athens, N.M.
345: Domitian

c.

PLATE 17

a. Athens, N.M. 3725: Titus Flavius
Onesiphoros

b. **5**: top view

c, d. **5** (Agora S 847): head

PLATE 18

a, b. **6** (Agora S 455): fringed mantle

c. **7** (Agora S 2551): right shoulder

PLATE 19

a. Athens, N.M. 1233: Mousaios and Amaryllis

b. Eleusis relief

c. Herakleion Museum 260+259: Isis and Sarapis

d. Herakleion Museum 260 (detail)

PLATE 20

a, b. Athens, N.M. 420

c. **8** (Agora S 202): figure with situla

d. Athens: Hilara

PLATE 21

c. Piraeus Museum 222: Paramonos and Alexandros

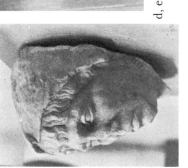

a, b. Athens, N.M. 3724: Melisia

d, e. Athens, N.M. 3552

f. Athens, Agora S 1118

PLATE 22

a. Athens, Philopappos Monument: lictors

b. Grenoble relief

c. **9** (Agora S 437): torso

d. Mantua, Ducal Palace 6677: Attikos

PLATE 23

a. Athens, E.M. 10040

b.

c.

d.

b–d. Athens, Third Ephoria 1160: Methe

PLATE 24

a, b. Athens, N.M. 1193: Alexandra

c. Sabratha: Isis

d. Athens, N.M. 1308: Epigonos and Elate

PLATE 25

a, b. **10** (Agora S 486): sistrum

c. Piraeus Museum: Neikias and Aristo

d. Marathon Museum: Zosas and Nostimos

PLATE 26

b. **12** (Agora S 1728): torso

a. **11** (Agora S 428): torso with garland

PLATE 27

b.

a.

c.

a–c. Piraeus Museum 1160:
Lamia Viboullia

d. Cyrene Museum: Faustina the
Elder

PLATE 28

a. Athens, N.M. Ἀπο. 237

c. Athens, N.M. 1249: Eisias

b. **13** (Agora S 2393): torso with garland

PLATE 29

a. **14** (Agora S 2543): legs and hand with situla

b. Laurion Museum: Sosipatros and Epiteugma
(drawing published as Conze 1967)

c. **15** (Agora S 754): right arm with sistrum

PLATE 30

a–c. Boston, M.F.A. 1971.209: Sosibia

d. 16 (Agora S 1920): fringe

PLATE 31

a, b. Rome, Museo Capitolino 744: Faustina the Younger as Isis

c–e. Athens, Agora S 2864

PLATE 32

e. London, B.M. 630: Agathemeris and Sempronius

b. Piraeus Museum relief

d. Athens, N.M. 1775: Telesphoros

a. Athens, N.M. 1243: Eukarpos and Philoxenos

c. Athens, N.M. 1303: Neike

PLATE 33

a. **17** (Agora S 1584): right leg

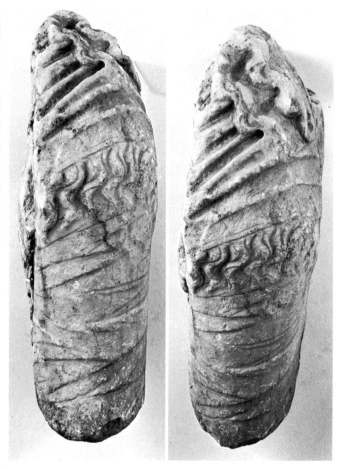

b, c. **17** (Agora S 261): left arm

d. **18** (Agora S 2544): torso

PLATE 34

a. Naples, M.N. 124325: Achilles sarcophagus

b. Naples, M.N. 124325: detail

c, d. Athens, N.M. 1617: Isis

PLATE 35

a, b. **19** (Agora S 2771): left shoulder

c. **19** (Agora S 2771): legs

d. **20** (Agora S 262): torso

PLATE 36

b. Athens, N.M. 3316: Timokrates

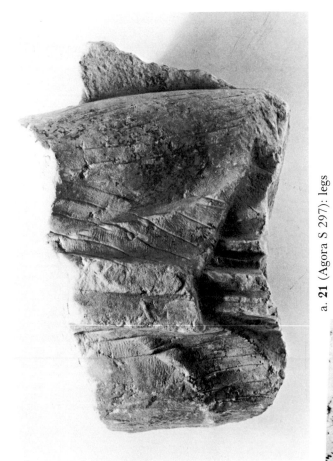

a. **21** (Agora S 297): legs

d. Athens, E.M. 9730: cist

c. Athens:
Praxiteles

PLATE 37

a, b. Athens, N.M. ’Aπο.
54+231

c. Paros: Kleitomenes (upper right)

d. Salamis: Aphelia and
Zosimos

e. Athens, N.M. 1214: Sophia and
Eukarpos

PLATE 38

a. Athens, N.M. 1223: Son of Soterion

b. Athens, N.M. 1247

c. Athens, N.M. 1266

d. **22** (Agora I 4776): sistrum

PLATE 39

a. **23** (Agora S 1917): torso with garland

b. **24** (Agora S 2029): sistrum

c. Broom Hall: Aphrodeisia

PLATE 40

b. Tarragona: Hippolytos sarcophagus

a. Athens, Kerameikos (Riemann, no. 62)

c. **25** (Agora I 3348+I 3532): cist

PLATE 41

b, c. Rome, Vatican, Museo Gregoriano Egizio 83:
   Julia Maesa
   as Isis

a. Athens, Agora S 1354

d. Detail of b, c

e. **26** (Agora S 2451): torso

PLATE 42

a. Athens, N.M. 2014

b. Athens, Agora S 2698

c. Brussels, Musées Royaux d'Art et d'Histoire:
   Aphthonetos

d. Piraeus Museum: Blastos

PLATE 43

a. **27** (Agora S 2280): knees

c. Trieste, Mus.Civ. 2214

b. **27**

PLATE 44

a, b. Athens, Akropolis Museum 3194

c. Rome, Pretextatus Catacomb: Balbinus sarcophagus

d. Zagreb, Archaeological
Museum 34: Isis

PLATE 45

a. **28** (Agora S 2900): torso

b. **29** (Agora S 434): torso

c. Piraeus Museum 278: Balbinus

d. **30** (Agora S 984): torso with garland

PLATE 46

a. Athens, N.M. 1176: Pelops sarcophagus

b. Athens, N.M. 3256

c. Athens, Kerameikos (Riemann, no. 59)

d. Verona, Museo Lapidario

PLATE 47

a. **31** (Agora S 2396): torso with garland

b. Detail of c

c. Thessaloniki, Archaeological Museum 1247: Dionysiac sarcophagus

PLATE 48

a. Naples, M.N.: "Brother" sarcophagus

b. Athens, N.M. 3669: Julios Ephebos

c. Athens, E.M. 10038: ephebic decree

PLATE 49

a, b. **32** (Agora S 341)

c. Rome, Piazza Venezia: Isis

PLATE 50

a. **33** (Agora S 1987): torso

b. Athens, N.M. 1244: Parthenope

c. Athens, Kerameikos (Riemann, no. 61)

d. Detail of b

PLATE 51

a. **34** (Agora S 1281): pediment with cist

b. Athens, Kerameikos
(Riemann, no. 46)

c. Naples, M.N.
2929: Balullia
Varilla

d. Athens, N.M. 274: Athena

e. Rome, Vatican, Loggia
Scoperta: Galatea

f. Palermo, M.N. 704

PLATE 52

a. Alexandria Museum
25783: Isis

b. Tunis, Bardo Museum
C 982: Isis

c. Naples, M.N.: black-stone Isis

d. Luxor, Sarapieion: Isis-
Fortuna

e. Naples, M.N.: Isis Barberini